The Command and
Control of
Nuclear Forces

The Command and Control of Nuclear Forces

PAUL BRACKEN

YALE UNIVERSITY PRESS
NEW HAVEN AND LONDON

Published with assistance from the
Kingsley Trust Association Publication Fund
established by the Scroll and Key Society of Yale College.

Designed by James J. Johnson
and set in Electra Roman type.
Printed in the United States of America by
Vail-Ballou Press, Binghamton, New York.

Library of Congress Cataloging in Publication Data

Bracken, Paul J.
    The command and control of nuclear forces.

    Includes index.
    1. Atomic warfare.   2. Command and control systems.
I. Title.
U263.B7   1983   355'.0217   83–42874
ISBN 0–300–02946–2

10   9   8   7   6   5   4   3   2

To Kathleen and James

Contents

List of Figures

Acronyms and Abbreviations

ADM	Atomic Demolition Munition
ASW	Anti-Submarine Warfare
AT&T	American Telephone and Telegraph Company
BMEWS	Ballistic Missile Early Warning System
CIA	Central Intelligence Agency
CINCSAC	Commander in Chief, Strategic Air Command
COMINT	Communications Intelligence
DEW	Distant Early Warning Line
DIA	Defense Intelligence Agency
DSP	Defense Support Program
ELINT	Electronic Intelligence
EMP	Electromagnetic Pulse
EORSAT	ELINT Ocean Reconnaissance Satellite
ERCS	Emergency Rocket Communications System
EUR	European (Command)
FOSIC	Fleet Ocean Surveillance Information Center
ICBM	Intercontinental Ballistic Missile
IONDS	Integrated Operational Nuclear Detonation Detection System
IRBM	Intermediate-Range Ballistic Missile
JCS	Joint Chiefs of Staff
LANT	Atlantic (Command)
MIDAS	Missile Defense Alarm System
MIRV	Multiple Independently Targeted Reentry Vehicle
MRBM	Medium-Range Ballistic Missile
NATO	North Atlantic Treaty Organization
NCA	National Command Authority
NCS	National Communications System

NEACP	National Emergency Airborne Command Post
NMCC	National Military Command Center
NMCS	National Military Command System
NORAD	North American Aerospace Defense Command
NSA	National Security Agency
NTM	National Technical Means of Verification
PAC	Pacific (Command)
PAL	Permissive Action Link
PSI	Pounds per Square Inch (Blast Overpressure)
QRA	Quick Reaction Alert Aircraft
RORSAT	Radar Ocean Reconnaissance Satellite
SAC	Strategic Air Command
SACCS	SAC Control System
SACEUR	Supreme Allied Commander in Europe
SAGE	Semi-Automatic Ground Environment Air Defense System
SALT	Strategic Arms Limitation Talks
SAM	Surface-to-Air Missile
SIDAC	Single Integrated Damage Assessment Capability
SIGINT	Signals Intelligence
SIOP	Single Integrated Operational Plan
SLBM	Submarine-Launched Ballistic Missile
SOSUS	Sound Surveillance System
SRF	Strategic Rocket Forces (Soviet)
SSBN	Strategic Nuclear Ballistic Missile Submarine
TACAMO	Airborne Command Post for the Ballistic Missile Submarines
TELINT	Telemetry Intelligence
WP	Warsaw Pact
WWMCCS	World Wide Military Command and Control System

1 A Perspective on Nuclear Forces

The purpose of this work is to examine concepts and realities in the management of nuclear forces in peace and war. Understanding the dynamics of how Soviet and American nuclear forces do what they do, of why they are organized the way they are, and of what institutional factors shape their use may be the best way to prevent disaster. The arsenals of both countries are now so large that reductions in nuclear armaments, even deep reductions, would leave so many remaining weapons that the difference might be negligible should a war break out. As the systems analysts of the 1960s were fond of pointing out, the mathematical equations of nuclear destruction top out beyond a certain point. For the United States, the Soviet Union, and Europe the point of diminishing returns in population destruction in a nuclear war has long since been passed.

If we focus instead on the management of forces at the moment they would go on alert, and as they would perform during a war, perhaps we can identify potential flashpoints and triggers that might lead to catastrophe. Ideally, these flashpoints and triggers can be removed by changes in strategic doctrines and acquisition policies. At least their number might then be reduced, making the world a little safer.

Rules of the road need to be established for operating nuclear forces, though rules cannot eliminate the danger that a crisis between two countries might escalate to the killing of tens of millions of people. If any nuclear state in the international system of nations is dedicated to starting such a war, or even to risking a war, rules alone cannot stop it. A late-twentieth-century Hitler in control of nuclear weapons could not be halted by nuclear rules of the road, arms control treaties, or even threats of nuclear deterrence. Nuclear weapons seem to be designed for such a leader, allowing him or her to bluff and threaten to achieve any gains he or she wishes. This was the great fear of the 1950s, when waves of articles on the theory and practice of blackmail in the nuclear age raised the possibility that such a leader might emerge.

The pessimism of the 1950s has proven incorrect on this point. As yet no nuclear Hitler has appeared on the world scene, and the world has not played stage to a never-ending sequence of Munichs with full alerting of forces. Some people consider it remarkable that no nuclear weapons have been fired since 1945. Far more remarkable is the absence of a full Soviet-American alert. No American bombers have been launched in anticipation of enemy attack, at no time have nuclear weapons in Europe been dispersed from their peacetime storage sites, nor have all of the Soviet nuclear submarines been dispatched from their ports at one time. Instead of the Munich world of blackmail backed by nuclear alerts that was predicted, we have had more than thirty-five years in which nuclear forces have been handled with kid gloves, because national leaders have understood the dangers.

Fear of nuclear weapons does not eliminate the potential for disaster, however. The likelihood of nuclear Munichs has been exaggerated, but the possibility of nuclear Sarajevos has been understated. No dictator singlehandedly pushed Europe into war in 1914; indeed, the national leaders of the major countries did not even want a conflict. Some even searched for last-minute alternatives to war. But during the preceding decade an institutionalized potential for catastrophe had been built on interlocking alerts and mobilizations that finally swamped the political process in 1914. It was a disaster waiting to happen.

The most appalling feature of World War I was not the destruction, nor was it the preview it offered of the evils that the linkage of science and war was to produce later in the century. Rather, it was the war's pointlessness. Ten million men died and monarchies were swept from power simply because government leaders did not think through the implications of either their actions or the institutions they had constructed for war. European security systems were engineered from provincial perspectives. War initiation, especially landing the first blow, was built into the system at the expense of flexibility and safety. Even precautionary protective actions appeared threatening, driving the actors into a frenzy of mutual stimulation once certain alerting thresholds were exceeded. As Jean Paul Sartre tells us, World War II had the clear purpose of stopping Hitler; even with its vastly greater destruction and its death camps, it had some meaning, however horrible and tragic it was for the participants. World War I had nothing comparable.

The lesson from the outbreak of World War I was less that war can come about from the actions of obtuse leaders than that a nation's actions in a crisis are profoundly influenced by the security institutions built years before the crisis occurs. The process of alerting and mobilizing forces, and of applying those forces, outran the political control apparatus. It even outran the strategies of the states involved. Even if leaders today understand the enormously destructive consequences of war, which are far more apparent now than in 1914, the construction of fantastically complex nuclear command organizations in the United States and the Soviet Union parallels the conflict institutions built in the decade before 1914, but on a far more spectacular and quick-reacting scale. A thoroughgoing examination of these organizations, and their governance, is clearly in order.

I deal in this book with the management of the institutionalized conflict systems erected in the nuclear age. I examine specifically, the command and control of nuclear forces—both the structure of command organization and the control over nuclear weapons.

In military circles, the subject is referred to as command and control. This is an arrangement of facilities, personnel, procedures, and means of information acquisition, processing, and dissemination used by a commander in planning, directing, and controlling military operations.[1] The phrase *command and control* has been used to de-

1. Some references in the past few years employ the phrase "command, control, communications, and intelligence," or even "command, control, communications, computers, intelligence, and informational processing." An understanding of the definition of command and control will show these additional terms to be redundant.

scribe the varied problems of force management; it distinguishes operational from acquisition problems. The earliest use of the term I have found was in after-action reports from the Battle of the Bulge in 1944, where breakdowns in command and control were identified as the leading cause of the collapse of American resistance.

My approach is to explore the evolution of nuclear command and control over the almost forty years since its inception, rather than focusing on a particular technical system at a given point in time. Coming to grips with the existence of nuclear weapons, at least to the extent that this is possible, is fundamentally different today than it was at the dawn of the atomic age. In 1945, concerned scientists and government leaders could center their dread on the levels of destruction produced by atomic energy. Today, we must account not only for this destruction but also for the legacy from the evolution of mature complex organizations charged with commanding nuclear forces. As in the decade preceding 1914, these organizations are the key to triggering catastrophe.

It is essential to my approach to examine the most vulnerable and dangerous aspects of nuclear command organizations in order to isolate especially reckless operating tactics. However, the process can also instruct about how to actually fight a nuclear war. I know of no alternatives that would allow my case to be made without bringing up some extremely unpleasant and sensitive subjects. On balance, we must be realistic. An understanding of how nuclear forces are managed, of how they are alerted, and of how they would be used is necessary if these forces are to be governed in a democratic, or any other kind, of society. That is what this book is about.

2 Warning and Intelligence

Early warning information provides decision makers with a description of enemy forces as they prepare for or actually initiate an attack. The sensors used for this purpose include overhead satellites, ground-based radars, communications intelligence systems, and other highly secret means. Information from these many different sources is transmitted to "fusion centers," where it is processed, synthesized, filtered, and distributed to political and military command centers for action.

Generally a distinction is made between tactical and strategic warning. The terminology of this distinction differs somewhat from the meaning one would ordinarily attach to strategic warning, so it is important to point out the difference. Strategic warning is warning of impending attack prior to its actual execution. Tactical warning, in contrast, refers to warning of an executed attack. As an example of this distinction, if the United States somehow got word that the Soviet Union was going to launch an attack in twenty-four hours, this would constitute strategic warning. If a launch of missiles had been carried out, and U.S. leaders detected the incoming missiles, this would constitute tactical warning. When the term warning is used without qualification it includes both the strategic and tactical varieties, including the intelligence inputs necessary to both.

Warning information is essential for the survival of many parts of the American and Soviet nuclear arsenals and their related control systems. For example, the American bomber force is dependent on timely early warning information so that it may scramble from ground alert to airborne stations where it is less vulnerable to nuclear attack. A principal design feature of a modern bomber, such as the B-1B, is

5

its ability to get off the ground quickly. Airplane designers are willing to make major concessions in other areas of performance in order to minimize what is known as a bomber's "escape time." There is little point to having a sophisticated plane if it is destroyed in a first-strike attack; this particular problem began to reach major proportions for the United States Air Force in the early 1970s when the Soviet Union began routinely to base strategic nuclear ballistic submarines (SSBNs) off America's coast. In these positions submarine-launched ballistic missiles (SLBMs) could reach inland bomber bases in twelve to fifteen minutes after launch, substantially reducing the allowable bomber escape time.

But the use of warning to save the bomber force, or any other weapon for that matter, addresses only a narrow aspect of warning. Over the years both the United States and the Soviet Union have built systems of incomprehensible complexity to give advance notice of attack. Intelligence systems have merged with warning systems, and the overall system has been vertically integrated with military forces to a degree unparalleled in military history.

The best way to show what has been happening is to describe the technical and organizational evolution of the warning system. Bit by bit, incremental additions to America's warning system over the last thirty years have dramatically changed the nature of nuclear forces as well as the Soviet-American relationship. What has happened is that the nuclear forces of both the United States and the Soviet Union have matured from their undeveloped stages of the late 1940s. This maturation has proceeded at a different pace in each country, but its chief effect has been to slow down the revolutionary rate of change which characterized nuclear force organizations in the 1950s and 1960s. Their basic structure has now been determined and it seems highly unlikely that any dramatic changes of the kind produced by the ICBM or the SLBM will occur any time soon. Two developments define this maturation. The first, vertical integration of warning and intelligence systems with actual nuclear weapons and their offensive control machinery, is detailed in this chapter. The nuclear forces of both nations have been closely tied to specialized intelligence agencies in a process that has taken nearly thirty years to achieve. The second element of maturation, horizontal integration, is discussed in the following chapter. It deals with the integration of nuclear weapons of geographically dispersed commands into a single centralized whole, with corresponding centralized war planning. These trends in vertical and horizontal integration are the major determinants shaping the modern nuclear arsenals of the superpowers, both today and for the remainder of the century.

Integration of warning and intelligence with nuclear forces arose from a need to establish control over the operating environment in which these weapons found themselves. Since intelligence, and the particular parts of intelligence which encompass warning, provides information about impending enemy attack, these information resources were a crucial part of a policy to stabilize and control the threats which confronted nuclear organizations. But the enormous amount of such information, and the peculiar way in which it came in continuously from electronic sensors, necessitated a heavy investment in information processing technology and a mechanization and rationalization of how it was handled. Standard operating procedures, rules embedded in computer software, and carefully delimited spans of authority all had to be devised to achieve this vertical integration. The idea behind this monumental task was that external threats of attack could be managed by changing the preparedness, or alert, levels of the offensive and defensive nuclear forces. Managing this alerting process was problematic because it was so complicated, involving thousands of nuclear weapons and hundreds of near real-time information channels which carried vital information about the enemy's state of preparedness.

The U.S. Air Force was the first to realize the profound change in warfare which had come about. The Air Force understood that military organizations must design their formal organizational structure to fit the type of information technology they rely on if they are to successfully prosecute a war. With the inception of the North American Aerospace Defense Command (NORAD) in 1957, a major step was taken to vertically integrate America's nuclear weapons with a specialized intelligence and warning management center. It is important to note that for warning of nuclear attack the United States was not to depend on a civilian staff group such as the CIA, but instead on a military organization which was much more tightly coupled to the direct control of atomic weapons.

Among the consequences of this vertical integration was the need to have instantly ready wartime organizations operating in peacetime twenty-four hours a day. The historical tendency of the United States and the Soviet Union to set up high commands and mobilization agencies after war had commenced would no longer be a safe policy in the era of surprise nuclear attack. Another effect was that political leadership would be constrained by this wartime command system. In World War II and even into the 1950s the size and complexity of nuclear command systems was not great enough to hamper the freedom of maneuver of national leaders had they ever been called upon to use nuclear weapons in some limited or discriminating way. Truman simply ordered that individual attacks be directed at Japan. The earliest civilian conceptualizations of nuclear command and control in both the United States and the Soviet Union continued the idea that tight control of atomic weapons by the highest political levels of government was the only safe way to govern this dangerous new technology. Yet in both a democracy and a communist state this conceptualization eroded and eventually broke down.

The military organizations created to manage the integration of warning with the weapons entered into the political control apparatus. In neither country do political leaders have the tight central control over nuclear arsenals offered in public relations statements. Instead, they rely on the vast organizations which are needed to manage the complex integration process. This has profound implications for maintaining coherent political control over nuclear forces as they go on alert and operate in war. It also has disturbing implications for a nation's vulnerability to surprise nuclear attack.

Recounting the historical evolution of the warning and intelligence systems for nuclear war drives home a point whose importance cannot be emphasized enough. Only recently has the full effect of the trend toward vertically integrated nuclear forces been realized. The piecemeal additions of the 1950s and 1960s moved in this direction, but it was not until the 1970s that the accumulated legacy matured into the current organizational structure. Never has there been a Soviet-American confrontation during this modern period, and in this chapter I raise some fundamental questions as to whether in a crisis stability could be either controlled or maintained in this new environment. The Cuban missile crisis of 1962 was the highest-level alert ever declared by the United States. At that time only rudimentary warning and intelligence systems were in use, and the interactions in that crisis could be very bad predictors of what would happen in a similar confrontation today or in the future.

The developments discussed in this chapter also pave the way for the examination of other issues of nuclear force management, ranging from why theater nuclear conflict is a uniquely important and dangerous matter to how the U.S. strategic nuclear command is structured to avoid being destroyed by Soviet attack. Therefore, this chapter includes extensive descriptive details, in order to set the stage for the subjects to follow.

THE AMERICAN SYSTEM

The original reason for America's development of a warning system is found at the beginning of the nuclear age. Because of the large disparity in the ground forces of the Eastern and Western blocs in the late 1940s, all American war plans called for the immediate use of atomic weapons at the outbreak of another war. It was thought, reasonably enough, that the only way to halt an invasion of Western Europe was to destroy the Soviet armies before they could overrun the continent.

In 1948, following the Czechoslovakian crisis and the beginning of the Berlin blockade, the National Security Council (NSC) authorized the military to draw up contingency plans on the presumption that nuclear weapons would be available. This was embodied in National Security Council Memorandum 30, which has guided virtually all subsequent military planning:

It is recognized that, in the event of hostilities, the National Military Establishment must be ready to use *promptly* and effectively all appropriate means available, including atomic weapons, in the interest of national security and must therefore plan accordingly.[1] [emphasis added]

Supporting a policy of prompt use of nuclear weapons against conventional attack required a warning system that could give the earliest possible signal that the Soviet Union was preparing for war. Defense planners first turned to what at the time was a highly secret propaganda and intelligence program.

In the 1940s British and American aircraft began overflying the Soviet Union and its East European satellites.[2] Originally, these flights were used for dropping propaganda leaflets or for parachuting agents into Soviet territory. But the lack of success in stirring up anti-Soviet revolts in the Ukraine and Eastern Europe created disenchantment with this idea, and gradually the overflights were used for monitoring Soviet military radio traffic and radar signals, photographic observation, and general intelligence collection.[3] Following the detonation of the first Soviet atomic bomb in 1949, the Department of Defense formalized a systematic program of flights around (and sometimes inside) Soviet borders.[4] Pieces of information were put together about operating patterns so that the United States could learn when Soviet forces were preparing for war. Once Soviet alerting patterns were learned by the United States, intelligence probes could be used to supply early warning and targeting information and, in the event of war, damage assessment, to American nuclear commanders. Various scraps of information were pieced together to permit American intelligence experts to locate the positions of Soviet army and air force units. This was long before the surprise attack era of thirty-minutes warning, and monitoring Soviet radio transmissions was one of the most useful ways to detect preparations for war. The information

1. "United States Policy on Atomic Weapons," NSC 30, September 10, 1948. Reprinted in Thomas H. Etzold and John Lewis Gaddis, *Containment* (New York: Columbia University Press, 1978), pp. 340–43.

2. Thomas Powers, *The Man Who Kept the Secrets* (New York: Alfred A. Knopf, 1979), p. 39.

3. Ibid.

4. Lawrence Freedman, *U.S. Intelligence and the Soviet Strategic Threat* (Boulder, Colo.: Westview Press, 1977), p. 6.

could be relayed to American military commanders for action, providing days of strategic warning of attack and meeting the needs of prompt nuclear defense of Western Europe. Flights over or near the borders of the Soviet Union have continued to the present day.[5]

The growing Soviet nuclear weapon capability further stimulated the United States into building a full-scale air defense protection system, which was initially studied and planned in the early 1950s. In 1952 the Pinetree Line of radars was begun in Canada, to be followed in 1953 by the Distant Early Warning (DEW) Line. These ground-based radar systems with their rearward transmission networks provided the American Strategic Air Command (SAC) with one or two hours' tactical warning of any approaching Soviet bombers. This time could be used to get SAC airborne and to launch it on its retaliatory mission.

The intelligence-collection flights around the Soviet border begun in the late 1940s were a source of strategic warning of impending attack on the United States. The DEW and Pinetree lines provided tactical warning. The intelligence flights would have provided much more reaction time than DEW or Pinetree, time that could be used to move SAC bombers to airbases in the northern United States or to Europe, where they would be in better positions to strike the Soviet Union. However, in a case where strategic warning was not available, or where it was interpreted incorrectly, as at Pearl Harbor, the air defense warning system would backstop SAC, preventing it from being destroyed on the ground by Soviet bombers.

The DEW and Pinetree lines themselves were, in the 1950s, pieces of a fantastically complex system of air defense known as SAGE (Semi-Automatic Ground Environment). SAGE was the largest data-processing system ever devised at the time of its inception. Its basic function, however, was simple: to use digital computers to coordinate the use of fighters and missiles with radar warning information. SAGE was a technologically updated version of the air defense system used in the Battle of Britain in 1940. The speed of jet aircraft cut down

5. For recent American intelligence flights see "Planes' Covert Role Is to Monitor Soviet Space Flights, Missile Tests," *Baltimore Sun*, May 7, 1981, p. 1.

on the ability of human operators to make the needed decisions quickly enough, so only through computer-directed decisions could air defense forces be used in an effective way against incoming high-speed Soviet bombers.

SAGE was the first truly complex warning and control system of the nuclear age, and it revealed a number of interesting things about the place of human beings in such a system. It was impossible to specify in advance all of the contingencies that would be faced in the course of actual operations. Reliance on formal written procedures proved impractical, and unwritten work-arounds soon developed among the human operators of SAGE. Controllers were even reluctant to specify to engineers the exact operating procedures they would employ in particular situations.[6] Time and time again in complex military systems informal and usually oral understandings circumvent the procedures contained in the rule books. This showed up in a major way in SAGE.[7] For example, small amounts of radar jamming could paralyze SAGE if rule book procedures were followed.[8] Oral agreements between operators could fix this, but these never showed up in official reports.

Given the complexity of air defense it is not surprising that informal understandings would evolve to fix problems unanticipated by the system's planners. Very few complex systems would ever run if rule books were followed to the letter. The lesson is important and SAGE showed it very well. Military command and control cannot be understood as the sum total of official rules and procedures. The most stressing and potentially dangerous nuclear command problems arise when no rules cover the situation, either because no one anticipated that it could arise or because unanticipated shocks fundamentally change the operating environment in which the system is designed to work. The SAGE experience is only a tip-off to a much larger set of phenomena, namely the extensive degree to which any nuclear command organization circumvents official procedures in order to carry

6. N. F. Kristy, *Man in a Large Information Processing System—His Changing Role in SAGE* (Santa Monica, Calif.: Rand Corp., 1963), pp. 8–9.

7. Ibid., p. 31.

8. Ibid., p. 10.

out its assigned mission. Such rule shortcutting is likely to be oral and informal, and therefore invisible to outside observation except under the high-stress conditions of actual war or crisis.

In the mid-1950s, at the same time SAGE was developed, there was a significant expansion of the radio monitoring begun earlier. In the winter of 1954–55 American technicians began work on a listening post and line-of-sight radar at Samsun, Turkey, on the Black Sea, and a bit later at Meshed and in the Elburz Mountains of Iran.[9] These sites allowed observation of Soviet missile tests at nearby launching sites, but they also permitted a much more extensive monitoring of Soviet military radio traffic, an invaluable source of strategic warning.

More significant still, in June 1956 the first U-2 overflight of the Soviet Union took place.[10] The overseas listening posts and the U-2 provided SAC with a much better picture of the location and status of Soviet military forces than had previously been possible. The proliferation of listening posts and the U-2 constituted a forward deployment of warning sensors, which followed by a few years the forward deployment of nuclear weapons to NATO and overseas SAC bases. The U-2 and the listening posts around the Soviet border were intended to serve the warning needs of the military every bit as much as they did those of the CIA. Fierce jurisdictional battles between SAC and the CIA were fought as a consequence.[11]

By the mid-1950s the American warning system for nuclear war was still in a developmental stage. The decision to emphasize warning made sense, because the very small size of the Soviet nuclear threat to the United States, in the form of its Long Range Air Armies, made it possible for SAC to plan a swift counterstrike with some hope of destroying a large proportion of the Soviet bombers before they could take off. But this could occur only if strategic warning of attack were given to SAC. The offensive striking power of SAC, plus the defensive

9. Freedman, *Soviet Threat*, p. 69.
10. Ibid. It is not known when the last non-U-2 overflight of the Soviet Union took place. Soviet advances in surface-to-air missiles would have made non-U-2 overflights dangerous by 1956, but the B-36 bomber was widely available and had been initially designed for high-altitude operations.
11. Powers, *The Man Who Kept the Secrets*, p. 96.

capabilities of SAGE and the DEW and Pinetree lines, offered a good chance, in the estimation of senior planners, of limiting nuclear damage to the United States even though it was daily growing less possible to blunt an attack on Europe itself.

SAC was far from being the only U.S. force concerned with warning in the 1950s. By 1957, the U.S. Navy's Sound Surveillance System (SOSUS) was in extensive operation.[12] Designed in the early 1950s, SOSUS was a collection of underwater acoustic sensors that could detect and locate Soviet submarines and ships. It gave shore-based centers the approximate location of enemy vessels by matching the noises of ships and submarines against the known patterns of American and Soviet vessels. The approximate location was relayed to U.S. Navy coastal airbases and ships at sea so that they could close in for the final precise detection needed to destroy the vessel in question. SOSUS has been expanded and improved over the years, and it is now deployed off the American Atlantic and Pacific coasts, in the Barents Sea, throughout European waters, and in the seas of northeast Asia.[13] It provides information to the U.S. Navy about Soviet naval buildups and played a crucial role in the 1962 Cuban missile crisis, when every Soviet submarine in the area was found and closely trailed.

SOSUS has attracted considerable Soviet attention, especially since the Cuban missile crisis, when Moscow was forced to use nuclear-firing submarines as a surrogate for the missiles removed from Cuba. The large number of Soviet "trawlers," intelligence-gathering ships disguised as fishing vessels, that forever patrol America's coastline are likely in a conflict to disrupt the underwater network of hydrophones, sonars, and communication lines that make up SOSUS. Apparently these trawlers break SOSUS communication lines with

12. Report to the President from the Security Resources Panel of the Scientific Advisory Committee, *Deterrence and Survival in the Nuclear Age (The Gaither Report)* (Washington, D.C., November 7, 1957), p. 27. This report was declassified in January 1973.

13. Joel S. Witt, "Advances in Antisubmarine Warfare," *Scientific American*, February 1981, pp. 36–37.

grappling hooks from time to time, both to test American reactions and to collect a sample of the cables for careful inspection.[14]

In addition to the deployment of SOSUS, the late 1950s also saw the original design work for the U.S. Air Force's "Big L" systems. These were the project names of over a score of computerized warning and control systems designed to accomplish a wide variety of tasks. The following is a selective list of the most important ones.

Air Force Big L Systems of the Late 1950s

117 L	MIDAS (Missile Defense Alarm System), satellite-based missile warning
416 L	SAGE (Semi-Automatic Ground Environment), air defense
425 L	NORAD (North American Air Defense), air defense, warning, and assessment
438 L	AFIDHS (Air Force Intelligence Data Handling System), intelligence and warning
465 L	SACCS (SAC Control System), status monitoring of ICBMs and bombers
474 L	BMEWS (Ballistic Missile Early Warning System), missile warning[15]

The stimulus for construction of most of the Big L systems was the threat of Soviet intercontinental missile attack. The successful launching of Sputnik in October 1957 caused American planners to take the threat of ICBM attack seriously for the first time and led to the BMEWS (Ballistic Missile Early Warning System), which consisted of large ground-based radars in Alaska, Greenland, and Great Britain, along with a complicated system of rearward communication lines to bring the information to commanders in the United States. It was able to detect Soviet missiles and could provide SAC and the

14. Thomas S. Burns, *The Secret War for the Ocean Depths* (New York: Rawson Associates, 1978), pp. 152–59.

15. Some of the systems on this list have been replaced since the 1950s. The old 425 L was combined with certain space tracking radars into the 427 M system in 1969, for example.

White House with about fifteen to thirty minutes' tactical warning of attack.[16] Construction of the radars began in the summer of 1958, and the first (in Greenland) began operating on December 31, 1960.[17]

MIDAS, the Missile Defense Alarm System, was an infrared radiation detector placed aboard a satellite that was positioned over the Soviet Union.[18] The theory was that a Soviet missile launch would be detected by the heat of the plumes from the booster lofting it skyward. The MIDAS program suffered from the reliability problems of the early days of satellite reconnaissance. However, the concept proved itself, and the descendants of MIDAS are today among the most critical warning sensors the United States possesses.

Big L programs such as BMEWS, MIDAS, and SAGE had major consequences other than the obvious one of improving America's ability to detect when a Soviet bomber or missile attack was under way. In purely physical terms, these systems increased the amount of warning time for American decision makers. Yet even before the Big L systems went into operation they produced some major conceptual changes in how people thought about operating under the threat of nuclear attack. First, and most obvious to the Air Force, the vast increase in information about Soviet military activity meant that SAC had to streamline its own procedures for managing its offensive forces. A balance had to be maintained, so that status information about the Soviets gained from warning and intelligence sensors would not overwhelm SAC headquarters. Therefore SAC had to develop automated command and control systems in order to make use of the new warning and assessment information available to it.

The SAC 465 L and 438 L systems were responses to the new requirement for more rapid control of the offensive nuclear forces. These were not warning systems but were necessitated by improvements in warning. Prior to 465 L, worldwide status information about bombers was sent to SAC headquarters by voice telephone or teletype. Similarly, worldwide intelligence information on enemy status and

16. BMEWS is described in Stanley L. Englebardt, *Strategic Defenses* (New York: Thomas Crowell, 1966), pp. 105–22.
17. Ibid., p. 118.
18. John Prados, *The Soviet Estimate* (New York: Dial Press, 1982), pp. 106–09.

location and on weather conditions over the Soviet Union was also transmitted by telephone. With better early warning, these slow-reacting systems became extremely cumbersome. The basis of both 465 L and 438 L was computer-generated transmission and display of information. The idea was to have automatic, rather than human, procedures for sending information to the bases and commanders who needed it. The details of designing these procedures, and writing them into computer programs, were extraordinarily complex. The development of computer software for the 465 L system, for example, is estimated to have taken over fourteen hundred man-years of computer programming effort.[19] During the late 1950s America's largest technology corporations, firms like AT&T and ITT, were undertaking massive systems-engineering and computer-programming projects to develop the Big L systems that would bring all of the nation's command and control up to speed with the improvements in warning.

It was at this juncture that the overall nuclear command system first began to shift from a relatively slow-reacting and loosely coupled system to a quick-reacting and more tightly coupled one. In purely physical terms the amount of decision-making time available in a potential crisis was increasing, as new warning sensors made it possible to detect threatening activities earlier than was previously the case. But the responses made possible by warning systems like BMEWS made it advantageous to integrate the nuclear forces with the warning systems. The United States did not move to a fully integrated and automated nuclear command system in the late 1950s and early 1960s, but a step was taken in this direction with the conceptualization of the Big L systems in the late 1950s and their actual operation in the 1960s. The process picked up speed in the 1960s and became fully mature only in the late 1970s.

Electronic warning systems caused another seminal change by the way they produced data and information. Historically, warning information had been delivered to national leaders in batches. As the

19. Taken from *Air Force Command and Control Information Processing in the 1980s: Trends in Software Technology* (Santa Monica, Calif.: Rand Corp., 1974), p. 76.

twentieth century progressed, the batches of information analyzed by
warning and intelligence staffs had been getting larger and larger as
military and political organizations relied more and more on electronic communications. The difference between the size of warning
and intelligence staffs in world wars I and II shows how the dimensions of this information processing grew. Still, in both wars most
analysis was characterized by mass processing of information, albeit
on a larger scale as measured by either the amount of information or
the number of individuals required to analyze it. Reading studies of
the outbreak of war in general, and surprise attack in particular, we
find that intelligence signals and reports of enemy activity were digested piecemeal by recipient groups. In 1941 the U.S. Army and
Navy had special units monitoring Japanese diplomatic cable traffic,
the famous "purple codes." Cryptographers and analysts would process
information for report to higher headquarters on what they had found.
Also in World War II, the Ultra codes of the Germans were cracked
and analyzed in Britain for distribution to political leaders and commanders at the front. Here too large amounts of data and information
were processed, in this case at Bletchley Park in England.[20]

The impact of the electronic warning systems developed in the
late 1950s and early 1960s was to alter how warning and intelligence
information were managed. Instead of piecemeal analysis dictated by
political requests, a *continuous* process was required, because warning
sensors like SOSUS and BMEWS spewed out data in real time. It
was impossible to shut down these sensors overnight, or for any period
of time during the day, because a surprise attack might be planned
for just such a time. If these data were to have any use in warning,
standing organizations, staffed around the clock, had to be formed
that could, through complicated integration with the political leadership, go to war on only a few minutes' notice. Vertical integration
of the warning system with the nuclear forces thus became essential.
Fully mobilized forces had to be constructed in peacetime that could

20. Descriptions of these activities are numerous. See David Kahn, *The Codebreak-
ers* (New York: Macmillan, 1974); and Ronald Lewin, *Ultra Goes to War* (New York:
Simon & Schuster, 1978).

go to war on short notice, and these forces had to remain fully prepared for war for years on end without any degradation in their ability to respond instantly to attack. Furthermore, this fully mobilized force must not go to war, either accidentally or inadvertently, except on direct political orders to do so.

Neither the United States nor the Soviet Union had ever faced such strenuous organizational requirements. Historically, military forces were mobilized in war and demobilized in peace. They were not required to stay mobilized for years, prepared to respond in a few minutes to warning and intelligence information that came in continuously in real time.

There were some precursors to this trend. During the Battle of Britain in 1940 a system of radars, communication lines, and fighter aircraft remained fully mobilized for months on end, prepared to meet German attacks instantly. But this defense network, although it produced warning information as a continuous process, was a system designed and built in wartime. The transition from the relatively slow batch processing of warning and intelligence to continuous processing was therefore not altogether sudden. Yet in the United States in the late 1950s it took on a new dimension, making it the central feature of the structure of nuclear war–fighting organizations.

The U.S. Air Force was closest to the technology of continuous warning information and was quick to realize its organizational implications. Only by redesigning their formal organizational structure to fit the information technology they relied upon could the Air Force prosecute a war successfully. The result was the creation in September 1957 of the North American Aerospace Defense Command (NORAD). NORAD is important because it was the first major institutional response to the continuous flow of warning information. As the central processor of real-time warning information, located in Colorado Springs, Colorado, it was set up as a joint U.S.-Canadian command because of the location of radars and fighter bases in Canada. Its job was to integrate the BMEWS, SOSUS, DEW Line, and other information sources for an overall warning estimate that would be relayed to other major command centers, such as SAC and the Pentagon. It also had responsibility for air defense against Soviet attack.

The continuous flow of information, and the time pressures of the nuclear age, made it impossible to coordinate warning and alerting via an interagency committee or working group. Most nations historically have used such loose mechanisms for coordinating their wartime plans with intelligence and warning. But by 1957 it was clear that full-time organizations tightly integrated into the chain of military command were needed to guarantee that warning and intelligence were effectively linked with the standing forces. Warning and intelligence information had to be monitored continuously as it came in from multiple sources. NORAD was to be the central "fusion center" for this information, and, as such, it would be the central coordinating institution responsible for determining when the United States was under attack.

One cannot adequately discuss the American command and control system, or its warning component, merely in terms of its physical apparatus such as radars, satellites, or communication lines. Much of the confusion that exists in this field arises from an attempt to do so. Instead, the organizational structures of command and control, which are critical to the way America's institutions for nuclear conflict work, must be carefully examined. Therefore it is revealing to explore in detail some of the reasons why certain institutions, like NORAD, were set up in the first place.

One obvious question is why the nuclear early warning function was given to NORAD rather than to the CIA or to SAC. The CIA was an organization established in 1947 that reported to the president and was responsible for coordinating American intelligence activities. Although extensive coordination between the CIA and the Defense Department took place, the U.S. Air Force in the 1950s understood that there was a world of difference between *coordination* and *command*. The CIA was an intelligence, not an operations, organization. It had neither authority nor responsibility for the command of any military forces. There is an age-old military principle known as "unity of command" stating that the locus of authority and responsibility in an organization should coincide. The Air Force had responsibility for strategic retaliation in the form of SAC, and therefore to give the warning job to anyone else, even the agency charged with *central* intelligence as the CIA was, would have violated the principle of unity of command.

The warning function was not turned over to SAC either. While NORAD, like SAC, is an Air Force command, and is highly integrated with SAC, it remains a separate organization. This organizational structure has two interesting aspects. First, it reduces the possible biases in the warning decision that stem from putting too much decision-making responsibility in the hands of any one organization. During the Korean War the United States was overly dependent on warning assessments from the intelligence, or G-2, branch of the army fighting on the scene. G-2's repeated predictions that China would not enter the war were later felt to have been distorted by the desire of the overall commander, General Douglas MacArthur, to believe that this was the case. It was difficult, if not impossible, in such circumstances for a two-star general to argue persuasively against his four-star superior on a subject as fraught with ambiguities as warning of a potential surprise attack. Separating SAC from NORAD, therefore, was done to lessen the likelihood that bureaucratic considerations would influence the warning process. In 1958 this separation was formalized into law by the Defense Reorganization Act, which placed SAC and NORAD on an equal hierarchical level. Both were established as specified commands, and each headed by a senior Air Force general.

The command separation of SAC and NORAD is by no means an academic distinction. Today there are misgivings that NORAD's authority has been eroded because of budget cutbacks arising from the phase-out of air defense fighter and missile forces that formerly came under its jurisdiction. Recently a congressional committee undertook an informal survey of opinion among military officers on whether the warning function should be moved from NORAD to SAC, and found a general consensus that it should remain separate in NORAD. The reasons given were that under conditions of extreme pressure, as in a nuclear crisis, each command would be affected by different factors and make different evaluations, and it was imperative to bring all such considerations to bear equally on whatever actions the United States might take.[21]

The second reason for separating the warning function from SAC, and indeed from all other offensive commands, has to do fundamentally with the way that nuclear control is integrated with warning in the United States. NORAD serves a critical alerting role in an elaborate system of *institutional* checks and balances to prevent unauthorized or inadvertent use of nuclear weapons, either of which could lead to nuclear war. As is widely known, the SAC commander has the authority to order the launch of the bomber force in order to prevent its destruction on the ground by incoming enemy missiles. The bombers, once airborne, do not proceed to targets in the Soviet Union but instead go to airborne holding positions, where they await orders either to proceed with an attack or return to base. In military jargon, this is known as a *positive control launch*. This authority depends crucially on the threat of incoming enemy attack, a condition determined by the NORAD commander.[22]

Although the exact details of how America's nuclear forces would go to war are justifiably classified, this example suggests the broad institutional character of the checks and balances that govern that decision. Certain alerting actions might be allowed, or certain prearranged emergency authority might come into effect, only on condition that a particular level of alert had been declared by a separate and *different* command.

In discussions of the need to prevent accidental war and unauthorized actions involving nuclear weapons, most attention has been given to things like the "two-man rule," the requirement that at least two persons act in concert in dealing with nuclear weapons, or to the electromechanical locks that are attached to certain weapons. However important these might be, the institutional system of checks and balances developed in the late 1950s is far more important, because

21. U.S. Congress, Senate, *Recent False Alerts from the Nation's Missile Attack Warning System*, by Gary Hart and Barry Goldwater, Committee Print (Washington, D.C.: Government Printing Office, 1980), p. 10.

22. David A. Anderton, *Strategic Air Command* (New York: Charles Scribner's, 1977), pp. 16–17.

it determines the way in which high-level control over nuclear forces is structured. How the United States uses warning, and indeed how it exercises command over its nuclear arsenal, is more affected by the organizational structures established for this purpose than it is by any specific electronic communication or physical command and control system.

For ensuring that a military commander does not start a nuclear war on his own, the nightmare of fiction and movies like *Dr. Strangelove*, the restraints are more institutional than physical. In other words, the checks and balances of one institution on another restrain a particular commander from taking any significant unilateral actions on his own. This is worth recalling, because there is a tendency to believe that locks and codes are the basis for controlling nuclear weapons, a view that misses the intimate relationship between warning and alert levels on the one hand, and control of offensive weapons on the other.

We need to understand the organization of the nuclear warning process in the latter 1950s because it was then that the management structure for handling warning was established. This was a watershed period, one in which major decisions affecting the structure of the United States nuclear forces were made. We are still living with many of these decisions, so it is essential to appreciate their significance. The decision, for example, to place the warning function with the Air Force, rather than with the CIA or a specially created organization reporting directly to the president, meant that the United States would *not* have a "presidential nuclear force." By this we mean a highly centralized nuclear force that is exclusively under political control. The earliest conceptions of nuclear command systems in the United States (and the Soviet Union) were of just this kind. Not until the early 1950s was the American military even allowed to have hands-on possession of nuclear warheads. Nuclear war was thought to be so radically different that a cadre of special Atomic Energy Commission civilians held physical possession of the warheads, which were to be turned over to the military when they were needed, and then only upon direct presidential authorization. In the Soviet Union, nuclear warheads were held by special KGB units and were not given to the military until the 1960s. Interestingly, in both nations there has been an evolution from direct political to military control. Other aspects of this evolution will be examined in chapter 6.

In the 1960s the U.S. nuclear warning system was influenced by both the Kennedy administration's strong desire to take more active political charge of events and the continuation and expansion of the trend toward a continuous flow of information from warning and intelligence sensors. President Kennedy's demand for methods to exercise more direct political control over military-related events arose from several sources. On an intellectual level he desired to move from the doctrine of "massive retaliation" to one of "flexible response." What this implied as far as warning was concerned was that political leadership had to become directly involved in the alerting process itself. Kennedy was deeply troubled by Barbara Tuchman's description of the outbreak of World War I in *The Guns of August*.[23] Recalling a conversation in it between two German leaders on how that war started, he said, "If this planet is ever ravaged by nuclear war—if the survivors of that devastation can then endure the fire, poison, chaos and catastrophe—I do not want one of these survivors to ask another, 'How did it all happen?' and to receive the incredible reply: 'Ah, if only one knew.' "[24]

At a more immediate level, President Kennedy faced a series of crises early in his administration that demonstrated to him the need for detailed political control of military forces. The Cuban missile crisis of 1962 has been extensively analyzed in this context, but it also seems clear that the Bay of Pigs events of 1961, coming less than two months after he took office, deeply impressed him. This CIA-backed invasion of Cuba by Cuban exiles went awry, leading to the capture of many prisoners on the beach at the Bay of Pigs and to humiliation at the White House. The sorry story of the CIA's planning and coordination of the invasion has been told many times, but the lesson learned at the White House was that in the decision-making process then in effect there was an enormous gap between concept and ac-

23. Theodore C. Sorensen, *Kennedy* (New York: Harper & Row, 1965), pp. 577–78.
24. Ibid.

tuality.[25] To solve this problem, more direct political control of military actions seemed essential, along with a technically competent staff loyal to the president and equipped with the information and management tools necessary to support such high-level intervention.[26]

A distinction between concept and actual execution is basic to the way military men think about the managemet of forces. In the traditional view, the president's job is to form concepts and broad policy guidelines, and the military's, to carry them out in actuality. But the Bay of Pigs debacle, and Kennedy's own proclivities, pointed to a disconnection between the two. For the political arm of government to bridge this gap by intervening in the execution of policy was a revolutionary idea, and one that the military resisted.

Whatever the impact of the Kennedy administration's intellectual attraction to political control of the military, or the lessons from the Bay of Pigs, the Cuban missile crisis of 1962 drove home once and for all the need for a restructuring of the U.S. command system in general, and the warning process in particular. During the Cuban crisis the implications of something going wrong became all too apparent. The warning and alerting system set up in the late 1950s to guarantee that American forces could immediately counter Soviet strikes was used during the Cuban crisis as much to communicate political intention and resolve as for the military purpose of preparing for attack. If it were to be used in such a political way, it was imperative that control of warning and alerting systems not be turned over to military decision-makers. Any gap between concept and actuality here could mean more than losing a thousand prisoners, as at the Bay of Pigs—it could mean World War III.

In June 1962, four months before the Cuban crisis, the National Military Command System (NMCS) was established.[27] Housed in the Pentagon, in a headquarters known as the National Military Com-

25. Ibid., p. 338.

26. See Frank Armbruster, "Command and Control for Crisis and Escalation," Hudson Institute, HI-421, September 1964.

27. Kenneth V. Johnson and Eston T. White, *National Military Command and Control* (Washington, D.C.: Industrial College of the Armed Forces, 1972), p. 1.

mand Center (NMCC), it was designed to be the central portal through which the president would interact with the warning system and with the commands responsible for nuclear weapons. Previously there had been no single place where the White House could receive detailed information on warning or issue orders to the nuclear forces. Indeed, there had been no need for such a facility, because the function of the president was perceived as setting guidelines of concepts and policy, without direct involvement in the details of warning and operations.

Following the establishment of the NMCS, other changes greatly increased presidential involvement in the details of operating the nuclear forces. The communications capabilities of the White House Situation Room were upgraded. After the Cuban crisis a direct reporting channel from the National Security Agency (NSA) at Fort Meade, Maryland, was brought into the White House.[28] NSA had been founded in 1952 to be the principal collector of communications and electronics intelligence (COMINT and ELINT respectively), and it reported through the Pentagon. Bringing information from NSA directly into the White House bypassed the chain of military command and was an early example of how more direct political control over the nuclear forces was gained by bringing the information used to alert and command them into the presidential domain.

The NSA's role in warning had been growing steadily prior to this, and giving the White House warning information about Soviet attack on the United States was an important political check on the alerting process. The system of institutional checks and balances begun in the late 1950s involving NORAD, SAC, and other nuclear commanders was a system of *military* checks and balances. Now a direct check on the military alerting process was supplied by political, not just military, leadership.

The COMINT and ELINT intelligence supplied by NSA to the White House was not strictly tactical warning, as were sensors like

28. Raymond Tate, "Worldwide C³I and Telecommunications," in *Seminar on Command, Control, Communications, and Intelligence,* Center for Information Policy Research, Harvard University, 1980, pp. 30–34.

BMEWS and the DEW Line. COMINT might supply early notice that an attack was in preparation well before it was actually launched. By the time BMEWS, the DEW Line, or even overhead satellites had detected an attack it would probably be too late to do much about it, except to order a retaliatory strike. Using COMINT, however, the president would be far less likely to be surprised than if he relied on sensors producing only tactical warning. In addition to the NSA inputs into the system of political control for nuclear forces, in 1963 the CIA upgraded a round-the-clock alert operations center for receipt of intelligence information from all of its varied sources.[29] While use of this facility was not restricted to warning of the threat of nuclear attack, it undoubtedly had great capability for this function.

The other major factor shaping America's warning system in the 1960s was the acceleration in the shift from batch to continuous processing of information that began in the 1950s. The continuous flow of information required setting up many additional real-time fusion centers to correlate the vast outputs of data from several different flows to get maximum value from the information. But the data fusion centers that began to appear in the 1960s were by no means restricted to tactical warning, as they had been in the 1950s. The advent of reliable satellite reconnaissance and the expansion of the number of overseas listening posts run by NSA led to the fusion of warning and intelligence information.

Although much of the intelligence information collected was not related to the threat of nuclear attack, so much information was collected that a large spillover of categories occurred. For example, a reconnaissance satellite might be monitoring a tank factory in Russia to take pictures of the vehicles surrounding the plant. If on its path it also photographed Soviet army divisions moving forward to positions against Western Europe, this would be an indication of strategic warning, one that must be passed on promptly to nuclear commanders in the United States.

29. U.S. Senate, Select Committee on Government Operations, *Foreign and Military Intelligence*, S. Rept. 94-755, 94th Cong., 2d sess., 1976, p. 262. In fact, a National Intelligence Indications Center was set up within CIA in 1961 and later also by the DIA. John Prados, *Soviet Threat*, p. 127.

The emergence of arms control agreements as an important issue in the latter 1960s also promoted the fusion of warning and intelligence. The COMINT, ELINT, satellite photography, and telemetry intelligence (TELINT) used to verify these agreements are known as *national technical means* (NTM) of verification, and enormous sums were invested in these systems in the late 1960s and 1970s. Since inherent in NTM is the ability to give strategic warning of nuclear attack, its integration into the general warning system was both essential and crucial. Although most information about them is classified, we can say something about the integration of NTM and COMINT, ELINT, and TELINT into the general warning process because of the publicity generated both during the bureaucratic battles for control of these intelligence collection systems in the mid-1970s and later when verification of the SALT II treaty became a major political issue.

The intelligence systems of CIA, DIA, NSA, and other agencies can be "targeted," in the sense of being directed to pick up certain kinds of information. Broadly speaking, the Air Force is interested in high-resolution intelligence about the immediate threat from Soviet military forces. The CIA, however, is likely to be more interested in long-range strategic information, for example, on Soviet factory construction or on the early phases of development of a new missile.[30] Allocation of intelligence resources, then, is a very basic decision, and a bewildering, ever-changing array of offices and interagency coordinating committees have been set up over the past two decades to decide the allocation mix of these expensive intelligence collectors. Certainly, if the White House were to decide that it wanted to know more about a particular subject, then the collectors would be "aimed" accordingly. In the absence of White House intervention, the state of tension or alert would have a great influence on this decision. During conditions of increased Soviet-American confrontation, intelligence-collection resources such as COMINT and ELINT would

30. See "History of the Central Intelligence Agency," in U.S. Senate, Select Committee to Study Governmental Operations, *Supplementary Detailed Staff Reports on Foreign and Military Intelligence*, S. Rept. 94-755, 94th Cong., 2d sess., 1976, pp. 75–76.

be shifted from long-range general information to an early warning function, either strategic or tactical depending on the particular collection system. Therefore there is an intimate and direct relationship between warning and intelligence systems, on the one hand, and the alerting process, on the other. As tension rises, and an alert of a particular level is declared, military commands may seize control of intelligence systems to exploit their early warning and high resolution capabilities. Again, the check-and-balance mechanism for integrating warning with control of nuclear forces applies: one of the reasons for declaring an increased state of alert is to automatically gain control of intelligence sensors for early warning purposes.

If my description of these trends seems abstract, it is because these intelligence programs, and even more so their connection with warning of possible nuclear attack, are wrapped in official and bureaucratic secrecy. From time to time, however, reports do surface that illustrate the connection. The U.S. Navy, for example, reportedly operates an ocean surveillance satellite intended to monitor Soviet nuclear-firing submarines.[31] Unlike its American counterparts, the Soviet Navy operates only a very small percentage of its total SSBN force at sea at any given time. Over 80 percent of its SSBNs are routinely kept in port. If the Soviets were to send all, or even most, of their SSBNs to sea this would be an ominous indication of strategic warning, and it would be information absolutely vital to SAC in order to know the threat facing its bombers. Once a Soviet submarine leaves port, as detected by the U.S. Navy satellite, cues are sent to other higher-resolution collectors to track it or to determine exactly what vessel it is.[32] These collectors could include photographic reconnaissance satellites or U-2 aircraft launched from Norway or Britain. Eventually the submarine in question would pass through the SOSUS network in the North Atlantic and ultimately to the SOSUS network off the U.S. Atlantic coast. If we think for a moment we see the staggering problems of worldwide coordination needed to keep track

31. Nicholas Danieloff, "How We Spy on the Russians," *Washington Post Magazine*, December 9, 1979, p. 24; idem., "How We Spy on Argentina," *New Statesman*, April 30, 1982, p. 5.

32. Ibid.

of multiple submarines from Soviet bases in the Arctic and the Pacific. They would involve real-time control of different kinds of satellites and aircraft, together with correlation with SOSUS information, for relay to NORAD and SAC. Throughout the latter 1960s, and into the 1970s, the creation of a large number of technical systems of this nature was one of the most important developments in the U.S. warning system.

The extent of U.S. intelligence coverage of the Soviet Union is never openly discussed by American defense officials for obvious reasons of security. The indicators used in warning are matters of common sense as much as anything else, however, and it seems entirely plausible that these would be among the principal targets of American intelligence collection. Things like the movement of Soviet SSBNs out of port, increased radio traffic among combat units, establishment of new military headquarters close to potential conflict areas, unusual changes in the pattern or amount of railroad or shipping traffic, reinforcement of understrength military units, an increase in the number of reconnaissance satellites orbited, or variations in the pattern of radar usage could all be indications of pending attack.[33]

The organizational mechanisms that manage the warning and intelligence process must collect information about these activities, analyze it, and distribute it to those commanders who need it. They must rely on radio listening ports, signals interception, spy satellites, and aircraft and submarine probes near Soviet borders. The coordination of all this data collection has become a monumental management task, one which has not kept up with the pace of development of sensor technology or the rate at which information is churned out. Synthesizing the information, rather than analyzing it, is the difficult problem; it has been likened to deriving "fingerprints" of the Soviet Union under various conditions. American military commanders in SAC and NORAD, for example, ideally would like to know how the fingerprint of the Soviet Union changes as it goes through its alerting process.

33. See Edmund Brunner, Jr., *Perception and Strategic Warning* (Santa Monica, Calif.: Rand Corp., 1979).

The pace of development of these technical intelligence systems was gradual. They did not spring into full bloom overnight in the 1960s. Not until the 1970s did they become numerous.[34] Just as BMEWS and SOSUS supplied a continuous stream of information in the early 1960s, so in the late 1960s were intelligence systems beginning to do the same. In addition, the development of communications satellites in the 1960s also made it possible to receive data from remote regions of the world instantly.

The development of standard operating procedures, correlation methods in fusion centers, communication linkages, and organizational routines all had to be carefully worked out over many years for this vertical integration to work effectively and smoothly. Moreover, all of these had to be specified as functions of tension and alert levels, so that the vast organizational resources in the American warning and intelligence system could be directed to the most urgent priorities. The vertical nature of this integration meant that warning and intelligence were fused and then interrelated to the control of the nuclear weapons themselves. A corresponding *horizontal* integration of the nuclear forces, in which the war plans of the different unified and specified commands were coordinated one with the other, was also being developed at the same time as vertical integration. The two forms of integration constituted the maturation of the American nuclear force.

Almost immediately after the introduction of intelligence collectors capable of spewing out information continuously, some unintended institutional impacts were noticed. The impact of information technology on organizational structure is a subtle thing, but several trends became evident to observers who had the security clearances needed for a review of these sensitive operations. Beginning in the middle 1960s, a technologically produced "information overload" inundated the warning and intelligence process. As a response to this, more and more fusion and operations centers were established to manage the glut of data. More information processing technology was

34. See John Lyttle, "Evolution of Intelligence Information Processing," *Signal*, October 1981, pp. 17–19.

also acquired, yet by all accounts management was never able to keep up with the continuously expanding flow of information.

A sampling of official reviews of the intelligence process between 1966 and 1971 testifies to these management difficulties and to other problems arising from the new information technology. A 1966 study, known as the Cunningham Report, undertaken by the inspector general of the CIA, concluded:

- Like the rest of the intelligence community, it [the CIA] makes up for not collecting enough of the right kind of information on the most important targets by flooding the system with secondary matter.

- The information explosion has already gotten out of hand, yet the CIA and the community are developing ways to intensify it. Its deleterious effects will certainly intensify as well, unless it is brought under control.

- The quantity of information is degrading the quality of finished intelligence.

- Great technological advances in storage and retrieval of information can do more harm than good if drastically higher standards for what is to be stored and retrieved are not initiated.[35]

Two years later, a special report to the director of the CIA concluded:

After a year's work on intelligence requirements, we have come to realize that they are not the driving force behind the flow of information. Rather, the real push comes from the collectors themselves—particularly the operations of large indiscriminating technical collection systems—who use national intelligence requirements to justify what they want to undertake for other reasons, e.g., military readiness, redundancy, technical continuity and the like.[36]

35. "Foreign Intelligence Collection Requirements: The Inspector General's Report," December 1966, as quoted in U.S. Congress, Select Committee on Governmental Operations, *Foreign and Military Intelligence*, S. Rept. 94-755, 94th Cong., 2d sess., 1976, p. 343.

36. This was known as the Taylor report, after its author, Vice Admiral Rufus L. Taylor, as quoted in U.S. Senate, *Foreign and Military Intelligence*, p. 346.

In 1970 a Blue Ribbon Panel on Defense elaborated on similar findings:

- There is a large imbalance in the allocation of resources which causes more information to be collected than can ever be processed or used.

- Collection efforts are driven by advances in sensor technology, not by requirements filtering down from consensus of the community's products.

- Production resources can make use of only a fraction of the information that is being collected. There exists no effective mechanism for balancing collection, processing and production resources.[37]

And in 1971, the (then) director of the Office of Management and Budget, James R. Schlesinger, found that it was

> not at all clear that our hypotheses about intentions, capabilities and activities have improved commensurately in scope and quality as more data comes in from modern collection methods.

> There is a strong presumption that additional data collection rather than improved analysis will provide answers to particular intelligence problems.[38]

The overload of information and the proliferation of fusion centers also had a fragmenting effect on the national security establishment, as the number of individuals with a broad overview of the functions of the entire establishment declined. It was common in the 1950s and 1960s to find project engineers or particularly knowledgeable generals with a grasp of the entire defense establishment's activities. By all accounts this kind of individual began to disappear in the late 1960s and 1970s. Other factors undoubtedly reinforced this trend, such as the rapid transfer of individuals from one post to the next before they had time to fully learn their jobs. But the very nature of intelligence necessitates secrecy, which is usually achieved through

37. Ibid., p. 342.
38. Ibid., p. 274.

the strict compartmentalization of information. Rigid compartmentalization of information within an organization can have unanticipated consequences, creating deep segmentation and parochialism
where a free exchange of ideas is essential. It can restrict both discussion and assessment to certain narrow factors and concerns only.
One estimate in 1979 was that there were between 150 and 200
specialized security classifications in the U.S. Defense Department,
each requiring particular clearances.[39] Such compartmentalized
channeling of information can make breadth of vision, not to mention
coordination, extremely problematic.

During this period the U.S. warning system had a poor record
of success, despite the increase in sophistication of the information
technology available to it. The Soviet intervention in Czechoslovakia,
the Tet offensive in Vietnam, and later the 1973 Yom Kippur War
were all missed by the system. No one can point to the definitive
causes of any of these failures, although a cottage industry has grown
up trying to do just that. Despite this, it does seem fair to remark
that, in the minds of many people inside the defense establishment,
sometime after the mid-1960s the quality of the organization began
to deteriorate. They also believe that the organization itself, rather
than individuals or ideologies, was to blame.[40]

One very threatening influence on the evolution of the American
warning system was the stationing of Soviet nuclear-firing submarines
near the Atlantic coastline. Since the 1950s, the Soviet Union has
had the ability to launch nuclear cruise missiles from submarines off
the Atlantic coast of the United States. This ability was preserved
throughout the 1960s, but the deployment in 1969 of the newly built
Yankee class of Soviet submarines marked a turning point in the
nuclear threat posed to the United States. Depending on tactics and
firing position, the Yankees were now able to fire SLBMs at U.S.
bomber bases and command centers with flight times ranging between
four and fifteen minutes. Since bomber bases and command centers

39. Edmund Brunner, Jr., *Perception and Strategic Warning*, p. 19.
40. This kind of comment is hard to document by its very nature. However, see
the interesting remarks of Admiral Elmo Zumwalt (U.S.N., ret.) in Roy Godson, ed.,
Intelligence Requirements for the 1980s: Analysis and Estimates (Washington, D.C.:
National Strategy Information Center, 1980), pp. 211–14.

were targets very sensitive to short flight time attacks, a new order of danger faced American nuclear forces. The danger was that Soviet Yankee-class submarines would fire their SLBMs and destroy the bombers before they could escape their bases and would further aim at Washington, NORAD, and at SAC headquarters in an effort to paralyze the retaliatory forces of the United States. Even if American forces could be paralyzed only temporarily, this just might be enough time to follow up with an all-out ICBM attack from Soviet missile fields.

Although the U.S. Navy's SOSUS network in the Atlantic could reasonably be expected to determine that Soviet SSBNs were within firing range of U.S. targets, the Soviets produced enough Yankees by 1971 to maintain a continuous presence of submarines. At any given moment a few submarines could be at sea, able to decapitate the American political high command from the body of its strategic forces. If the Soviets used tactics known as depressed trajectory launches, the political nerve center so carefully established during the Kennedy administration to control the nuclear forces could be lopped off in about five minutes' time. The fact that U.S. Navy antisubmarine forces would be able to destroy the Yankees after they fired their missiles would be little consolation.

The threat posed by the continued presence of Soviet SLBMs off the Atlantic coast has generally been underappreciated by students of the arms race. The efforts to establish reliable political control over the nuclear forces undertaken in the early 1960s were jeopardized because the White House, the National Military Command Center in the Pentagon, the CIA and NSA operations centers, the president's emergency airborne command post at Andrews Air Force Base, and all the other paraphernalia of the political high command could be wiped out in five minutes. The White House recognized the threat posed to the political command structure by September 1970, although the government had already begun efforts to manage this problem to the extent that it could be managed at all.[41]

Within the government, the military operations research com-

---

41. See H. R. Haldeman, *The Ends of Power* (New York: Quadrangle, 1978), pp. 86–88.

munity went to work on nuclear exchange modeling, which included simulating attacks on time-sensitive targets in order to develop a better understanding of the utility of different amounts of warning time.[42] The most important American response, however, was to expand and upgrade the sensors capable of detecting the launch of a Soviet SLBM. In the early 1970s early warning satellites were orbited. These satellites, descendants of the old MIDAS program, use infrared sensors to detect the hot boost plumes of either SLBMs or ICBMs. The current satellites go under the euphemism of the Defense Support Program (DSP) and are far more reliable than satellites of the early 1960s.[43] There are apparently three DSP satellites in orbit, providing overlapping coverage of the Soviet Union and China (for ICBM launches) and the Atlantic and Pacific oceans (for SLBM launches). The satellites transmit real-time information because of the nature of the SLBM detection problem. Two major ground stations, one near Denver and one in Alice Springs, Australia, are used to process this data before it is forwarded to NORAD and other command posts. Because of the extraordinary time pressures involved in warning of SLBM attack, data from the two ground stations is sent directly to SAC and the NMCC in the Pentagon and simultaneously distributed to NORAD.[44] The extent to which this erodes the system of checks and balances established around NORAD in the late 1950s is not known. It does illustrate, however, how the extraordinary compression of decision time may force organizational changes as well as changes in physical electronic networks.

In addition to the DSP satellites, two phased-array radars were constructed in the 1970s in Massachusetts and California to provide radar coverage of possible SLBM attack from either the Atlantic or the Pacific. Known as Pave Paws, they replaced an earlier radar system from the 1960s known as the FSS-7. One FSS-7 in Florida is cur-

42. See, for example, Jerome Bracken and James T. McGill, "A Convex Programming Model for Optimizing SLBM Attack of Bomber Bases," *Operations Research* 21 (January–February 1973): 30–36.

43. See "Improved U.S. Warning Net Spurred," *Aviation Week and Space Technology*, June 23, 1980, p. 38.

44. U.S. Senate, *Recent False Alerts*, p. 3.

rently planned to be maintained, along with a converted space-track-
ing radar known as the FPS-85, for ground-based coverage of SLBMs
launched from the Gulf of Mexico or Caribbean regions.

The evolution of American warning systems in recent years continues to follow the trends already under way, reinforced by technological advances. The merger of intelligence and warning networks
into a comprehensive early warning system has continued. The rising
political concern with arms control, and especially with arms control
verification, has enabled budgets for NTM verification systems to be
almost open-ended, and these systems can and do have important
spillover capabilities for warning. For example, a ground-based radar
known as Cobra Dane on Shemya Island, Alaska, was built in 1977.
Cobra Dane can track dozens of targets simultaneously and is used
to monitor Soviet missile tests of multiple independently targeted reentry
vehicles (MIRVs), providing information on the size and shape of
reentry vehicles launched in the Soviet Pacific Ocean test range.
Although Cobra Dane is an NTM intended to help monitor Soviet
missile developments, it has been described in declassified congressional studies of the American warning system.[45] Since other NTM
intelligence systems also possess important warning capabilities, we
could logically expect that they too had been integrated into the American warning system. Cobra Judy, for instance, is a smaller floating
version of Cobra Dane used aboard a Navy vessel. It is usually described as an NTM verification system to monitor Soviet missile tests,
but one would expect that at a certain level of alert or tension it would
be used for warning. In a crisis, a wide variety of reconnaissance
aircraft, ships, and submarines could also be switched from general
intelligence gathering to early warning. Were this switch to occur, it
would be instantly picked up by the Soviet warning and intelligence
system because of the altered radar patterns and communications traffic
of the American systems.

Another recent trend is the extension of the most modern warning technology to U.S. conventional and theater nuclear arms. The
U.S. Navy's satellite-based ocean surveillance system, which has al-

45. Ibid., p. 2.

38   WARNING AND INTELLIGENCE

ready been mentioned, is only one piece of a broader U.S. Navy
intelligence and warning network of data fusion centers that are known
as Fleet Ocean Surveillance Information Centers (FOSICs). FOSICs
receive data from satellites, ships, aircraft, agents in the field, and the
SOSUS network and compare the diverse information for warning of
buildups and for patterns of Soviet naval activity. A FOSIC for the
entire North Atlantic is located at U.S. Navy headquarters in Gros-
venor Square, London. It continuously transmits assessments to other
U.S. and NATO command posts.[46] Other FOSICs cover the ocean
regions of the world and coordinate information from hundreds of
land-based intelligence collection sites around the world. Facilities
for the Western Pacific are in Kamesya, Japan, and for the Mediterranean in Rota, Spain.

Other military services have data fusion networks comparable to
the Navy's FOSICs. The Army has the Beta project, begun in the
late 1970s, oriented toward warning and intelligence regarding Warsaw Pact army activities. The U.S. Air Force has similar networks to
monitor the Soviet Air Force. The warning and intelligence systems
have become so vast and produce so much specialized data that a
multilayered reporting and fusion organization has evolved to manage
the glut. These military warning and intelligence systems are tied in
to higher-level command centers responsible for warning of nuclear
attack, of course; they can also be targeted to collect information about
particular activities depending on the alert and tension level.

The extension to the armed services of sophisticated, interconnected warning and intelligence networks has led to a highly integrated coupling among forces designed for strategic, theater nuclear,
and conventional warfare. Although it has been possible, and even
fashionable, to make intellectual distinctions among the three kinds
of forces, in fact all three have become tightly integrated and interdependent, in large measure because they are bound together by the
same complex warning and intelligence system.

Finally, breakthroughs in computer technology and information
processing in recent years have made it possible to do things that were

46. "How We Spy on Argentina," p. 5.

never possible before. The Navy is able to mount a worldwide ocean surveillance program because computers can be used to correlate the vast amounts of data such a program generates. Sophisticated signal-processing routines, fast, reliable data transmission lines, and artificial intelligence methods applied to satellite photographs all depend on very large computers or, more likely, networks of geographically dispersed computers. Advances in software are a greater determinant of the viability of an ocean surveillance program than technological advances in the sensors themselves. One major reason that the Soviet Union lags the United States in this and related areas is that its computer industry is inferior to ours.

Some hint of what the modern computer can do may be gleaned from the COMINT programs of NSA. In a country as large as the Soviet Union, the number of daily electronic communications, both military and civilian, is astronomical. Computer storage, however, allows the instantaneous retrieval of information based on keywords. Voice transmissions still cannot be monitored without human listeners, although technological advances are being made in this area as well. The COMINT programs consist of receiving stations that are linked to analysis centers where computers are used to assist in interpreting the millions of messages that flow through the Soviet military and political bureaucracies. The technique used, described as random scanning dragnets or fishing expeditions, is made all the more effective by the growing reliance on microwave relays to transmit ordinary telephone calls.[47] In the early 1970s, reportedly, the United States was able to tune in on conversations between Soviet leaders as they drove around Moscow and talked via two-way radio.[48]

The application of computers to the task of collection and analysis of COMINT, satellite photographs, TELINT, and SIGINT can advance the state of the art of warning and intelligence greatly, if used properly. In the past, the greatest warning breakthroughs have relied chiefly on communications intelligence and cryptography to analyze

47. See "Colby Says N.S.A. Tapped Phone Calls of Americans," *New York Times*, August 7, 1975, p. 16; also James Banford, *The Puzzle Palace* (Boston: Houghton Mifflin, 1982).
48. Nicholas Danieloff, "How We Spy on the Russians," p. 25.

a tiny portion of an enemy's communications, generally high-level messages. In 1941, for instance, the United States was able to break the Japanese diplomatic codes but not the more critical ciphers of the Japanese Navy. Had the Japanese Navy's codes been systematically collected and cracked, strategic warning about the attack on Pearl Harbor might have been gained. As it was, the diplomatic communications between Tokyo and the Japanese embassy in Washington contained no direct hint of the military attack, so the communications intelligence that was gained gave an incomplete picture of the events of the final critical weeks before the attack. The Japanese, quite wisely, simply compartmentalized information about the surprise attack. Only the military knew of the timing of the attack on Pearl Harbor, and only parts of the diplomatic corps were informed about the diplomatic end game. As a result, this compartmentalization of information prevented the United States from seeing the whole picture. Similarly, the Ultra codes used against Nazi Germany often proved ineffective because the British were unable to penetrate most parts of the German Army. In addition, orders were often changed and plans revised at a lower level following the issuance of the high-level German orders.

Computer technology now makes it possible for intelligence to penetrate an enemy command organization on a system-wide basis, rather than just to insert a few probes into it here and there. The most important intelligence has typically come from proper interpretation of routine, low-level military activities. In World War II, for example, statistical techniques were applied to serial-number tracking of captured German equipment that enabled intelligence to estimate German war production and strength.[49] The Germans never thought to encrypt the serial numbers placed by manufacturers on tires, trucks, tanks, and planes, probably because to do so was not considered important, compared to the communications security needs of Hitler and the high command. These serial numbers, however, gave inval-

49. Richard Ruggles and Henry Brodie, "An Empirical Approach to Economic Intelligence in World War II," *Journal of the American Statistical Association*, 41 (March 1947): 72–91.

uable information about Germany's true strength, revealing which factories produced the lion's share of different kinds of military equipment. A few factories produced a majority of tanks, for example, and the serial numbers told which ones. This information was duly relayed to the strategic bomber forces, which could then target the most important industrial centers.

In the 1980s the aggregate collection and comparison of information from hundreds of programs across an enemy's entire command has been made possible using computers. Their ability to keep track of a variety of low-level activities enables them to give critical strategic warning. As a mundane, and hypothetical, illustration, if we could monitor the communications of the laundry facilities at Soviet ports we could probably get excellent strategic warning of when the surface and submarine forces were about to put to sea or had returned to port.[50] Correlated with other intelligence about the status of the Soviet Army and Air Force, such information could provide warning and insights about enemy intentions of a kind inconceivable in previous wars.

THE SOVIET SYSTEM

Looking at the Soviet warning system raises deeply troubling issues. Indeed, so does looking at the entire Soviet command structure. When it is examined as a system, and not merely as a physical collection of radars and computers, we see a consistency between doctrine and capability. The concept is a doctrine of preemptive attack, and the capability is a system of warning and command that supports just such a strategy.

The Soviet infatuation with preemption undoubtedly has strong ties to the stunning surprise of the Nazis' attack in 1941. However, not until after the death of Stalin did Soviet military literature begin to emphasize the importance of surprise and preemptive attack in the nuclear age.[51] Ever since that time, though the distinctions are not

---

50. This illustration was provided to the author by Admiral Noel Gaylor (U.S.N., ret.), August 10, 1982.

51. See John M. Caravelli, "The Role of Surprise and Preemption in Soviet Military Strategy," *International Security Review* 6 (Summer 1981): 209–36.

always precise, there has been a general attraction in the Kremlin to the concepts of surprise attack, preemptive attack, and automatic firing. During the mounting tension over the status of Berlin in 1959, for example, Premier Nikita S. Khrushchev warned Averill Harriman:

> Your generals talk of maintaining your position in Berlin with force. That is bluff. If you send in tanks, they will burn and make no mistake about it. If you want war, you can have it, but remember, it will be your war. Our rockets will fly automatically.[52]

The term "automatically" was emphasized later as Khrushchev's colleagues echoed this part of the threat. Further evidence of Soviet attraction to automatic firing policies occurred during the 1960 U-2 crisis. Deputy Secretary of Defense Roswell Gilpatric, when questioned in 1961 about Soviet control of their nuclear weapons, stated:

> With regard to top-level control over the use of nuclear weapons, the Soviets have not explicitly and formally identified where the responsibility for authorizing use resides, as has the United States. It can be presumed that in the U.S.S.R. this authority is in the hands of Khrushchev alone, or in the Presidium of the Central Committee. At the same time, Soviet statements have indicated that this authority may be delegated to the military under some circumstances. For example, shortly after the U-2 incident, Khrushchev said that Marshal Malinovsky was empowered to respond instantly with missile attack on any bases from which further U-2s might be sent.[53]

It would be a mistake of awesome proportions to discount such Soviet statements as mere political bluff. Soviet threats contain exaggeration, but they also have a rationale that gives us insight into their mentality. Although Khrushchev surely did not give nuclear use authority to one of his generals during the U-2 crisis, the threat is one that would have been inconceivable for a U.S. president to utter. It reflected a logic of war that has shown up in many other areas of Soviet nuclear force

---

52. The primary source for this is *Life* magazine, July 13, 1959, p. 33.

53. Letter from the Deputy Secretary of Defense to Senator Hubert Humphrey, August 23, 1961, contained in Disarmament Agency Hearings, U.S. Senate, Committee on Foreign Relations, Hearings on S. 2180, August 14, 15, 16, 1961, pp. 110–11.

development. Automatic or quick-launch systems have been a preeminent design goal for Soviet ICBM forces. Automatic quick-launch capabilities are not a by-product of Soviet technology; they are a guiding principle, and they have been an integral feature of the Strategic Rocket Forces (SRF) since their inception. In his memoirs, Khrushchev writes that one of the reasons he disliked the early SS-6 missile, tested in 1959, was that it could not "be fired at a moment's notice."[54] This was the missile that the West originally expected would form the backbone of the Soviet rocket force, the one that led Western intelligence agencies to predict the existence of a missile gap. The SS-6 was never deployed in substantial numbers. A considerable period went by without major deployments until the SS-7s and SS-8s were introduced in 1962 and 1963 respectively. Khrushchev recounts that the designers of these systems "tackled the problem of perfecting a rocket that could be launched on short notice."[55] Unlike the SS-6, the SS-7 and SS-8 had storable liquid fuel that gave them a quick-launch capability. These missiles were the kind needed by a warning system geared for preemptive attack.

General Daniel O. Graham, former director of the U.S. Defense Intelligence Agency, has stated that the Soviet Union actually adopted a launch-on-warning policy in the mid-1960s. This does not mean that the decision to launch nuclear weapons was turned over to a computer wired to a warning system. Rather launch on warning can include cases where military operators are given emergency authority to use nuclear weapons in advance of hostilities, and are further instructed to use this authority if there are indications of attack. Strictly speaking, a launch-on-warning strategy does not require any computers or radars, although as a practical matter these are necessary to implement it smoothly. One policy that could be pursued by a nation is to create everything necessary for a launch-on-warning strategy except giving out the emergency use authority to the military. No po-

54. *Khrushchev Remembers: The Last Testament* (Boston: Little, Brown, 1974), p. 50.
55. Ibid. See also Karl F. Speilmann, "A Multiple Approach Analysis of the SS-6 Program," in "Analyzing Soviet Strategic Arms Decisions," Institute for Defense Analyses, IDA Paper P-1256, Arlington, Va., April 1977.

litical leader in the Soviet Union (or the United States for that matter) is going to allow nuclear forces to be operated in a launch-on-warning mode in peacetime. It is far too dangerous, and literally begs for accidental war. But what can be done is to create the personnel and hardware organizations needed for launch on warning, things such as quick-reacting missiles, radars, and smoothly functioning command chains, while withholding the emergency authority to actually launch. In a crisis this authority can then be given with a simple prearranged codeword. It is this kind of arrangement that General Graham refers to when he states that the Soviet Union adopted a launch-on-warning policy.[56]

More doctrinal elaboration of the benefits of preemptive nuclear strikes could be seen in the 1970s. Soviet military writings began to stress the detection and countering of an opponent's attack *before* it is initiated. Not to be confused with a bolt-from-the-blue surprise attack, this amounts to getting in the first blow, immediately prior to an enemy's planned attack, and disrupting the opponent's first strike. In his 1974 book, *The Initial Period of a War*, General S. P. Ivanov emphasized the need for large preemptive strikes at the outset of conflict. This necessitates, in his view, the transfer into the prewar period of various planning functions that formerly occurred after a war's outbreak, because during the initial period of conflict it is unlikely that there would be sufficient time for proper planning.[57] As recently as July 1982, Defense Minister Dimitri Ustinov reiterated the idea that the United States should be denied the freedom of first use of nuclear weapons. At the same time he hinted at renewed Soviet interest in launch-under-attack policies:

> With the *present-day state of systems of detection, and the combat readiness of the Soviet Union's strategic nuclear means*, the USA will not be able to deal a crippling blow to the socialist countries. The aggressor will not be able to evade an all-crushing retaliatory strike. . . . The state

56. Daniel O. Graham, *Shall America Be Defended?* (New Rochelle, N.Y.: Arlington House, 1979), pp. 87–88 and p. 257.

57. General S. P. Ivanov, *The Initial Period of a War*, translations on U.S.S.R. Military Affairs, Joint Publications Research Service, Washington, D.C., January 1976.

of military potential and the military-technological potentials of the sides are such that the imperialist forces will not succeed in ensuring for themselves military superiority either at the stage of preparing a nuclear war *or at the moment when they try to start that war* [emphasis added].[58]

Imperatives of organization and time in the nuclear age have ruled out central control of Soviet military forces by the political leadership, as was the case in World War II under Stalin. The creation of peacetime institutions to monitor threatening events had as a necessary side effect a decentralizing effect on high-level information and authority. The very willingness of Khrushchev twenty years ago to suggest delegation of nuclear authority demonstrates a fundamental evolution from the Stalin era.[59] The widespread dissemination of a nuclear doctrine calling for intensive, coordinated military planning before a conflict, as suggested in General Ivanov's book, also reflects a less adversarial relationship between civil and military groups. These kinds of actions could hardly occur if the civil leaders of the Soviet Union still held the military in such deep distrust as is sometimes believed. Stalin's distrust was attested to by his military purges and his refusal to form a high military command (Stavka) until *after* the German invasion of his country. However, in recent times a smoother working relationship has developed between political and military leadership. The rising influence of the Soviet general staff, not only in bureaucratic terms, but also in gaining operational control over the military in peacetime, reflects the change. A great deal of authority is now delegated to the general staff. It is a matter of practical necessity, given the massive scale of the Soviet defense establishment.[60]

All evidence now points to the existence of peacetime institutions in the Soviet Union charged with monitoring the strategic and tactical

58. Remarks of Soviet defense minister Dimitri Ustinov, "For Averting the Threat of Nuclear War," *Pravda*, July 12, 1982, translated by the Information Department of the Soviet Embassy, Washington, D.C.

59. For arguments along similar lines, see Ross O'Donoghue, "A Viability Analysis of Stavka via Function," Defense Intelligence School, June 1977.

60. Some of this material is based on discussions from the Aspen Institute Seminar on Command and Control, Aspen, Colo., August 9–13, 1982.

warning situation for use in directing counteractions. The volume of intelligence and warning information streaming into the Soviet Union would alone require such institutions, since, in addition to the information from radars and satellites, the Soviets have constructed a large strategic warning system over the past twenty years. As far back as the 1962 Cuban missile crisis, the intelligence arm of the military, the GRU, was able to supply Khrushchev with information from telephone intercepts in Washington during the actual course of the crisis.[61]

Advances in computer storage enable the Soviets to choose from a list of stored telephone numbers that match activated microwave circuits, to select calls by computer, and to tape them for later analysis.[62] Although the most senior U.S. government officials have access to "scramblers" to encrypt their conversations or are able to use specially protected communications lines, the vast majority of middle managers who run the American security establishment have no access to this technology. Neither do the thousands of defense consultants and contractors. Computers enable the Soviets to piece together millions of these conversations, thus providing invaluable warning of impending events—just as they do for the U.S. in monitoring Soviet communications.

The Soviet trawlers forever "fishing" off America's coasts likewise play an important role, active as floating listening posts in conjunction with aerial reconnaissance flights from Cuba over the Atlantic coast of the United States.[63] Soviet photographic and ferret satellites also routinely monitor U.S. military activities. Indications are that these satellites are especially directed to watch the network of airborne command posts used for emergencies by SAC and the White House. A multiple launching of these special aircraft, which is unusual, could indicate that U.S. military preparations for a possible nuclear strike were underway.

In Europe, the Soviets' emphasis is on interception of NATO

61. Harry Rositzke, The KGB (New York: Doubleday, 1981), pp. 197–98.
62. Ibid.
63. See "Two Soviet Bombers Spy on New U.S. Carrier off Virginia," Baltimore Sun, January 27, 1982, p. 9.

communications and penetration of the highest levels of Allied governments. A reading of the spy history of the last decade alone should convince anyone that virtually all NATO European governments have been compromised. Less appreciated is the extent of the penetration, from the senior ministerial level all the way down to the lowly tactical communications clerk. Soviet military exercises actually estimate the point that the United States issues orders to use nuclear weapons and then preempt before such an action can take place.[64] The Soviets are said to have an uncanny ability to determine the exact timing of U.S. release of atomic weapons to military commanders.[65]

What is noteworthy about this ability is *not* the Soviets' thoroughgoing penetration of the NATO command. Rather, it is that they are able to make timely use of this information in exercises for preemptive attack by Soviet offensive forces. This reveals a vertical integration between their warning and intelligence systems and their nuclear forces, as has occurred in the United States.

The emphasis on preemption in Soviet peacetime doctrine is, of course, no guarantee whatsoever that preemption would actually be used in a crisis. Furthermore, it is unimaginable that the Soviets would operate their nuclear forces in a launch-under-attack mode during peacetime. Rather, one must consider how their nuclear doctrine might affect operating policy in a crisis, with information pouring into Moscow about American military buildups, and with Soviet forces placed on high alert. People do what they are trained and organized to do. The chief consequence of their emphasis on preemption may be that it serves as an indoctrinating force throughout their defense organization. Once such a view of war has been incorporated into the planning process, competing theories of conflict stand a diminished chance of receiving much attention, either in studies, in training, or in the competition within the bureaucracy for funding for alternative warning and intelligence systems. By building an arsenal and a training system directed toward preemptive attack, the

64. See "Improving Defense Concepts for the NATO Central Region," European-American Institute for Security Research, Report, April 1978, p. 23.
65. Ibid.

Soviets have precluded alternative strategies from consideration. Thus, it becomes ever more unlikely that plans would be changed at the last moment in a crisis.

IMPLICATIONS

Sophisticated systems to warn of nuclear attack are necessary for the protection of the United States. They are necessary not only for the protection of vulnerable strategic forces, such as bombers and sub-marines, but also because if an enemy knows that the United States has an effective warning system, it is less likely to attack in the first place. When both the United States and the Soviet Union possess effective warning systems, both sides have less incentive to launch an attack and the world is more stable as a result.

Therefore, if warning systems are built for the narrow purpose of protecting one's own strategic forces, stability appears to increase as a bonus side effect. The greater the investment in warning, it might seem, the greater the investment in peace. The immense investment in warning systems over the last two decades attests to the power of this perception. The sophistication of these systems, and their inter-connection, has advanced in a manner that defies comprehension. And this may be the heart of the problem.

Better warning may mean better security. But not always. There is more to it than the simple principle that "more warning means more stability." During the past twenty years both the United States and the Soviet Union have built highly interactive warning systems of incomprehensible complexity. With these systems tightly coupling the nuclear arsenals of each side, the effect of small perturbations is amplified throughout the entire nuclear force system.

The average person seems to realize, or at least intuit, the pos-sible consequences of such a situation. Since the early 1950s the specter of nuclear war by technical accident has been a pervasive theme of popular novels and movies. Indeed, the story from the 1950s of a flock of Canada geese that triggered the DEW Line into mistak-enly interpreting the event as an attack by Soviet bombers has been enshrined in the lore of the nuclear age. As warning systems became more sophisticated, variants of the story inevitably followed. In 1960, meteor showers and lunar radar reflections, rather than Canada geese, excited the new BMEWS, temporarily leading NORAD to believe that a Soviet missile attack was en route. In 1980, a 46-cent computer chip failed in the computer warning system, producing an image of a Soviet SLBM attack on the United States.

The official reactions to these stories tend to be defensive. Corrective actions are taken to prevent a repeat. Persons in the know about how the warning system actually functions take a dismissive attitude as well. Nobody wants accidental war, least of all the military. The system has been designed to make sure that the decision to go to war is not driven by a flock of geese or a defective computer chip. The arguments offered by experts as to why such an incident could not cause a nuclear launch seem persuasive to anyone who bothers to make even the most rudimentary investigation. Man is always in the decision loop, positive control is exercised at every point, and man will commit our country to whatever we do; computers won't. For whatever it is worth, I am convinced of the validity of these propositions, at least in the narrow sense in which they are offered.

Nonetheless, many people still remain unconvinced that all is well. There is a latent fear, almost an intuitive or folk wisdom belief, that any high-risk, tightly coupled military system built to control nuclear forces just cannot be all that safe, that something just has to go wrong in anything that complicated. These fears about the complexities of the nuclear warning system do not really have to do with specific design flaws. They are not engineering critiques about the radar cross-sections of Canada geese versus Soviet bombers or of redundancy levels in computer chips. Rather, they are intuitive statements based on living in the world.

Broadly speaking, people believe in Murphy's law ("if anything can go wrong it will"). They believe in it because it applies to the world of experience, and it applies with special force to large, technically complex systems. In the world in which people live, power grids fail, trains derail, bridges and dams fall down, DC-10 engines fall off, and nuclear power plants come close to meltdown. These things don't happen often, but they do occur. Recalling the chain of events behind some of these incidents is enough to convince one that the devil must be at work. A power failure in the Northeast in 1965 was studied and traced to a single inexpensive switch. It was said repeatedly after 1965 that such a cascading power blackout could never occur again, since the freak accident had been carefully considered in new designs based on the lessons of 1965. But it *did* happen again, in 1977 in New York.

The Ford Motor Company had every incentive to avoid the bad publicity that stemmed from its exploding Pinto gas tanks. However, even with sophisticated testing systems, computer simulations, and an army of quality control procedures, engineers, and inspectors, somehow the gas tank vulnerability problem slipped through cracks of all the layers of the Ford organization responsible for guarding against it.

The case of the DC-10s reinforces the popular belief in Murphy's law (which has led to Murphy's corollary, that is, "Murphy was an optimist"). Engines fell off an inspected airplane, leading to public outcry, high-level attention, and lawsuits. But then, even after repeated warnings, the same type of engine fell off the same type of plane two months later. Similarly, the cargo doors of the DC-10 blew out, not once but three times. Somehow word didn't get out to fix the doors, or it didn't get to the right people. Ultimately the blown-out cargo doors caused a plane crash with major loss of life.

The failures at the Three Mile Island nuclear power plant in 1979 came after innumerable engineering studies had been made on the safety of these plants. Nuclear power advocates had claimed, for instance, that getting hit by a meteor was far more likely than a major nuclear plant accident. Yet in retrospect we know that these analogies were invalid.

Intuitive notions of danger, of something "going wrong," do not address the same issue as an expert's narrow statement about a system working properly. When an expert states that a flock of geese or a lunar radar reflection will not trigger the automatic launch of a nuclear weapon, he or she is making a particular remark about a particular possibility. Our intuition, on the other hand, takes the flock of geese triggering World War III as an example of a wider concern.

In the world of experience, we feel, complex systems are bound to go awry, precisely because they *are* complex.[66]

Systems can go awry in many ways, *not* just in inadvertently starting a nuclear war. For warning systems, the danger of wrongly predicting a surprise attack, or indeed any kind of attack, haunts military people in the know. And their intuition about this potential failure, in an interesting way, parallels the average man's concern that the system will contribute to the initiation of war. It is not hard to understand why many persons in the U.S. security establishment, both military and nonmilitary, have doubts about the ability of the warning system to predict attack. Quite simply, the record has been terrible, despite all the technological improvements of the last twenty years. The Soviet intervention in Czechoslovakia, the Yom Kippur War, and the Argentine takeover of the Falkland Islands all caught the American government by surprise.

The experts fear that a Soviet attack on Europe or the United States will not be discerned by the warning system not so much because the attack might occur without indications, but because the indications might be confusing or ambiguous, or because the attack that takes place might not fit our preconceived notions of a Soviet attack. For a small number of stylized and highly practiced attacks, the warning system is likely to work well, just as it works well when a NORAD computer chip fails. However, within the Pentagon many people intuitively fear that even if a Soviet attack is detected in enough time to do something about it, the sheer incomprehensibility of the event may either paralyze political leaders or induce such chaos that no actions will be ordered in the brief time available. Over the past two decades, the movement toward direct involvement of political leaders in the warning process, bypassing the chain of military command, has created a centralization of authority which, in certain circumstances, makes the vast nuclear arsenal of the United States

66. For fascinating discussions of this, see Charles Perrow, "Normal Accident at Three Mile Island," *Society*, 18 (July/August 1981), pp. 17–26; also Perrow's *Complex Organizations* (Glenview, Ill.: Scott, Foresman, 1972). The investigations into the power blackouts in 1965 in the northeast and in 1977 in New York also drive home this point.

dependent on the actions of a single man. While there are positive reasons for organizing the system in this way, it is not without its vulnerabilities.

Every study of major failure in a complex technical system has one thing in common with studies of failure to react to surprise military attack: in retrospect, the cause of failure is always clear. Of course, this misses the point. The very nature of complex technical systems means that events are incomprehensible at the time something unusual is occurring. Even if years later someone will be able to sift through the evidence to sort "signals" from "noise," that is irrelevant to the problem of designing these systems for dependability and safety. As President Kennedy remarked about the origins of a World War III, it is of no consolation to say "if only we'd known." The logic of the situation will not be understood until after the damage is done.

Turning to the world of power plant failures, DC-10 failures, and nuclear power station accidents can reassure us of the validity of our intuitive concerns about these problems. In each of these examples, it was not the *isolated* accident that led to trouble, but a series of compound, and highly correlated events, which triggered a sequence of human, bureaucratic, and technical reactions. These reactions resulted in incorrect diagnoses of what was going wrong, which led to the initiation of actions that either had nothing to do with the problem or, even worse, exacerbated it. Taking the wrong corrective actions directed the limited available management attention to the wrong problem and allowed precious time to slip by.

Thus, we can see why a technical failure has never caused the inadvertent launching of a nuclear attack, despite the vast complexity of the warning and control system. The flight of geese, the lunar radar reflection, and the imperfect computer chip are all isolated events; they are not part of a compound or correlated sequence of failures and stimuli. Discrete accidents are easy to design against. With so many checks and balances, procedures for authentication of orders, and independent human interventions overlaid onto the control system for strategic weapons, the likelihood of accidental or inadvertent war is very, very low in peacetime. As each piece of the warning system is integrated with other pieces and with nuclear forces, a searching reappraisal of the decision mechanisms to launch the weapons is also undertaken. Each layer of the warning and intelligence system inspires new checks, new balances, and new authentication procedures. Indeed, the more complex the warning and control system the less the chance of an inadvertent launch, because of the disproportionate increase in the number of checks and balances designed to prevent this from occurring. Against the discrete accident, malfunction, or operator error the total system is massively redundant. The more complex, the more redundant. I believe the likelihood of nuclear war by pure technical accident is much lower today than it was twenty years ago, precisely because of today's more complex warning and control system.

While the complexity of the system has made us safer from accidental war it protects us only against the discrete, isolated failure. Multiple errors or malfunctions are a different matter altogether, because they invoke reactions by humans and involve organizational procedures and computers. The problem with compound accidents, especially those involving human behavior, is that the number of possible reactions is enormous and no design can protect against all of them. The likelihood that multiple events will lead to trouble increases when there is increased military activity. Thus, when forces are placed on alert, the complexity of the warning system may not only cease to provide redundancy; it may also amplify the mistakes. What set off the interlocking alerts of the European armies in 1914 was not the isolated assassination of the archduke in Sarajevo but the decision to mobilize. The effect of the thousands of orders issued was to create an unstoppable chain reaction of reinforcing alerts. The alerts acted like ratchets, step by step moving Europe into war but unable to function in reverse toward peace. In the summer of 1914 everything functioned the way it was supposed to. There were no accidents in the usual sense of the term. Accidents were not needed to drive Europe into conflict, because the war systems of the day stimulated each other into a frenzy. Political leaders lost control of the tremendous momentum built up when their armies went on alert. Only in retrospect, *always* in retrospect, can we see that the institutions designed to protect the peace moved the nations of Europe into war. Let us examine some of the implications of this theme for nuclear forces.

Tightly Coupled Forces

A major element in the evolution of both American and Soviet warning systems has been their thoroughgoing vertical integration with the nuclear weapons themselves. The transition from massive batch processing of warning and intelligence information to a near real-time continuous flow of information made the integration necessary. The result was a tightly coupled system in which a perturbation in one part can in short order be amplified throughout the entire system. The greatest single change in nuclear forces during the past twenty years is this shift from *loose* to *tight* coupling.

Two false alerts in 1979 and 1980 illustrate the strong interconnectedness of different parts of the nuclear forces. Both occurred at the NORAD headquarters inside Cheyenne Mountain, near Colorado Springs, Colorado. In the first, an operator mistake led to the transmission of an erroneous message that the United States was under nuclear attack.[67] This information was sent to NORAD fighter bases, and ultimately ten fighters from three separate bases in the United States and Canada were scrambled and sent airborne. Furthermore, U.S. missile and submarine bases across the nation automatically switched to a higher level of alert.

Several months later, in 1980, a failed chip in a minicomputer led to the transmission of a similar message to American forces. This time about a hundred B-52 bombers were readied for takeoff, as was

67. This particular incident took place on November 9, 1979. See "Error Alerts U.S. Forces to a False Missile Attack," *New York Times*, November 11, 1979, p. 30; "U.S. Aides Recount Moments of False Missile Alert," *New York Times*, December 16, 1979, p. 25. A description of the two NORAD false alarms that occurred seven months later can be found in "Brown Says False Alarm Cannot Activate Missiles," *New York Times*, June 18, 1980, p. A16; "False Nuclear Alarms Spur Urgent Effort to Find Flaws," *New York Times*, June 13, 1980, p. A16; "Missile Alerts Traced to 46¢ Item," *New York Times*, June 18, 1980, p. A16; "Pentagon Identifies Cause of False Missile Alerts," *Soviet Aerospace*, June 23, 1980, p. 58.

the president's emergency aircraft, the so-called NEACP (National Emergency Airborne Command Post), which is held at Andrews Air Force Base near Washington, D.C. The airborne command post of the U.S. commander in the Pacific actually took off from its base in Hawaii.

These incidents suggest some of the problems of a tightly coupled nuclear force and also illustrate how different nuclear forces are from conventional armies, navies, and air forces. For conventional forces of the kind used to wage world wars I and II and the wars in Korea and Vietnam, quick reaction was sometimes needed, but it was only essential when it was used to save a part of the force. For conventional armies, the key to survival was loose coupling. A part of the force could be sacrificed to save the whole, and pieces could be cut off without destroying the cohesion of the whole. When the U.S. Eighth Army was attacked by Chinese Communist forces in November 1950 it was able to save itself in long retreat because it sacrificed front-line units to protect itself. The command of the front-line units was left to the units involved, out of both necessity and military design. S. L. A. Marshall tells us that the battle between Chinese forces and the Eighth Army broke down into a series of relatively independent small fights, some of which were related and some of which were not.[68]

For nuclear forces, however, everything affects everything else. A seemingly small threat in one area, say one Soviet submarine, could wipe out much of the American bomber force, or it could paralyze the entire force by striking Washington and SAC headquarters if organizational countermeasures were not taken. To protect itself a nuclear force does the opposite of what a conventional army does. It tries to "manage" every small threat in detail by centralized direction, reliance on near real-time warning, and dependence on prearranged reactions. The result is a system in which relatively small stimuli in one part produce vast reverberations throughout the rest of the system.

Tightly coupled systems are notorious for producing overcompensation effects. Because of the amplification that characterizes the information processing found in them this is not surprising. Over-

68. S. L. A. Marshall, *The River and the Gauntlet* (New York: Morrow, 1953).

compensation can be seen in the missile alert example. What turned out to be a malfunctioning 46-cent computer chip initiated a chain of events thousands of miles away in Washington and Hawaii. Had the accident proceeded a bit longer the president of the United States would have had to be awakened, in this particular case at 2:30 in the morning, to be told he had fourteen minutes to get out of the White House and to decide on a retaliatory plan in the event that the attack was real, and even less time to get on the Hot Line to Moscow. Nearly a hundred B-52s would have been launched to airborne positions over the Arctic, alert messages sent to ICBM crews, and warning messages sent to U.S. military units from Korea to Germany.

The missile alert in question, of course, did not lead to such actions, let alone to an automatic launch of American nuclear weapons. But to argue that the major lesson of the NORAD missile alerts of 1979 and 1980 is that the warning system proved itself is to miss the forest for the trees. They revealed a deeper, more fundamental truth about nuclear forces, that is, that over the past twenty years they have developed into highly interdependent synergistic systems. Under peacetime conditions, the system's massive complexity does prevent isolated accidents from leading to catastrophe. This is why NORAD and other commands were able to deal safely with some fifteen hundred false alarms in 1979.[69] In none of these incidents was the system in danger of going out of control. But during heightened military activity, such as an alert, the system is likely to become even more tightly coupled than it ordinarily is. Intelligence sensors will be switched on to their warning functions, and virtually every scrap of an already overwhelming amount of information will be reported to the various headquarters.

Even in peacetime, one can detect the entire system responding to a very small technical stimulus. On a full alert, with worldwide warning and intelligence sensors flooding the headquarters with information, it is safe to say that much stronger reactive dynamics would drive the system this way and that. Furthermore, under alert conditions the institutional checks and balances that ordinarily dampen the

69. U.S., Senate, *Recent False Alerts*, p. 4.

internal overcompensation dynamics would be removed, either totally or partially, depending on the level of the alert. That, after all, is what it means to go on alert. At the highest levels of alert, (which have never come close to taking place), the coupling might become so tight, and the checks and balances so removed, that the stability of the command system itself would be in doubt.

The tendency for the nuclear force system to become even more tightly coupled on alert also has implications for the centralized control of these forces. The problem is especially severe for the theater nuclear forces in Europe (see chapter 5) and at sea. Most military organizations do not send every small problem to the attention of the top hierarchy, but operate on a much looser basis, handling problems and incidents as low in the organization as realistically possible. Historically, military forces manage the complexity of battle through their hierarchical structure. Pieces of the organization concentrate their attention on the immediate local problem, ignoring what is occurring elsewhere on the front.

In sharp contrast to traditional military organization, the structure of nuclear command systems is nonhierarchical. Hierarchical structure, which divides an organization into units that are subdivided into smaller units and are again subdivided repeatedly, with a pyramidal authority structure imposed on each successive partitioning, is the prevalent system for business, military, and government organizations. The divergence from hierarchy in nuclear command systems should be an immediate tip-off that things really are different for these systems.[70] The warning and intelligence networks of the United States bypass much of the military command structure, reporting directly to the political leadership. Effective warning of nuclear attack depends on data fusion centers being linked with each other and with the nuclear forces, not according to hierarchical principles but according to compartmentalized channels in which timeliness and security matter more than pyramidal authority. The fact that the warning and intelligence system is operated by a hierarchical organization of peo-

---

70. For a discussion of the prevalence of hierarchical organization see Herbert A. Simon, *The Sciences of the Artificial* (Cambridge, MIT Press, 1969), chap. 4.

ple, namely the U.S. military, should not obscure the divergence from hierarchy caused by interlinked computers, sensors, communication lines, and compartmentalized intelligence channels. Even the many data fusion centers are designed to correlate information from distant parts of the organization, rather than to coordinate information in order to better control the units immediately below it in authority. With this kind of structure it is not surprising that tight coupling results. Stimuli to different parts of the organization instantly excite other warning centers, cutting across pyramidal authority lines and involving the entire organization in the management of potential threats to its safety—even small ones.

The appropriate models for nuclear command organizations, then are other tightly coupled complex systems, not the classical military organizations that fought World War II. A better analogy is a control system for a nuclear power plant, albeit on a microscopically small scale. The operators of a nuclear power plant are themselves organized hierarchically, but their complex power plant is not, and this results in an irreconcilable tension. The personnel all have pay and grade ranks, and each employee is aware of who his or her superior is. At the pinnacle is the president of the utility who is by legal and social custom empowered to direct all actions within the power plant and who therefore possesses central control over what does and does not happen. In most cases, this central control works smoothly. In a crisis, however, the utility president does not really have central control, even though lip service is given to the concept. He depends on a great many technicians, on the reactor's designers, and on those charged with keeping it in working order. Most of all, he depends on the reactor system itself not to go too far out of whack.

For nuclear forces under peacetime conditions or even mild tension, centralized political control may likewise be quite adequate. But during a very intense alert, or during a conventional or theater nuclear war, centralized control may become difficult or impossible. In such circumstances, the information from warning and intelligence systems will overwhelm political authorities and their staffs. Then, one could expect what usually occurs when centralized direction is artificially enforced on a system that is not compatible with it. Some parts of the system will continue executing long-planned standard operating procedures, regardless of their relevance to the situation. Other parts of the system may simply "hang" in the air, awaiting detailed orders from a higher headquarters that is unprepared or unable to provide them because it doesn't understand the situation or because it is inundated with incomprehensible warning and intelligence information. This "hanging" behavior can be expected to occur within parts of the organization that are close to the political control centers but lack their own command authority. In the United States this describes the very National Military Command System set up in 1962 to be the central portal through which the president commands the nuclear forces. In the Soviet Union it is likely that their general staff would be in a similar position.

Interactions

The interactions of American and Soviet nuclear forces are often seen as long-term moves in the arms race. The Soviets build an antiballistic missile system, and a few years later the United States counters it with MIRVs. Or the United States builds a fleet of Polaris submarines, and a few years later the Soviets deploy a new array of ASW systems. This has led to the characterization of the arms race as an action-reaction process. But there is another kind of action-reaction process that has been much less studied and is potentially much more dangerous.

The tight coupling of nuclear forces that has occurred over the past twenty years is not limited to American, or even to Soviet, forces. Along with the expansion of sophisticated warning and intelligence systems has come a tight coupling of American with Soviet forces, one to the other. In certain respects, American and Soviet strategic forces have combined into a single gigantic nuclear system. What cements the coupling is the warning and intelligence networks of each side. If the situation were not potentially so grave, we could dismiss this as science fiction.

This mutual coupling occurs because a threatening Soviet military action or alert can be detected almost immediately by American warning and intelligence systems and conveyed to force commanders. The detected action may not have a clear meaning, but because of its possible consequences protective measures must be taken against it. The action-reaction process does not necessarily stop after only two moves, however. It can proceed to many moves and can, and often does, extend from sea-based forces to air- and land-based forces because of the effect of tight coupling. In certain political and military situations, this action-reaction process can be described as a cat-and-mouse game of maneuvering for geographic and tactical position. In more ominous circumstances it may be seen as a jockeying for positions before the first salvo of an all-out war.

The linkup between American and Soviet nuclear forces has been accompanied by other developments. In addition to the improved American (or Soviet) ability to monitor enemy forces that has led to faster counterreactions, intelligence systems now have the ability to monitor not only enemy military units but also enemy warning and intelligence systems themselves. In addition the possibility exists that each side's warning and intelligence systems could interact with the other's in unusual or complicated ways that are unanticipated, to produce a mutually reinforcing alert. Unfortunately, this last possibility is not a totally new phenomenon; it is precisely what happened in Europe in 1914. What *is* new is the technology, and the speed with which it could happen.

By using COMINT, SIGINT, and other means, it has become possible to tap into an opponent's military warning and intelligence network. The full extent of this has been appreciated by only a handful of specialists. Some examples of current capabilities in this area have become public despite the blankets of security that justifiably cover the field. In 1969, for example, the North Koreans shot down an American EC-121 reconnaissance aircraft in international air space. At a news conference shortly thereafter, President Richard Nixon disclosed that not only was the aircraft in international air space, but the United States *knew* that the Soviets and the North Koreans were aware that it was. This (apparently) inadvertent presidential remark revealed the existence of an American ability to "read" Soviet radar scopes and to "listen" to the Soviet military as they tracked the EC-

121. Apparently, U.S. COMINT, SIGINT, and other sensors were penetrating the Soviet early warning and radar-tracking networks.[71]

Another instance of penetration of one intelligence system by another came to light in 1975 when the operation of the highly classified Holystone missions by the U.S. Navy became public. These missions employed specially fitted attack submarines to enter Soviet territorial waters in order to monitor their SLBM tests. Perhaps more important, according to one source, "the submarines were able to plug into Soviet land communication cables strewn across the ocean bottom and thus were able to intercept high level military messages and other communications considered too important to be sent by radio or other less secure means."[72] The use of hard wire lines for communication with their nuclear forces has long characterized Soviet operating procedure; it is a defining feature of what they consider to be their most important command information.[73] The ability to eavesdrop on highly secret communications about the Soviet nuclear control system could be exploited to great advantage for warning of attack. It might constitute the ultimate early warning information, if integrated with American nuclear forces. Not only might it tell of impending attack but it could also detail the characteristics of the oncoming attack.

An example of mutually interacting strategic moves occurred in April 1978, when two Soviet Yankee-class submarines moved unusually close to the eastern coastline of the United States. In such close-in positions these nuclear-missile-equipped submarines had the capability of launching attacks with minimal warning on bomber bases, command and control centers, submarine bases—and on Washington itself. Their movements were tracked by the underwater SOSUS acoustic detection network operated by the U.S. Navy.

The American response to this provocation was to "let the Soviets

71. This description was given on ABC television network's "20/20" on December 12, 1979.

72. "Submarines of U.S. Stage Spy Missions inside Soviet Waters," *New York Times*, May 25, 1975, pp. 1, 42.

73. See, for example, Norman Polmar, "Soviet C³," *Air Force Magazine*, June 1980, pp. 58–66.

know that we know" how close in they had moved, which was done by raising the alert level at several SAC bomber bases and ultimately by dispersing the aircraft to other bases. Such an action in a crisis might suggest that the bomber force was preparing to launch against the Soviet Union. Presumably, these actions were detected almost immediately by Soviet electronic reconnaissance satellites or by other technical means. The Soviet submarines soon retreated from their close-in positions to their usual deployments farther out in the Atlantic.[74]

These examples suggest several problems of mutual interactions. The Soviet-American strategic forces are growing increasingly coupled in near real time by the integration that has developed between intelligence collection systems and the strategic forces. This development naturally and inevitably has arisen due to the emergence of continuous information collection and produces tightly coupled interactions between the two strategic forces, as suggested in figure 2.1.

Fig. 2.1 The coupling of nuclear forces

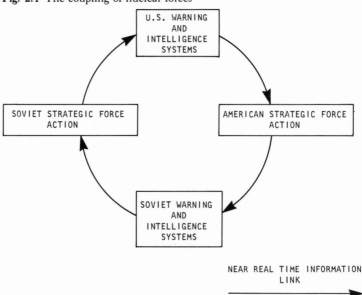

74. "A Soviet War of Nerves," *Newsweek*, January 5, 1981, p. 21.

The complexity of the warning system led to an increase in the number of checks and balances governing the use of nuclear forces, and for similar reasons a mutually reinforcing alerting process in peacetime does not escalate to the brink of war. More will be said about this shortly, but it is important neither to overestimate nor underestimate the consequences of such a process. In peacetime non-alert conditions, the response to a single discrete threat can be to take a small number of precautionary moves. If Soviet SSBNs move un-usually close to the Eastern coast, then SAC bombers can be removed to different airfields. One reason this peacetime cat-and-mouse game is controllable is that the United States simultaneously can observe that other Soviet arms are either dormant or are operating in expected fashion. Similarly, the Soviets observe that only American bombers are active, and that American SSBNs in port, for example, are in-active. On the respective warning and intelligence staffs, the human operators can observe this isolated event, which is potentially threat-ening but nonetheless stands out against the broader context of force deployments that are not especially threatening.

One additional reason that these interactions are unlikely to get out of control in peacetime is the relatively passive nature of the Soviet nuclear forces. On a day-to-day basis, the Soviet Union does not operate its nuclear forces with anything like the degree of readiness displayed by the United States. Over 80 percent of their nuclear sub-marines are in port on average, compared to only 30 percent for the United States. Their ICBMs and bombers also operate at much lower peacetime alert levels.[75] This trend is changing, however. Increas-ingly, Soviet forces operate on a worldwide basis distant from home ports and bases. They also employ a more active warning and sur-veillance system to monitor American forces, relying on aerial recon-naissance flights and spy satellites that increasingly supply continuous information directly to their combat forces.

In peacetime the interactions between the two forces are char-acterized by isolated threatening actions, which can be managed pre-cisely because of their isolation from the synergies and interdepen-

75. Ibid.

dencies within the nuclear forces. For more or less the same reason that the warning system is able to handle the Canada geese problem, institutional mechanisms can manage this kind of problem. Some countermeasures and precautions can be taken, without upward momentum driving the system to full alert.

But once warning and intelligence systems are stimulated beyond a certain threshold, or once a certain level of alert has been ordered by political or military authorities, the situation may alter dramatically. The interdependencies and synergies that were safely ignored during the peacetime cat-and-mouse game then begin to enter the picture. Tight coupling of the forces increases, information begins to inundate headquarters, and human, preprogrammed-computer, and organizational responses are invoked. Each response, whether it arises from a human operator or a computer, is intended to meet some narrow precautionary objective, but the overall effect of both Soviet and American actions might be to aggravate the crisis, forcing alert levels to ratchet upward worldwide. Although each side might well believe it was taking necessary precautionary moves, the other side might see a precaution as a threat. This would in turn click the alert level upward another notch.

Beyond a certain level not only is a mutually reinforcing alert possible, but there would be major political consequences as well. The alert itself undoubtedly would contribute to the political tension because, fundamentally, decision makers would know how impossible it is to separate military moves, however precautionary, from political ones. During the crisis it would not be clear that a certain enemy action was indeed precautionary, and this very incomprehensibility would drive the mutual stimulation. In particular, if the Soviet Union, which inactively operates its nuclear forces, actually seemed to be going on alert, this would be a shock that would trigger hundreds of preprogrammed American responses.

Whether or not such a chain-reaction alert could lead to war is highly uncertain and is probably not the right question. That the alerting process could cause someone to launch a nuclear weapon is difficult to imagine, stated in these terms. Unfortunately, it is not all that difficult to envision a political crisis leading to an alert, and the alerting process escalating until NATO was forced to disperse its nuclear weapons from their storage positions (see chapter 5) or until conventional attacks were authorized against Soviet or U.S. submarines patrolling near enemy coasts. It is also possible to imagine a mutual alerting process reaching the point where interference or direct attack of satellites was undertaken, or where spontaneous evacuation of Soviet and American cities would occur for civil defense reasons. Few people would disagree that operating nuclear forces at such high states of alert in this environment could easily tip over into preemptive attacks and all-out war. Each nation might not want war but might feel driven to hit first rather than second. Instead of war versus peace, the decision would be seen as either striking first or striking second.

It is perhaps too easy to exaggerate the nightmarish process described here. Were it not for the history of the outbreak of World War I, it might seem alarmist. Yet it is even more dangerous to underestimate the situation's hazardous potential, especially if this is done by extrapolating peacetime interactions into an environment of intense political crisis. This would miss some of the fundamental characteristics of nuclear forces.

Reactions to Compound Stimuli

An example of compound warning stimuli occurred in 1956 and illustrates how a warning system can contribute to the perception of danger. In early November at the same time as the British and French attack on Suez, the Hungarian uprising was taking place. TASS, the Soviet press agency, was drumming up fears of worldwide nuclear war. Moscow issued a communique to London and Paris strongly hinting that rocket attacks against these cities were being considered, and, in a separate communique to Washington, Moscow suggested that joint U.S.-Soviet military action should be taken in Suez.[76] This last message was received at the White House in the late afternoon of November 5.

Against this context, on the same night, the following fourfold

76. Herman Finer, *Dulles over Suez* (Chicago: Quadrangle, 1964), pp. 418–21.

coincidence took place. The headquarters of the U.S. military command in Europe received a flash message that unidentified jet aircraft were flying over Turkey and that the Turkish air force had gone on alert in response. There were additional reports of 100 Soviet MiG-15s over Syria and further reports that a British Canberra bomber had been shot down also over Syria. (In the mid-1950s only the Soviet MiGs had the ability to shoot down the high flying Canberras.) Finally, there were reports that a Russian fleet was moving through the Dardanelles. This has long been considered an indicator of hostilities, because of the Soviet need to get its fleet out of the Black Sea, where it was bottled up in both world wars. The White House reaction to these events is not fully known, but reportedly General Andrew Goodpaster was afraid that the events "might trigger off all the NATO operations plan." At this time, the NATO operations plan called for all-out nuclear strikes on the Soviet Union.

As it turned out, the "jets" over Turkey were actually a flock of swans picked up on radar and incorrectly identified, and the 100 Soviet MiGs over Syria were really a much smaller routine escort returning the president of Syria from a state visit to Moscow. The British Canberra bomber was downed by mechanical difficulty, and the Soviet fleet was engaging in long-scheduled exercises. The detection and misinterpretation of these events, against the context of world tensions from Hungary and Suez, was the first major example of how the size and complexity of worldwide electronic warning systems could, at certain critical times, create a crisis momentum of its own.

The fourfold compound events in the Suez incident did not lead to war. However, SAC was put on a heightened state of alert in response to the crisis. Furthermore, the fourfold coincidence was, in a probabilistic sense, independent. That is, the events were not correlated one with the other by an underlying decision in Moscow to place its forces on a heightened alert. Had this taken place the compound events interpreted by the United States would not have been coincidences at all. They would have been part of a general, and more ominous, Soviet response.

Even with these caveats the Suez incident shows an interesting feature of reliance on warning systems that cover a multiplicity of phenomena over a widespread geographic area. Turkish radars, listening posts in the Dardanelles, and communications intelligence from Syria and the Soviet Union each contributed to an overall picture of what was going on. In this manner the sensors all "worked." However, the simultaneity of the events, which was an unfortuitous and arbitrary accident, was interpreted as prima facie evidence that they were all related.

Once again, in retrospect it was easy to see that there was actually no danger of attack. Each individual event could be explained as independent of the others. But in November 1956, at the time they were happening, the compound events did not seem benign. There is a natural tendency for the United States to be suspicious of the Soviet Union and to expect the worst. When warning incidents appeared simultaneously, the simultaneity itself contributed to the belief in Washington that the situation really might be dangerous.

The warning and intelligence systems of 1956 were primitive compared with those built over the next twenty-five years. Not only have warning systems improved technically; more important, both in the number of phenomena covered and their geographic spread the U.S. coverage of the Soviet Union—and the Soviet coverage of America—has increased immensely. Conceptually, each additional system that covers a part of the Soviet Union contributes a piece of the overall picture to a central headquarters. At the headquarters, information from the many warning and intelligence information channels is superposed. The change over the quarter century since the Suez crisis has been in the increase in the number of input information channels feeding into the superposition.

This trend would seem to make it more likely that simultaneous events picked up by warning and intelligence sensors would, by the very reason of their simultaneity, be interpreted at headquarters as related. Even if the Soviets were to increase their military activity in some way, random *unrelated* events would still be occurring within their system which, when seen by the United States, could be taken as prima facie evidence of coordination and intimate relationship. Since no one in the United States has ever seen the Soviet Union go on alert, especially a nuclear alert, the task of discerning a pattern in observed events is difficult enough. But due to the proliferation of information channels that cover the Soviet Union, random events would superimpose a much stronger random pattern on the observations of a directed alert today than two decades ago.

The massive redundancy inherent in a system as complex as the American nuclear forces mitigates the danger of a war resulting from a single technical accident. It very likely mitigates the danger of war from even a handful of such isolated stresses. When the stresses occur together in time, the situation is a bit more dangerous. The situation becomes very dangerous, however, when the stresses occur in the midst of a Soviet-American crisis. The real danger during Suez occurred because the simultaneous incidents took place during a political crisis. In a future crisis, one in which nuclear forces are placed on increased alert as a demonstration of political resolve, the warning system may have to contend with a strong random input of simultaneously threatening events. Some of the events will be part of the directed alert and some won't, but the system will not be able to discern the difference. In such a future crisis, going to high levels of alert could be a much more dangerous game than it was in the 1950s or 1960s.

Ambiguous Warning

Ambiguity is defined in Webster's Dictionary as intellectual uncertainty and "the condition of admitting of two or more meanings." Anyone familiar with retrospective case studies of warning and surprise attack knows how easy it is to misread a threatening military situation. At Pearl Harbor, the ambiguity resulted from a fragmented intelligence bureaucracy's inability to centralize all the indicators at one time and in one place.[77] In 1941, although Stalin had repeatedly heard from many different sources that Hitler intended to attack, he

---

77. Which is not to imply proper centralization or coordination would have averted the surprise. See Roberta Wohlstetter, *Pearl Harbor, Warning and Decision* (Stanford, Calif.: Stanford University Press, 1962).

refused to take even basic precautions to lessen the vulnerability of his forward armies, for fear of provoking the Germans.

In both individuals and organizations there is a tendency to ignore warning of incomprehensible events. Day-to-day operations condition us to believe the worst will not happen, and generally it doesn't, making this a most effective kind of conditioning.

As we have mentioned previously, if there is evidence of an incoming enemy missile attack, the commander-in-chief of SAC (CINCSAC) has the authority and responsibility to launch the nuclear bomber force in order to protect it. This decision would have the most serious consequences, because a launch would be observed immediately by Soviet spy satellites and could trigger a dangerous counterreaction. When launched, the bomber force does not proceed with an attack upon the Soviet Union, but has orders to go to holding positions where it awaits orders either to continue with the attack or return to bases. This all sounds workable, and it is practiced repeatedly by SAC. There are hundreds of bombers with nuclear weapons aboard, and no one is going to launch this system into action frivolously. Nonetheless, especially if a crisis were underway, a full-scale launch of the SAC bomber force would have enormous international repercussions. A political storm was created over the sounding of false civil defense messages in 1970 and the missile false alarms in 1979 and 1980. In both cases newspapers and television carried editorials for weeks demanding an end to this sort of thing. And in these cases there was no launch of any nuclear forces. People just don't like to be reminded that the United States has a nuclear force that can instantly turn someone's pleasant afternoon into a traumatic confrontation with the apocalypse.

My guess is that if it turned out there was no real Soviet attack a precautionary launch of the SAC bomber force would still create, at a minimum, a congressional-media storm that could turn the U.S. Air Force inside out. It could give the Soviet Union its greatest propaganda device since World War II, and it could do incalculable political damage to any president who didn't disavow responsibility for it. For these reasons, and undoubtedly many more, there has never been a precautionary launch of American bombers since the founding of the Strategic Air Command in 1946.

Now one begins to see the problem. It is one thing to err on the side of caution, but caution can be carried so far that the bomber force might be wiped out in an actual Soviet attack. A more than half-serious chart is used at the MITRE Corporation to convey this notion, and to illustrate the powerful part that individual beliefs and incentives play when we try to interpret the meaning of a potentially threatening event. Figure 2.2 tries to capture the essence of the decision to launch the bombers as seen by CINCSAC, using the terminology of the MITRE experts. The entries in the boxes describe the "payoff" to the SAC commander.

If a surprise attack were to occur, say, on a peacetime winter night at 2:30 in the morning, perhaps with a snowstorm going on, the chance that U.S. bombers would be launched is at best not certain. Three or four Soviet submarines on each coast, appearing to be on routine patrol, could be ordered to fire upon hearing some prearranged codeword over Radio Moscow. Conceivably this surprise attack could be coordinated with the sabotage of the Defense Support Program ground stations in Australia and Colorado. The incapacitation of these "soft" facilities would tip off NORAD that something was wrong. However, even if it took only three or four minutes to check the problem, that might be enough time for the Soviets to catch the bombers on the ground.

How can a warning system be designed to prevent this kind of attack? The answer is, it can't. Because a Soviet surprise attack is

Fig. 2.2 The decision to launch the bombers

CINCSAC's CHOICE	SOVIET ATTACK UNDERWAY	NO SOVIET ATTACK UNDERWAY
LAUNCH THE BOMBERS	DEAD HERO	COURT MARTIALED, AT BEST
DON'T LAUNCH THE BOMBERS	DEAD BUM	——

virtually unimaginable in peacetime, human operators would hesitate and rely on the peacetime checks and balances designed to keep the force from accidentally going to war. The key vulnerabilities here are a mind-set in which nuclear attack and war are unthinkable and a peacetime system of institutional checks and balances that dampens the behavior of the tightly coupled network. Improving the physical warning sensors and their communication lines might alleviate this problem, but it would not solve it altogether.

What is more, not only might CINCSAC be unable to believe that it was a nuclear attack, so might other operators, including the president. Because decades have passed without attack, and because of the unthinkable implications of authorizing a nuclear war, they might be unable to act immediately on the news that the dreaded ultimate event had actually arrived. Undeniable authentication of Soviet attack would certainly become available eventually. But in the event of surprise attack, with only minutes in which to launch the bomber force and to launch the missiles before their destruction by incoming warheads, it is entirely conceivable that the president, mindful of the impact on the nation and the world of a misreading of the situation, might be paralyzed into inaction, or might desperately search for more information and advice while missile warheads exploded over Washington, Omaha, Colorado Springs, and missile and bomber fields across the nation. It is ironic indeed that the many peacetime checks and balances that prevent a mistaken warning from leading to a nuclear weapon launch and the centralized involvement of the president both in the warning and control system might actually increase the vulnerability to genuine surprise attack. The very procedures that prevent accidents in peacetime could lock the entire arsenal into the off position. Not just CINCSAC and the president, but many other operators throughout the command system, could be so stunned and disbelieving when told that the attack was real that they might also refuse to take immediate action. Because of the way the system is organized to prevent accidental war in the peacetime state, they could block retaliatory actions in a surprise attack.

Thus, vulnerability to surprise attack in peacetime increases because of the checks and balances intended to prevent accidental war.

When a crisis already exists, however, the system works differently. The president, CINCSAC, and everybody else are more able to believe an attack might take place. Also, as the alert level increases, the checks and balances are removed. This can lead to the other danger described: the dampening of stimuli is lessened, leading to overcompensation dynamics and mutually reinforcing Soviet-American alerts. Above some bilateral alert threshold, command stability itself might be in question, leading to accidental or preemptive war.

However, there are many gradations of alert, and the exact threshold when stability is lost is difficult to know in advance. Some increases in alert level would not threaten a loss of control but instead would reinforce in the minds of political leaders the dangers of going to a higher alert. For this reason, the role of the Soviet and American political leaders in an acute crisis might be to dampen the internal and mutual dynamics of an overstimulated warning and intelligence system. Long-planned precautionary and necessary countermeasures might be overruled at the last minute by a president who believed they would induce so much Soviet overcompensation, which would require still greater U.S. counterreactions, as to lead events beyond the president's, or anyone's, control.

This dampening behavior is not unusual. During the Soviet invasion of Czechoslovakia in 1968, NATO cancelled routine reconnaissance flights over West Germany to avoid giving the Soviets the impression NATO was increasing its military activities. Soviet fears were allayed, but valuable intelligence was lost as well. During the Cuban missile crisis President Kennedy reportedly ordered the fuses and warheads removed from American Jupiter missiles in Turkey to forestall any sort of accident in the tense environment. And during the Soviet-inspired crackdown in Poland in 1981, NATO cut back its intelligence collection efforts in order not to provoke Soviet counteractions. For low- and medium-level alerts, at least, there apparently is political pressure to "de-alert" some parts of the forces. Under certain circumstances this tendency could create a tempting opportunity for preemption, especially given the Soviets' fascination with this strategy.

Surprise nuclear attack on the United States is not a recommended course of action. Just as things can go wrong for the president and SAC, so too can they go wrong for the Soviet Union. But there is a point worth making here. In the 1950s, there was great concern about surprise attack in the United States. Probably this concern was exaggerated. The lesson learned, however, was that American nuclear forces should be designed not to depend on warning for their survival, that is, they should not be vulnerable to surprise enemy attack. Over the past twenty years the nuclear forces have become more vulnerable to sudden attack, and the force now depends on a complex warning and intelligence system for its survival.

In the past twenty years there has also been a sharp decline in discussion about and consciousness of surprise nuclear attack. The "bolt-from-the-blue" attack is now considered such an unfashionable topic that it is almost never discussed seriously by students of nuclear strategy. What is ironic, however, is that the price paid for the redundancy of checks and balances intended to dampen the strong dynamics within the forces has been a corresponding increase in the system's peacetime vulnerability to surprise attack. This increased vulnerability is less a function of any physical shortcoming, such as inadequate radar power or insufficient hardening to blast effects, than it is a consequence of the nature of the system. A highly centralized, tightly coupled system has very limited ability to respond to an unimaginable event whose occurrence is counted highly unlikely.

There is a lesson in the greatest surprise attack and disaster in American military history, Pearl Harbor. There, the American military establishment failed to predict the surprise attack and failed to take protective countermeasures. Since U.S. military forces were loosely coupled in 1941, however, their overall survival did *not* depend on a functioning warning system. America was able to go on to defeat Japan and Germany decisively because it had so much military and economic slack that it could afford to lose pieces of itself without dragging the whole system down to catastrophe. Although much of the Pacific Fleet and Army was destroyed in 1941, this shock was not enough to destroy America's military capability. Today, however, the danger is that the changes in the warning system over the past two decades may have created vulnerabilities of a kind undreamed of in 1941.

3   War Plans

In a nuclear attack, with thousands of warheads bursting, the decision-making system for national security will be subject to a level of disruption comparable to being on the scene at Pearl Harbor in 1941 or the Yalu River in 1950. The difference between a nuclear attack and those of the past is that then there was always time, at the national level if not in the theater, to look at the situation and plan responses. In the nuclear era, irrevocable decisions to launch, or not to launch, will have to be made in mere minutes. The urgency to launch nuclear weapons is a function of their destructiveness. By waiting out an attack, the victim risks losing a substantial part of his forces. More important, he loses the ability to destroy or disrupt follow-on enemy strikes, for there can be no guarantee that the enemy's initial attacks are not the precursors to more massive ones. A relatively small initial strike may be designed to paralyze the victim, to hold his forces in place while full-scale follow-up strikes are launched. Riding out even a small attack may foreclose the possibility of saving lives, by enabling the enemy to pinpoint attacks with his undamaged command system. In the 1950s, a SAC commander pointed out that a quick, all-out counterstrike could disrupt an enemy's attack enough to save tens of millions of American lives, and this logic has guided thinking about nuclear war ever since.

One effect of the quick counterstrike strategy on war planning is that momentous choices will have to be made in an extraordinarily short time. We know of no literature that shows how an American president would be able to absorb warning information, assess the battlefield nuclear situation in Europe, including strikes on the Soviet

74

Union with NATO aircraft and missiles, monitor damage inflicted on the United States, and simultaneously plan a retaliatory response—all in the space of twenty to thirty minutes. Not only are the communication and computation obstacles overwhelming, but the human aspect of the situation defies comprehension. When we add to the problem the unanticipated consequences of using these tightly coupled systems, the outline of the real vulnerabilities in a nuclear force begins to take shape.

Much has been made of the compression of decision-making time in the nuclear age, which surely presents major obstacles. But an equally stressing factor is that so many things would be going on at once that the president, or indeed any single human being, could not be expected to absorb them all. Man by nature is a serial processor of information, analyzing problems piece-by-piece, one at a time. Organizations are much better than individuals at parallel information processing, that is, analyzing several problems simultaneously. Because of the absence of extensive decision-making time, nuclear war plans must be structured to initiate many actions at the same time, and these multifaceted plans must be prepared well ahead of the event. A war plan is a coordinating mechanism. For the United States there has been a horizontal integration of the nuclear weapons of the various commands, coordinating the individual plans into one super war plan, which became known as the SIOP. Increased weapon deployments aboard submarines, naval vessels, ICBMs, bombers, and in Europe created strong economies of scale in war planning. A single plan which integrated the forces of the constituent commands could achieve efficiencies unattainable through decentralized coordination, and promised more destruction for the same budget. American nuclear war planning has therefore pursued grand optimization schemes over many commands, areas, and types of military operations. The number and diversity of nuclear weapons, and the push toward optimizing the pieces, was greatly dependent on information technology allowing centralized computations. This fit in nicely with the vertical integration trends described earlier because centralized fusion centers were a fundamental part of that trend too.

A consequence of the centralized planning requirements of the horizontal integration trend was the shift from a "bottom-up" to a "top-down" planning style. Over thirty years, war plans evolved from being purely military expressions of strategy to plans which contained a very high level of political civilian input. Each new administration in the White House feels obligated to put its own stamp on nuclear war planning, and this is feasible because it is so easy to intervene in such a centralized process. Whether or not this political input to the planning process translates into central control is a different matter, especially during a crisis or war. Indeed one of the most striking features of American nuclear strategy is the presumption that a war will be run between two actors in full central control of their forces. Some of the stresses working against this will be described as they pertain to American war plans.

PLANS FOR NUCLEAR WAR

Early Years, 1949–53

America's earliest nuclear war plans were influenced mainly by the limited number of atomic bombs available. Only about fifty atomic bombs existed in 1949, and this dictated target selection.[1] The target list of the time, drawn up by American intelligence experts, consisted of just seventy targets, mainly industrial centers.[2] Strategic thinking was still greatly influenced by the experience of World War II bombardment, and since the Soviet Union did not possess its own nuclear arsenal there were no targets that required quick destruction in order to limit damage to the United States.

Soviet forces were, however, posing a threat to Western Europe and Japan. Large Soviet armies and naval forces were then considered the major threat to the West, and they received considerable attention from American nuclear planners. But with so few atomic weapons available, it seemed more effective to target Soviet industrial areas

1. Desmond Ball, "Counterforce Targeting: How New? How Viable?," *Arms Control Today* 11 (February 1981): 1.
2. Ibid.

WAR PLANS 77

than to attack military forces. Consequently, U.S. war plans in the late 1940s emphasized strikes against industrial areas in the belief that destroying them would also destroy the supplies essential for Soviet ground and naval operations.[3] One 1949 war plan, known as "Drop-shot," called for SAC to mount six thousand sorties against the Soviet Union and occupied territory, using three hundred atomic bombs and twenty thousand tons of high explosives.[4] Targets for nuclear attack were in the hundred largest Soviet cities.[5]

As the Korean war buildup of 1950 made larger budgets for nuclear forces available, a rapid expansion in the number of atomic weapons became possible. Between 1950 and 1953, spending for strategic forces increased from $9.6 billion to $43.3 billion, measured in constant 1981 dollars.[6] Weapons that formerly had been too expensive to build now fit easily into the new buildup, and in addition major new programs could be launched as well. SAC was modernized and expanded, a growing nuclear role was developed for carrier-based naval aircraft, and research was initiated on a new generation of army nuclear weapons.

Nuclear doctrine remained based on the counterindustrial targeting plans of the late 1940s, which were reflected in the action policies of the early 1950s. However, as the arsenals grew, so did interest in countermilitary targeting, and the services began to think about what to do with all of the additional weapons. Accordingly, plans were drawn up for attack of tactical military targets. Within the Air Force, and especially within SAC, nuclear targeting was viewed as an extension of World War II strategic bombing, but exploiting the more powerful effects of nuclear weapons. Targets included industrial facilities, transportation links that supported operations of the

3. Aaron L. Friedberg, "A History of the U.S. Strategic Doctrine, 1945 to 1980," *The Journal of Strategic Studies* 3 (December 1980): 40.
4. Anthony Cave Brown, ed., *Dropshot* (New York: Dial, 1978), p. 24. The United States did not possess three hundred atomic bombs in 1949. Dropshot was intended for a mid-1950s conflict.
5. Ibid.
6. U.S., Office of the Assistant Secretary of Defense (Comptroller), *National Defense Budget Estimated for FY 1981* (Washington, D.C.: Department of Defense, 1981), p. 68.

Soviet Army, and the bases of the long-range Soviet Air Force. Population damage was viewed as a necessary by-product to such attacks.[7] There was no direct counterpopulation targeting, as advocated by the British in World War II. The distinction was, of course, academic; vast population damage would have occurred if any of these war plans had been implemented.

Another aspect of nuclear targeting shows up if we look beyond Air Force plans. In November 1950, in the midst of the confusion and shock caused by the Chinese intervention in Korea, President Truman responded to a press question by saying that the atomic bomb was being considered for use there. When questioned about targets, he responded, "It's a matter that the military people will have to decide. I'm not a military authority that passes on those things. . . . The military commander in the field will have charge of the use of the weapons, as he always has."[8] The statement expresses the view that targeting decisions belong to the military commander on the scene, who alone would have detailed knowledge about what was going on, and alone would be able to evaluate the military consequences of its use. The statement followed a long tradition in the American military of leaving battlefield choices to the military. The momentous consequences of using *nuclear* weapons would be thought to change this tradition; however, this begs the question about detailed knowledge of local conditions and military consequences. Demanding that a president retain tighter control over nuclear targeting begs the same question. Indeed, by 1950 and 1951 there were strong pressures to give U.S. military commanders more direct access to these weapons.

At the time of President Truman's remarks, nonnuclear atomic bomb components were ready to be deployed on aircraft carriers in the Mediterranean. The nuclear components, which were under the

7. Henry S. Rowen, "The Evolution of Strategic Nuclear Doctrine," in Laurence Martin, ed., *Strategic Thought in the Nuclear Age* (Baltimore: Johns Hopkins University Press, 1979), p. 137.

8. President of the United States, *Public Papers of the Presidents of the United States* (Washington, D.C.: Office of the *Federal Register*, National Archives and Records Service, 1965), Harry S. Truman, 1950, p. 727.

physical control of civilian employees of the Atomic Energy Commission, were to be flown to the carriers immediately prior to use. There they would be assembled for delivery by the new AJ-1 Savage and the P2V-3C aircraft. Apparently by February 1951 these aircraft were making shuttle flights between the United States and Morocco and then on to the carriers stationed in the Mediterranean.[9] By the end of 1951 the entire set of nuclear and nonnuclear bomb components were deployed on several American carriers.[10] They were targeted against Soviet submarine bases and other Soviet military targets within a 600-mile radius of the Mediterranean.[11] Nonnuclear atomic bomb components were also deployed in Britain in 1950, and apparently also in Guam.[12] Had a decision to go to war been made, these components would have been fitted with nuclear components for delivery against targets in Europe and Asian Russia.

Knowledge of the details of Soviet army operations was crucial in order to understand how to stop the Red Army. Stockpiles of railroad flatcars, seemingly innocuous in peacetime, might be used to bring Soviet tanks to the front; thus, it was necessary to target those particular marshaling yards. A certain Baltic port might have been designated as a major transportation center in wartime, so it too had to be targeted. Targeting plans were closely tied to intelligence operations, which alone could determine *which* ports, and *which* rail yards, were intended for use in war. As best they could, American targeteers pieced together scraps of information from defectors, captured documents, electronic and communications intelligence, and every other source to find out how the Soviet Army planned to wage war. This knowledge was put into targeting plans and represented our best understanding of the dynamics of war. Had U.S. plans been revealed to the Soviets, they would have been provided with a picture of their own intelligence breakdowns, as well as our action plans against them.

9. D. A. Rosenberg and F. D. Kennedy, *History of the Strategic Arms Competition, 1945–1974* (Falls Church, Va.: Lulejian & Associates, 1975), II-174; Norman Polmar, *Strategic Weapons* (New York: Crane, Russak, 1975), p. 19.

10. Ibid., pp. 19–20.

11. Rosenberg and Kennedy, *Strategic Arms Competition*, p. I-175.

12. Polmar, *Strategic Weapons*, p. 13.

For this reason, targeting information was highly sensitive, and the targeting process was rigidly compartmentalized in order to prevent security breakdowns.

In the process, it became difficult, if not impossible, for political leaders to fully understand the process and plans. They could be given only the broadest guidance, and, for what was given, it was difficult for political leaders to verify that it had been put into effect. Targeting plans became enormously complex, as they attempted to capture the dynamics of combat, of how one thing affected another in wartime. The outlines of these interdependences were specified in the Dropshot war plan of 1949, and were a major component of NATO war plans.[13] In one plan, for example, atomic bombs were to be dropped on downtown Warsaw in order to destroy the bridges over the Vistula River, which would slow down a particular army for days. Other East European and Soviet urban areas were targeted for similar reasons, to destroy important military-supply and industrial facilities.[14]

Although Korea was the trigger to the nuclear weapons buildup, there is no doubt that Europe was the main concern, and tightly coupled plans for conflict there governed most of the general war plans. Even attacks planned by SAC against urban-industrial areas in the Soviet Union were seen as one element of this concern for Europe. Some nuclear attacks were designed to blunt a Soviet ground force's advance into Europe; others were intended to destroy the war-making capacity of Soviet industry. Nuclear attacks from SAC bases in Europe and aircraft carriers in the Mediterranean each had their own objectives, but the concern to blunt a conventional Soviet attack into Europe shaped them all.

Political leaders in Washington had no realistic way of deciding the targeting of Soviet submarine bases and rail lines in Poland. Only the responsible military organizations had the necessary knowledge about target vulnerabilities, campaign dynamics, and intelligence to

13. Brown, *Dropshot*, p. 200. Interview with two former NATO planners.
14. Ibid. American targeteers assigned to NATO in the early 1950s were so pessimistic about the West's chances of stopping the Soviet army before it reached the English Channel that they systematically collected data on targets in *Western* Europe so they could better attack Soviet units that had smashed through NATO's defenses.

engage in the complex targeting process. Consequently, nearly all of these decisions had to be delegated to the military, with political leaders providing only the broadest guidance. The plans did *not* call for exclusive targeting of cities as a deterrent to Soviet aggression, despite widespread rumors to the contrary and statements by political and military leaders who should know better. Such "countervalue" attacks played no part in early war plans, nor did they later.

Formative Years, 1953–61

In the middle 1950s the number of nuclear weapons increased greatly relative to 1950, especially the number of delivery vehicles for getting weapons to their targets. The chief delivery vehicles were the B-47 and B-52 bombers, which were stationed in the United States but capable of staging through Britain, Turkey, Italy, Libya, and bases in the Far East. The advent of the H-bomb, with its substantially greater killing radius, also produced major changes in targeting because it allowed the easy destruction of entire urban areas. Because cities could now be destroyed so easily, the objective of neutralizing Soviet war-supporting industries was now accomplished. Consequently, weapons were freed for other kinds of attacks, especially for attacks to blunt a Soviet invasion of Europe and attacks on the nascent stockpiles of Soviet atomic weapons.

War plans in the 1950s divided targets into three classes: "Bravo," "Delta," and "Romeo."[15] Bravo targets consisted of the time-urgent nuclear and projection forces of the Soviet Union. Long-range air armies, submarines in port, and medium- and intermediate-range ballistic missiles were in this category. Such forces were vulnerable only during the period prior to launch, before they had been used against NATO or the United States. Thus the only realistic way to destroy them was to fire at them as soon as was practical. This necessity produced consequences not so much in targeting, as in com-

15. Desmond Ball, *Deja Vu: The Return to Counterforce in the Nixon Administration* (Santa Monica, Calif.: California Seminar on Arms Control and Foreign Policy, December 1974), p. 10.

mand and control. For action to be taken very quickly in a war necessitated, as a practical matter, preemptive attack.

Delta targets were the factories, transportation centers, ports, and cities that were used to support the war-making capacity of the Soviet Union. Destroying them would prevent any Soviet aggressive initiatives from recurring, hopefully forever in the eyes of American war planners. Delta targets were mainly in the interior of the Soviet Union, and an attack on them would produce horrendous casualties. One study even concluded that with the American arsenal growing in size and yield, damage was growing insensitive to targeting. Such large nuclear weapon campaigns would produce so much radioactive fallout that "random targeting," the selection of weapon aimpoints to cover the country uniformly rather than fire directly at cities, was almost as effective as other tactics.[16]

Romeo targets consisted of the less time-urgent military forces of the Soviet Union that were usable in a ground advance into Western Europe. Typical targets here included army divisions and logistic centers. The large number of American nuclear weapons in the late 1950s meant that it was impossible to avoid massive collateral damage in the event of strikes against any target class. Even Bravo targets, generally thought of as purely military targets, could be, and indeed often were, in major urban areas. Moscow itself was the foremost Bravo target of all, because it served as the command and control center for directing armies and defending Soviet airspace.

In 1954 Secretary of State John Foster Dulles announced the doctrine of "massive retaliation," in which the United States would respond with large-scale attacks at a time and place not necessarily commensurate with the Soviet provocation.[17] "Massive" was construed by one and all to mean a full-scale nuclear attack, although Secretary Dulles never specified the details of his threat. It is only possible to conclude from this doctrine, together with the U.S. warn-

16. Hugh Everett and George E. Pugh, "The Distribution and Effects of Fallout in Large Nuclear Weapon Campaigns," *Operations Research*, 7 (March–April 1959): 243–44.

17. See Samuel F. Wells, "The Origins of Massive Retaliation," *Political Science Quarterly* 96 (Spring 1981): 31–52.

ing system's emphasis on getting word of impending attack on Europe as soon as possible and the target classifications of the day, that the United States had organized its nuclear forces essentially for launch on warning. This is not to say that launch on warning would have been the actual policy in a crisis, but only that the forces and plans were structured to this end. The president could have vetoed any such strategy at the last moment.

Other evidence reinforces a launch-on-warning interpretation, and here we emphasize the ambiguity concerning the different kinds of warning. On the question of whether tactical or strategic warning would have been sufficient to trigger a U.S. response, different people probably held different beliefs. The actual distinction between tactical and strategic warning, however, is less clear in practice than theory. The strategy of launch on warning could be dependent on there already being a conflict going on (for example, a Soviet conventional attack on Europe). If a nuclear attack were launched at such a point, it could still qualify as a defensive or second-strike use of nuclear weapons. General Curtis E. LeMay, the commander of SAC in the mid-1950s, reflects this logic in commenting on proposals to hold back certain weapons in a strike:

> If one were in the President's position, would one give orders for bomb- ers to attack and at the same time hold back "second strike" Polaris and Minuteman missiles until the enemy weapons had actually struck? Or would one attempt to blunt the enemy attack and destroy as many weapons on the ground as possible? . . . Granted, the President could not eliminate the enemy attack altogether nor protect all of the popu- lation. But, as some strategists have calculated, he might save as many as fifty million lives by rapid retaliation with all available weapons.[18]

A more telling piece of evidence supporting the launch-on-warn- ing interpretation came in a top secret 1954 briefing given by General LeMay that has recently been declassified. Asked how SAC's plans fit in with the stated national policy that the United States would never strike the first blow in a war, he responded:

18. Curtis E. LeMay, *America Is in Danger* (New York: Funk & Wagnalls, 1968), p. 58.

I have heard this thought stated many times and it sounds very fine. However, it is not in keeping with United States history. Just look back and note who started the Revolutionary War, the War of 1812, the Indian Wars, and the Spanish-America War. I want to make it clear that I am not advocating a preventive war; however, I believe that if the U.S. is pushed in the corner far enough we would not hesitate to strike first.[19]

As the 1950s came to a close, American nuclear doctrine was increasingly criticized on the grounds that it was too extreme ever to be put into practice. According to a 1960 estimate, a spasm attack by the United States would inflict 500 million fatalities on Russia, China, and Eastern Europe.[20] Such incomprehensible destruction would result from the fallout produced by the large-yield weapons then in the arsenal. But beyond this, the growing criticism was directed less at the technical makeup of the nuclear weapons arsenal than at the politicians who accepted such massive retaliation, and military organizations that advocated it. It was clear to critics like Herman Kahn that SAC in particular had turned the military plans into a strategy of all-out deterrence. In the late 1950s SAC advocated being able to wipe out the Soviet Union so overwhelmingly that there would not be one iota of doubt in the Kremlin about the consequences of attacking the West. Destruction would be immediate, overwhelming, and total, encompassing military and urban targets alike. This was as pure an expression of massive retaliation as could be had. Yet because retaliation would be so total, the doctrine did not appear credible either for dealing with lesser provocations, or for dealing with a Soviet Union capable of returning a massive attack of its own.

The Search for Options, 1961–76

One of Secretary of Defense Robert S. McNamara's first actions after taking office was to review American plans for waging nuclear war.

19. This is not a verbatim quote, but is drawn from notes made at the briefing by an audience member. See D. A. Rosenberg, "A Smoking Radiating Ruin at the End of Two Hours," *International Security*, 6 (Winter 1981–82): 27.

20. Ball, *Return to Counterforce*, p. 11.

The intercontinental missile was just being phased into operation in 1961, and the existing war plans inherited from the 1950s received strong criticism from the Rand Corporation analysts who were now working in the Pentagon.[21] It was a unique opportunity for restructuring war plans. In addition, a new targeting plan, known as the Single Integrated Operational Plan (SIOP), which integrated all of America's nuclear weapons into a single plan, had been organized in 1960. This created for the first time a single framework for making changes.

As far as targeting was concerned, the basic change was to select targets that did not overlap with Soviet cities and to provide for some targets to be exceptions from the basic plan which could be fired on later in battle if it was desired. In contrast to the plans of the 1950s, the new arrangement organized different *packages* of targets and provided for *not* firing on the unselected ones. It is known that packages were drawn up in 1961 and 1962 for attacking each of the East European nations, China, and the Soviet Union—specifically Moscow, industrial-urban areas, nuclear military targets *not* located near cities, and all nuclear military targets regardless of location.[22] The plan had other options, but fundamental to it was the ability, if desired, to avoid firing at Soviet cities. The reason for this was the belief that the best way to limit damage to the U.S. population was to hold Soviet cities hostage to follow-on attack, an idea central to many of the academic writings on nuclear strategy of the late 1950s. As long as the United States could not actually destroy Soviet nuclear forces before they fired, the best hope for avoiding escalation to urban attacks in atomic war was to bargain with Moscow during the war. The instruments of bargaining would be the weapons exploded on an enemy's territory, and those as yet unexploded, which could hold Soviet cities hostage to follow-on attack.[23]

At a far lower level of tension, the Berlin crisis of 1961 demonstrated the need both to find alternatives to massive attacks and to

21. Ibid., p. 11.
22. Ibid., p. 12.
23. Peter C. Wagstaff, "An Analysis of the Cities-Avoidance Theory," *Stanford Journal of International Studies* 7 (Spring 1972): 162–71.

involve civilians in war planning. At the onset of the crisis President Kennedy inquired about the plans prepared by NATO and the Joint Chiefs of Staff (JCS) for responding to Soviet closure of the autobahn connecting Berlin to West Germany. Under these plans a series of military probes down the autobahn would be attempted. If these probes were rebuffed, which was not unlikely, given the overwhelming Soviet and East German troop advantage, then nuclear weapons were to be used.[24] Plans such as these were, in a sense, more dangerous than no plans at all, because they provided the illusion of having usable courses of action open to the president. It was this search for usable limited military options that led to the high-level civilian intervention in the war-planning process in the early 1960s.

Although Secretary McNamara ordered that limited options be put into the SIOP, they were not as far-reaching as is generally believed. Even the smallest SIOP options against the Soviet Union consisted of thousands of weapons in the 1960s and early 1970s.[25] It was left to Secretary of Defense James R. Schlesinger in 1974 to complete the McNamara program by organizing a large number of "small" options in the SIOP. The thinking behind this was that as the Soviet nuclear threat grew it would become increasingly difficult to limit damage by destroying the Soviet nuclear forces that could attack the United States. The theory behind so-called limited nuclear options was that America needed the ability to attack target sets in order to influence the actions of Soviet leaders, especially in a war in Europe.[26] As an example, a nuclear strike against the Soviet petroleum industry and its supporting facilities would be useful in blunting an attack by conventional forces that depended on petroleum for fuel. Special attention would be given to keeping urban damage at a minimum in these attacks, in order to encourage reciprocal Soviet behavior.

The full implementation of limited nuclear options in targeting plans in the mid-1970s represented a victory for the bargaining and

24. Theodore C. Sorensen, *Kennedy* (New York: Harper & Row, 1965), p. 662.
25. Rowen, "Evolution of Nuclear Doctrine," p. 145.
26. See Lynn E. Davis, *Limited Nuclear Options* (London: International Institute for Strategic Studies, 1975).

escalation-control view of nuclear war. The plans were partially implemented by Secretary McNamara in the early 1960s; the new options developed ten years later by Secretary Schlesinger can be interpreted as a fine tuning of the idea. Whether or not we accept this strategy as realistic, we need to understand that it was developed in reaction to the strategy that posited an all-out attack at the outset of hostilities. It was an attempt to avoid catastrophe, and as such it was not a bad idea.

A Search for Advantage, 1977–83

By the late 1970s, the U.S. arsenal had grown to over nine thousand strategic warheads, and disillusionment about the entire subject of targeting had set in. The weapon technologies were no longer new, and neither were the issues. Even the number of people who paid any attention to these matters declined, and, of those, only a handful were concerned with the subject of targeting.

In the 1950s, when there was a relatively small Soviet arsenal, it appeared possible to achieve some advantage in a nuclear war. Yet even by 1958 the Soviet buildup of long-range air armies and medium- and intermediate-range ballistic missiles (M/IRBMs) against Europe meant that any conflict would be devastating to the West. As a response to this, American target planners incorporated certain bargaining concepts into war plans. Soviet cities were not targeted for initial attack, in hopes of holding them hostage; China and the East European nations were also withheld from plans, as a move to dissuade them from joining in any Soviet-led attack. By the mid-1970s, the bargaining notion was refined to incorporate smaller, limited nuclear options against a large number of target sets. This limitation and restraint in target planning was an American recognition of the insurmountable difficulty of significant damage limitation against the Soviets. As the number of Soviet nuclear weapons grew, and as concrete silos were built to protect them, the chances of destroying enough missiles to reduce American urban damage to "only" 10 or 20 million fatalities vanished.

The official reaction to these trends in the late 1970s was Presidential Directive PD-59, signed in July 1980.[27] Although the text of PD-59 has not been released, it and other follow-on policy statements are generally regarded as highly ambiguous expressions of strategy. One view of PD-59 is that it represents a mandate for a nuclear "war-winning" strategy and contains the idea of how to achieve such a victory. This strategy would represent a shift in outlook about nuclear conflict from the U.S. statements of the 1960s and 1970s.

The war-winning interpretation of PD-59, however, is not the only one. Responsible officials in the Department of Defense have also treated it as representing only a marginal change from past declaratory policies.[28] Such inconsistent interpretations of the same document are quite common.

The Reagan administration seems to treat PD-59, as a bit of both, both in its emphasis on war-winning advantage and claiming that it too is only a slight modification of previous theories about nuclear war. National Security Decision Directive 13 (NSDD-13), which officially replaced PD-59 in 1982, contains the same emphasis on destroying political-control centers and preparing for a protracted nuclear war.[29] Whether the revisions in PD-59 and NSDD-13 represent a major change in American war planning depends on which interpretation is believed. At the coordinating level little has changed, but at the theoretical level there appears to have been a considerable change.

What is especially worth noting about PD-59 and NSDD-13 is the idea advanced as the key to victory over the Soviet Union in a nuclear war, which is to target the political and military control system of the Soviet Union, not just its military forces. The thread of this strategy was already expressed in 1975, when the SIOP specified four classes of targets—nuclear forces, conventional military forces, mili-

---

27. Ball, "Counterforce Targeting," p. 6; "The New Strategy for Nuclear War," *New York Times*, August 13, 1980, p. A3; "Carter Directive Modifies Strategy for a Nuclear War," *Washington Post*, August 6, 1980, p. A10.

28. See Walter Slocombe, "The Countervailing Strategy," *International Security* 5 (Spring 1981): 18–27.

29. "U.S. Plan Sees Extended Fight in Nuclear War," *Stamford Advocate*, August 15, 1982, p. A8.

tary and political leadership, and economic and industrial targets[30]—
which have become known as "building blocks." Although Soviet
military and leadership targets had always been included in earlier
plans, PD-59 for the first time declared open threats against them. As
a consequence, a spate of academic articles appeared about the benefits of "knocking out the Soviet control system."[31] Most of these were
superficial, almost nonsensical, for they never even defined "control
system," nor did they address what would happen if the Soviets shot
back. Still, this bizarre debate highlighted the important theoretical
change expressed in PD-59 and NSDD-13.

WAR PLANS IN A BROADER PERSPECTIVE

A summary of U.S. nuclear war plans ultimately raises this question:
Just how should one think about the problem of targeting? Most
histories of targeting, and even most studies of contemporary American nuclear strategy, define the problem of targeting as a matter of
selecting "things" for destruction. Typical questions include: Should
we target Soviet cities or military facilities? Will destruction of "control targets" deter Soviet escalation? Consequently the doctrines of
"counterforce" and "countervalue" have arisen, the first reflecting the
belief that in the event of a war America should aim to destroy military
(counterforce) targets; the second, that it should aim at urban and
industrial (countervalue) targets. Large, and mushy, intellectual debates between the advocates of counterforce and those of countervalue
have arisen. The very idea of deterrent effectiveness hinges on whether
one favors counterforce or countervalue, with a school of strategists
(and brief writers) organized behind each alternative. New weapons
are advanced on the basis of this debate as well.

Even though counterforce versus countervalue is a legitimate
avenue of analysis, the approach taken here does not follow this path.
We could have chosen, for example, to review targeting plans and

30. Ball, "Counterforce Targeting," p. 6.
31. For one example see Jeffrey T. Richelson, "The Dilemmas of Counterpower
Targeting," *Comparative Strategy* 3 (1980): 223–37.

might have concluded that counterforce attacks have always been the basis of American action planning, even when declaratory doctrine placed nearly exclusive emphasis on countervalue attacks, as it did under Secretary McNamara in the mid-1960s. But this kind of analysis is unable to account for a richer, and more important, collection of targeting phenomena. Nonetheless, I readily acknowledge that most writers on nuclear strategy, and most political leaders who have given any thought to the subject, have relied on this analysis and understand nuclear war planning to be the process of selecting things to be destroyed in the Soviet Union.

The counterforce-versus-countervalue approach to targeting is deficient, first of all, because it fails to say anything about coupling effects among targets. It also fails to deal with how knowledge about damage could be concentrated in order to assess the consequences of a targeting plan, or how a political leader could absorb the vast quantity of needed information in only a few minutes, or how the dynamic responses of the system attacked would interact with the attacker's war plan.

Three levels of targeting can be distinguished in the development of American nuclear war plans. At the individual level of analysis, cities, missile sites, buildings, stockpiles, dams, bridges, airfields, and other "things"—*individual* targets—are identified for destruction. Nuclear weapons are then selected on the basis of their accuracy, yield, reliability, location, delivery speed, and other technical factors so as to optimize the allocation of discrete weapons to discrete targets.[32] For example, an arsenal of one hundred nuclear weapons might be "applied" to two hundred Soviet military facilities, and decisions would have to be made on which facilities to target, how many weapons to assign to each target, and similar kinds of questions, depending on the detail considered.

At a higher level of analysis, targeting plans can be directed at a *group* of people. They are targeted not in order to obliterate them but

32. For detailed models on how to do this, see A. Ross Eckler and Stefan A. Burr, *Mathematical Models of Target Coverage and Missile Allocations* (Alexandria, Va.: Military Operations Research Society, 1972).

to influence their behavior. The term group is used here in a rather precise sense, to mean a number of persons, each of whom directly interacts with each other member of the group. Because of the requirement that each member be able to interact with each other member directly, such a group must be small. The term is used here to describe an entity such as the Soviet or American leaders who would make decisions in a crisis. The group has no fixed number of members, but it is likely to be small enough to be manageable when time is in short supply.[33] Even one person, the national leader, can constitute a group in this definition.

Since actually destroying the Soviet leadership group would serve no militarily useful purpose, targeting is a bargaining tool that is intended to *influence* the group. In the early 1960s, as the Soviet nuclear arsenal grew in size, American targeting plans were revised so that Soviet cities would not be destroyed.[34] The logic of this move was that the Soviet leadership group, observing American self-imposed restrictions, would be more likely to impose similar restrictions on their own targeting of nuclear weapons. In this model of a nuclear war, the two nations, or more precisely the two leadership groups, would bargain with each other before *and* during the war. The motivations for bargaining, thoroughly explored in the literature of the day, were believed to include mutual interest in survival and the desire to control escalation.[35] As we saw in the preceding section, the American SIOP was revised to conform to just this model in the early 1960s.

Targeting at the group level depends on the physical destruction of particular sites, as at the individual level, but there is more to it than this. Destruction of a bridge, for example, may have direct mil-

---

33. During the Cuban missile crisis President John Kennedy relied on an "Executive Committee" of fifteen persons. The Soviet Politburo today consists of fourteen persons. Both are examples of leadership groups in the sense intended here. See also Graham T. Allison, *Essence of Decision* (Boston: Little, Brown, 1971), p. 57.

34. Plans were also explicitly revised to withhold attacks against the Soviet leaders, in order to keep them alive so that the American leadership would have an entity to bargain with. See Ball, *Return to Counterforce*, p. 12.

35. Two of the classic works include Thomas C. Schelling, *The Strategy of Conflict* (Oxford: Oxford University Press, 1960); and Herman Kahn, *On Escalation* (Baltimore: Penguin, 1965).

itary consequences in that the bridge can no longer be used for river crossings. But it also shapes the perception of Soviet leaders. It has military value, but its symbolic political value can easily outweigh its military significance. If in a conventional confrontation with the Soviet Union the United States were to fire a single nuclear weapon at a bridge in Eastern Europe, the physical destruction of the bridge would pall in comparison to the fact that a nuclear weapon had been used for the first time since 1945.

Speculation about how the Soviet leadership would respond to different kinds of nuclear attack has filled volumes. Most often it concentrates on the perceived value of different kinds of targets. Military (counterforce) targeting might induce one type of behavior, urban (countervalue) targeting another. Soviet leadership reactions would depend on many factors over and above the military value of the target. Ethnocentric perceptions, Soviet heritage, and even social psychological dynamics like "group-think" also would play a part.

The third level of analysis of targeting is organizational. An organization is used here to mean groups of people and machines in which explicit procedures for coordination have been established in order to achieve specified objectives. Unlike a group, an organization has no necessary requirement that each member directly interact with each other member or machine. The key to an organization, and especially to a military organization, is its dependence on procedures for conducting its operations. Whereas the Soviet or U.S. leadership groups likely in a nuclear crisis are small, say less than twenty persons each, the size of an organization for waging nuclear war is large—indeed, very large compared to a group. It is not at all clear how to even measure the size of a nuclear warfighting organization, whether to count people, machines, weapons, or computers. The United States probably has about twenty-five thousand persons involved in its nuclear command and control system, including those in the warning and intelligence networks feeding into it. These people are stationed worldwide, from Guam to Omaha, and from Alaska to Turkey. Organizations of similar or greater size exist in the Soviet Union.

Thinking about targeting in organizational terms suggests some very different questions than thinking about the group or individual levels of analysis. For example, if one's theory of nuclear war is as a symbolic contest in pain bearing and bargaining advantage, it would do well to send clear signals to the enemy at least some of the time. This could translate into firing limited attacks in well-defined salvos rather than over extended periods of time, in order to give the enemy time to reflect on his position in the bargaining game. Alternatively, at the organizational level of analysis it might be better to conceal the meaning in one's attack plan, and to maximally disrupt the coordinating procedures used in the enemy command. Ground bursting of thousands of weapons on enemy territory would do this because the extensive fallout generated would disrupt his ability to reload missiles and reconstitute bombers.

One of the most compelling reasons for asking questions at the organizational level is that it comes closest to how military targeting plans are actually devised. What is more, the questions raised correspond to the problems arising from complex warning and control systems. We can illustrate this by recalling the plans for blunting a Soviet ground attack on Western Europe. There, the problem was not to destroy a number of bridges, ports, railyards, airfields, and stockpiles, it was rather to stop a Soviet ground invasion before it could penetrate deeply into Western Europe. Targeting for this purpose depends upon detailed understanding of the Soviet military organization, of how its logistic branch supplies forward units, of whether rail or truck transportation would be selected for moving tanks into staging areas, of how ground armies coordinate with air forces, of whether tank armies advance with mechanized infantry, of how long before second-echelon units exploit the breakthroughs achieved by advanced units, and of hundreds of other similar issues.

The military services alone can undertake targeting decisions about these matters, because they alone understand the details of military organization. And they alone have been given the task of stopping a Soviet offensive into Europe. Targeting is not an exercise in killing individual Soviet missile silos and military units in some sort of Vietnam-style body count; it is instead an intelligence-based activity that seeks to turn an understanding of combat dynamics into a plan that breaks up the attack into manageable pieces. If this influences Soviet leadership to change its behavior, then so much the better. But at the military-intelligence level where targets are selected, this is not likely to be an overriding concern.

When we consider a target, or collection of targets, as an organization, it suggests certain kinds of questions—and even new tactics. These questions are generally not posed if targets are understood to be merely a set of uncoupled facilities or a collection of sites that have only symbolic utility to a leadership group. For example, it poses the question of reaction dynamics. During World War II the British and American strategic bombardment of German industry and urban areas was based on the idea that destruction of factories critical to the war effort would demonstrably slow down the German armies in the field, and might further crack the morale of the German people and lead to a prompt capitulation. The actual results were quite different. As more bombs were dropped on Germany, production of war goods actually increased.[36] This happened because the target system was not just an inert collection of buildings, locomotives, and shipyards, but was a reactive organization directed by human beings. Although individual locations were destroyed by bombardment, the German decision-making system and its physical apparatus were not destroyed until very late in the war, when ground armies had overrun most of the country.

A similar phenomenon occurred in the air war in Vietnam. There, U.S. attacks could not significantly reduce North Vietnamese combat capability because there was always time for the enemy to regroup after a bombing attack, no matter how intense, and because there were few individual targets whose destruction affected ground operations.[37]

In both of these examples, a response by the organization more than made up for whatever damage was inflicted in air attacks. Plants were rebuilt, substitute materials were used, bridges were repaired, and alternate sources of supply and methods of production were found.

36. Mancur Olson, "The Economics of Target Selection for the Combined Bomber Offensive," *Journal of the Royal United Services Institute* (November 1962): 308.

37. See Herman L. Gilster, "On War, Time, and the Principle of Substitution," *Air University Review* 6 (October 1979): 2–19.

Different parts of the organization under attack made decisions and took compensating action. One of the reasons for the success of this approach was that it did not require detailed direction from political leadership. People in the organizations reacted to attack by making decisions based on their own knowledge and authority. The aggregate effect of these thousands upon thousands of actions was to offset the consequences of the bombardment.

We cannot predict the reaction dynamics in a nuclear war, but we can point out that reactive dynamics is an important question that is unlikely to be considered if targeting analysis attends only to individual facility destruction or to the reactions of the Soviet leadership group. With the long-standing mission of halting a Soviet attack into Europe, it does seem that the U.S. should give thought in its analysis of American targeting policy to the consequences of launching several thousand theater and strategic warheads at Soviet armies and logistic nets dispersed over a large part of Central Europe, including Russia west of the Urals. Many of these Soviet units have nuclear weapons under their physical control. From what we know about reaction dynamics, it is very plausible that many of these weapons would be fired in return. This action would be based on the Soviet units' military reasoning about unit survival and the need to destroy NATO's military capabilities. It seems far-fetched to believe that a military unit would behave like an inert building if it was attacked.

This line of analysis suggests another interesting point. One of the ways both Germany in World War II and North Vietnam in the 1960s overcame the effects of strategic air attacks was to make adjustments and institute countermeasures in the way they carried on their activities. The adjustments and countermeasures were, at bottom, procedural changes for coordinating the different wartime activities. Procedures are the essence of organization, and the modification of an organization's procedures takes time. In the bombing of Germany and Vietnam there was time after each attack to assess the situation and institute adjustments. However, the destruction in a nuclear war may be so vast that time will *not* be available unless the pace of reaction is speeded up enormously. In past air wars there were usually at least a few days, and more often a few weeks, between major strikes. In a nuclear exchange, either in Europe or intercontinentally, there may only be a few minutes—at most, a few hours.

An organization will respond in this speeded-up environment by taking account of its most important missions. In the bombardment of Germany and Vietnam the response was to produce needed war equipment and supply front-line combat units. In a nuclear war such economic and production requirements, because of the expected short duration of such a conflict, will be far less significant. However, the issuance of nuclear weapon firing orders and authorizations throughout the various military hierarchies may have to take place very rapidly. If it is not done early on, the necessary orders and codes could be isolated from the weapons by enemy attack. Thus, a nuclear-equipped army could be paralyzed into inaction if appropriate orders are not issued at the earliest practical time. Indeed, this threat may be so great as to force issuance of contingent authorizations to use nuclear weapons, as we will discuss later. A nuclear-armed military organization may react by making adjustments in the procedures for command and control of nuclear weapons, just as Germany and Vietnam reacted by making procedural changes when they were attacked. In both kinds of situations, it is an oversimplification to analyze the consequences of strategic attack only in terms of "things destroyed" or the effects on political leadership. This misses the critical *dynamics* of response, and the changes forced on *procedures*.

What does seem clear is that in the twenty or thirty minutes it takes for missiles to reach their targets there will be almost no feasible way for senior military commanders and political leadership groups to discuss and coordinate procedural changes. The one exception to this would be the nation that strikes first, which could do so with a carefully prepared SIOP. The nation attacked may have to undertake extensive calculations and assessments about what has happened to it, how the enemy target system has changed, and who has survived. The longer this takes, the more opportunity the first striker will have to reattack, disrupting again the reactions of the victim.[38] The im-

38. Edward W. Paxon, *Computers and Strategic Advantage: Games, Computer Technology, and a Strategic Power Ratio* (Santa Monica, Calif.: Rand Corp., 1975), p. 20.

plications for targeting are thus very different from those suggested in the bargaining approach at the group level of analysis. Targeting in order to improve one's bargaining position might lead to aiming at enemy missiles if a country were subjected to a first strike. This tactic would even up the firepower ratios.

However, at an organizational level a retaliatory response would be more likely to aim at the enemy's command and control system, which embodies its information processing and procedural operating rules. The reason is that the nation struck first would be threatened by follow-on attacks by an enemy who has an undamaged assessment and information processing system that could be used to exploit the disruption of the first strike. Thus, an attacked state would have a strong incentive to disrupt, mangle, and confuse the attacker's ability to engage in carefully planned restrikes. Here, a first strike would be met with a retaliatory attack against sensor and warning systems, command sites, and communication systems, as well as against military forces. Furthermore, such a retaliatory attack would have to be launched very soon after the first strike, or in the case of launch under attack, even during it.

4 Problems of Assessment

To make it feasible to wage a controlled nuclear war, that is, a nuclear war with political direction, was at the heart of the changes in American war plans undertaken in the early 1960s. It was a controversial subject then and is even more so today. During the past twenty years war plans have been revised further, and electronic equipment, airborne command posts, and reconnaissance satellites have been acquired at least partly to increase the nation's ability to do this. Over the same period, the character of the U.S. nuclear force has changed, becoming more interactive, tightly coupled, and synergistic. Yet before we can dismiss the possibility of controlled nuclear war, or before we can state dogmatically that controlled exchanges are likely in the event of war, we must examine the fundamental obstacles to limitation of a nuclear conflict.

In order to analyze the feasibility of controlled nuclear war, we first must avoid being confused by irrelevant details that give the appearance of technical realism but actually hinder our understanding. We must also beware of omitting other critical factors from the analysis altogether. Technically detailed accounts of the merits or the vulnerabilities of a new satellite communications system may be interesting on their own account, but the fundamental reason for communications within a strategic force is to bind the system into a coherent whole that can be directed by a central command mechanism. The command mechanism might tell the force to continue firing, or to stop firing, or it might order the forces to undertake a particular attack of enemy targets. To do any of these things, it needs communications, so it is the communications function, rather than technology, which needs examination.

The purpose of this chapter is to explore the problem of assessment in wartime. There is a beguilingly seductive trap here. It is often assumed that we would have as much information in wartime as in peacetime. But to determine the status of one's own forces, enemy forces, enemy capabilities, enemy intentions, and civil damage in wartime conditions might prove impossibly burdensome.

Given what we have said about the complexity of the warning and intelligence system when its checks and balances have been removed, it might seem that the very complexity of nuclear forces would guarantee breakdowns that would lead to all-out escalation. However, we have discovered that this complexity cuts both ways, making the command vulnerable to paralysis in certain circumstances. What makes centralized control most difficult is the lack of centralized assessment, that is, the ability to determine even approximately what is going on in a war.

The previous chapter concluded that an incoming missile attack would be likely to be met by an automatic response directed at the first striker's command and control system. This chapter explores the consequences of another way of reacting to attack—riding out the attack and then responding. I argue that wartime conditions will impose a radically different information regime on the victim's command system. Because of the destructiveness of nuclear weapons and the vulnerability of communication linkages, a command will be shattered into separated islands of disconnected forces once it is subjected to heavy nuclear attack. Each separated island will then face its own individual assessment problem. It will not only have to estimate the damage it has sustained, but also the damage sustained by the other separated units and the status of enemy forces. The independently made joint decision of all the isolated forces will determine whether a break in the firing will occur. If a single separated unit continues to fire, or is presumed to, it could be enough to destabilize a cease-fire.

Due to the absence of communication linkages among isolated

forces, assessment will be intrinsically decentralized. The question then facing decision makers will not be how much damage the enemy has sustained, but how much the isolated forces *think* it has sustained. As a practical matter, war termination might only be possible if some kind of equilibrium exists among the fragmented commands of each nation.

THE PEACETIME INFORMATION REGIME

By the term assessment I mean an appraisal of military forces and their capabilities, strategies, and goals, in a competitive interaction. Competitive interactions include wartime operations, but also refer to peacetime maneuvering to secure advantageous political or military effect. Alerts and mobilizations both qualify as competitive interactions because both might be met by counterreactions to offset whatever political or military gains were initially sought. Appraisals of this kind are routinely carried out in peacetime by civilian and military planning staffs, and have become known as net assessments. Net assessments place great stock in the way differences in cognition and perception influence the selection of actions. Can the Soviet Union's nuclear forces destroy a high percentage of American missiles on the ground, and if they can, what American retaliatory targeting assignments can maximize deterrence against such a first strike? is a typical question in a net assessment. The answer depends on the many factors influencing this particular attack, such as the number of Soviet and American missiles, their technical characteristics, Soviet goals as to the desirability of a nuclear war, and Soviet strategy as to whether an attack would try to minimize civilian damage (for example, through careful aiming and airbursting to decrease radioactive fallout).

Even a restricted assessment would include many factors. Here it is important to assess the number of missiles, their locations, and the damage sustained by military and civilian targets. This last factor is broad and includes whether leaders knew that an attack had destroyed the enemy's communications system connecting its political leaders with its military forces.

Although our concerns are not as all-inclusive as in a net assessment, we will discuss net assessment first because it establishes a comparative context for wartime assessment. For example, net assessments of nuclear war are often based on use of quantitative models of weapon exchanges that tabulate the amount of damage and number of surviving missiles for each side—but in wartime, knowledge about destroyed missiles might not be available, or it might be available only to local commanders. What kind of assessment process would replace the net assessments relied upon in peacetime? This is a critical question, and its elucidation requires an understanding of the alternative information regimes that rule in peace and war.

The objective of a net assessment, broadly speaking, is to develop a profile of the likely strategy changes each competitor might make, each side's probable response to a range of strategic moves, and each competitor's reaction to technological and environmental shifts. Sophisticated net assessments ask such questions as the following: How will deployment of long-range missiles to Europe affect overall targeting assignments, and how will the Soviets react, both in their own targeting and in development of new weapons? Do the Soviets possess enough raw military power in Asia to endanger the security of America's allies, and are their goals such that they might use this military power? How does nuclear deterrence depend on the existence of invulnerable retaliatory forces?

Figure 4.1 shows a convenient way to think about net assessment. Goals, strategies, and capabilities are each assessed separately. This information goes into an interaction profile, which determines how these diverse factors will affect overall outcomes. Each of the three components relies on its own peculiar methodologies and makes use of different kinds of data and tests of validity. The key feature of a net assessment is its *integration* of the different components. This is represented by the box entitled "interaction profiles." Net assessment is able to cut across traditional boundaries of academic and military disciplines because it integrates knowledge from all relevant sources. The need to formalize this process arises from the large number of factors that have to be dealt with. Without some order imposed

Fig. 4.1. Components of a net assessment

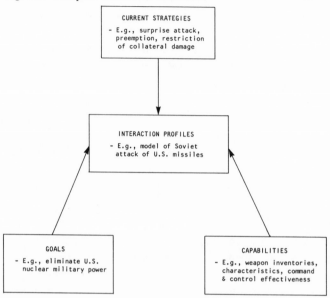

on this information, it is no more than data, that is, raw information deprived of a context.

The "national goals" component in a net assessment makes use of political analysis and foreign policy studies. In these fields, the methods used range from what can only be termed "revealed truth," to sophisticated content analysis, examination of political signals, and plain common sense.[1] Very different methodologies are used to determine Soviet and American goals, and hence results are also highly different. Because of this, considerable difficulties arise in assessing this component.

The second component, strategies, is closely related to goals. Strategies are the instruments for attaining goals. An example can

1. The goals of the Soviet Union in the Cuban missile crisis of 1962 have been exhaustively analyzed. See Arnold L. Horelick and Myron Rush, *Strategic Power and Soviet Foreign Policy* (Chicago: University of Chicago Press, 1965); and Graham T. Allison, *Essence of Decision* (Cambridge: Harvard University Press, 1971).

clarify the distinction. A goal of the Soviet Union could be to eliminate American nuclear military power, and one way to accomplish this would be through the strategy of preemptive attack on military targets. The attack might have several variants. Only land-based missiles might be targeted, on the assumption that the resulting imbalance of forces following attack would necessarily compel the United States to capitulate. This attack is a strategy, in the sense of meeting the goal of destroying American military power.

The most widely used method for determining Soviet strategy is to read doctrinal texts, field manuals, military journals, and staff reports. Despite security restrictions, there is usually more of this kind of material available than there is time to read it all. For the Soviet Union, there are compendia of digested Soviet writings that can also be synthesized for insights about strategies.[2]

Capability analysis for a net assessment must rely on the intelligence arms of the American military and civilian defense establishments. The CIA and the special intelligence groups of the Army, Navy, and Air Force all contribute estimates of deployed Soviet forces along with their technical characteristics. Enormous effort has been put into developing intelligence mechanisms for ascertaining this information. It is painstaking work to collect all of this information, and it is even harder to piece it together so that trends in capabilities can be predicted.[3] Since it now takes a decade or more to develop weapon systems, it has become necessary to ascertain Soviet capabilities not only today but for years into the future.

The final component of net assessment, the interaction profile, integrates goals, strategies, and capabilities, fitting them together to determine what may happen in a given interaction. The methods used for this include mathematical models, computer simulations, war games, analogies from military history, informal bargaining models suggested by game theory, and simple quantitatively based conjec-

2. An example is Joseph D. Douglass, Jr., *The Soviet Theater Nuclear Offensive* (Washington, D.C.: Government Printing Office, 1976).
3. See Lawrence Freedman, *U.S. Intelligence and the Soviet Strategic Threat* (Boulder, Colo.: Westview, 1977).

tures.[4] The last method may be the most widely used, and it some-times involves nothing more than concluding that victory will go to the side with more missiles, bombers, and submarines. The more sophisticated methods are based on the other inputs to net assessment, which sometimes are quite complicated. For example, creating math-ematical models of Soviet missile attacks on the United States can consume many hours of computer time, and preparing war games with human players can take months or even years.

We can summarize some of the broad aspects of net assessment as it is currently practiced in the United States. Most importantly, it is an integrative process that takes the results from several specialties and shows how their different effects affect the totality. In this sense, net assessment is more of a synthetic than an analytic undertaking. Analysis breaks a problem into its constituent parts, whereas net as-sessment synthesizes the separated pieces into a unified appraisal of a military interaction.

Because it is an integrative process, net assessment is greatly dependent on communicated information, and it is therefore reliant on lines of communication and all of the paraphernalia used in mod-ern information processing. This dependence is easy to overlook in peacetime when there is no danger of disconnected communications. Unless satellite reconnaissance is available for determining accurate, timely estimates of Soviet missile strength, however, it is impossible to exercise the standard calculating procedures used to assess strategic advantage.

Finally, there are ways to incorporate uncertainty into net as-sessment appraisals. For the most part, uncertainty is treated in the same way as it is handled by its constituent methodologies. For math-ematical models, this is probability theory; for computer simulations, it is statistics; and for war games, it is conjecture about the behavior

4. For a description of models, simulations, and games, see Garry D. Brewer and Martin Shubik, *The War Game* (Cambridge: Harvard University Press, 1979); for the military history approach see T. N. Dupuy, *Numbers, Predictions, and War* (India-napolis: Bobbs-Merrill, 1979); for game theory–inspired reasoning, Herman Kahn, *On Escalation* (Baltimore: Penguin, 1965); and for simple quantitative conjectures see John M. Collins, *Imbalance of Power* (San Rafael, Calif.: Presidio Press, 1978).

of people and nations. But there is little place in net assessment for uncertainty about the ability of the lines of communications to deliver input information. If there is uncertainty about the existence of this information, it would reduce, and might even remove, the integrative underpinnings of net assessment.

THE WARTIME INFORMATION REGIME

Wartime assessment differs in critical ways from the net assessment we have just described. Yet since it is quite difficult to articulate the details of these differences, there is a tendency to apply peacetime thinking to the analysis of wartime problems. This can result in a misunderstanding of war requirements, a tendency for peacetime descriptions of wartime behavior to be artificial, and, most ominously, an imposition of a peacetime design philosophy on systems that must do their job in war. The last tendency has led to a deemphasis on command and control factors and an emphasis on comparing the American and Soviet nuclear forces by their inventories of weapons. In a nuclear conflict, it is doubtful that the assessment systems of either the United States or the Soviet Union could survive very long. If we neglect this vulnerability, and pay attention only to weapon vulnerabilities, we may be in greater danger when war actually breaks out.

In war, information is often fragmented and incomplete, with bits of information being possessed by many groups. Experts have assumed that such dispersed information can be coordinated by a process something like net assessment. But net assessment is a difficult process in peacetime, even without the stresses that exist in war. Distortions, misestimates, and misperceptions can creep into any assessment. But the peculiar difficulties introduced by dispersal of information are very different, and they must be appreciated, because they can easily lead to dispersal of *authority*.

The systems built to determine what is happening in a nuclear conflict are essentially peacetime systems, constructed for a benign environment. It seems unlikely that they could survive even in a high explosive war. We can see how vulnerable the assessment process would be in war if we look at systems that tell what is about to happen in a war or what has already happened. We will leave aside for the moment the problem of what action would be taken in the event that sufficient centralized information were available.

The United States would rely on the warning and intelligence networks described in chapter 2 to inform the president, or the president's successor, of follow-on nuclear attacks that were in progress. For determining damage to its cities and military facilities the U.S. is dependent on a host of sensors and communication systems. The DSP infrared satellites used for early warning of ICBM and SLBM attack would to some extent be able to tell where nuclear explosions had taken place both in the United States and the Soviet Union, although they might not be able to give exact locations. The Vela satellites, launched in 1970, mainly verify the atmospheric test ban treaty. The Vela system is very unreliable, however. It was unable to differentiate the "incident" of a possible nuclear explosion off the coast of South Africa in 1979 from other atmospheric disturbances.[5]

More useful than Vela for damage assessment are manned aircraft. In the U.S. they could let us know what has happened to us, and in the Soviet Union they could let us know what we have done to the Soviets. SAC has over fifty planes specially fitted for reconnaissance and damage assessment for example. They could fly over America, Europe, and the Soviet Union, to survey the damage inflicted up to that point. The B-52 (or B-1B) bomber forces would also be able to provide useful information on what happened, as would other military or even civil aircraft. In the destruction and chaos of such a war it is possible that the only way the president might be able to find out quickly what had happened would be to order a SAC reconnaissance plane to Chicago, for example, to look out of the window and see if it was still there.

We should not discount information from individuals on the ground reporting what they see through the ordinary telephone sys-

5. "Neutron Bomb Is Suspected in South African Explosion," *International Herald Tribune*, March 15, 1980, p. 1.

tem. Part of the telephone system is nearly certain to survive any Soviet attack, no matter how large. The remnants of state and local civil defense agencies could also be expected to give status reports to higher headquarters, since the employees of these agencies have been trained to do so.

Because the government is concerned about the inadequacy of this hodgepodge of systems, it has recently embarked on a new, sophisticated damage assessment system to cover both America and the Soviet Union. Known as IONDS (for Integrated Operational Nuclear Detonation Detection System), it consists of visible-light sensors that detect a nuclear explosion's flash. The sensors will be placed aboard the Navstar Global Position System Satellites. Eighteen of these navigation satellites will be placed in deep space, meaning that in theory they cannot be quickly destroyed by Soviet antisatellite weapons.[6] They would give information on the number, yield, and location of above-ground nuclear explosions worldwide. The system is expected to be in operation in the late 1980s, contingent on Congress's funding not only the IONDS sensors but also the Navstar satellites.

A nation can determine the status of its strategic forces if the communication linkages that connect them to headquarters work. These links tend to work well in peacetime but in wartime their survival is in great doubt.[7] Most vulnerable links of all are with the SSBN force at sea. The problem is that most radio wavelengths are unable to travel through sea water. Only very long waves (VLF) can do this, and the submerged submarines must pick up these VLF signals via a "trailing wire" that floats near the surface. The United States has three principal and seven back-up VLF stations. In addition, an extremely low frequency (ELF) transmission system in Wisconsin has been proposed. It would permit communication with the

6. U.S., Congressional Budget Office, *Strategic Command, Control, and Communications: Alternative Approaches for Modernization* (Washington, D.C.: Government Printing Office, 1981), p. 24.

7. Details on the vulnerability of strategic communication systems can be found in Desmond Ball, *Can Nuclear War Be Controlled?* (London: International Institute for Strategic Studies, 1981).

SSBNs (and attack submarines as well) at greater depths. This would decrease the chances of a submarine being spotted by an enemy aerial patrol.

If the connection between headquarters and the submerged SSBN force is broken, headquarters is unable to assess what vessels have been sunk by the enemy. In peacetime, it can send a message to each submarine to count down. This is called polling the force. But in wartime, any electronic message sent from a submarine could give away its location. Submarines are easy to destroy if their location is known. Thus war conditions make it extremely dangerous to poll the submarines. The failure of a submarine to answer is not definite proof that a submarine has been killed by the enemy, of course. It may not be able to send a message because an enemy vessel is on its trail, preventing it from revealing its position.

The Soviets lag behind the United States in the ability to make assessments in war, partly because of technical deficiencies and partly because they have chosen to emphasize other projects. They have been experimenting and testing an infrared satellite for over ten years to monitor U.S. ICBM and SLBM launches, but as yet they have not fielded a reliable system. They have emphasized strategic, rather than tactical, warning; consequently, they are denied the spillover assessment capabilities provided by tactical warning systems.[8] I must emphasize that the relative inferiority of the Soviet wartime assessment system may not work to the U.S.'s advantage; it could be a major detriment to U.S. security. The absence of an assessment system that lets them know the damage inflicted upon the United States, for instance, severely reduces the Soviets' options for waging any form of limited nuclear war. They will have reduced information feedback, and this could reinforce their existing proclivity toward large spasm attacks.

The Soviet Union does possess photographic and electronic intelligence satellites, but they would be very difficult to operate and

8. See C. A. Zraket, "Technical Assessment of Current U.S. and U.S.S.R. Strategic C³I Systems in Normal Peacetime and Crisis Operations," MITRE Corp., August 1982.

coordinate during an actual nuclear war. Moscow also has ocean reconnaissance satellites—RORSAT (for Radar Ocean Reconnaissance Satellite) and EORSAT (for ELINT Ocean Reconnaissance Satellite)—that reportedly can locate American aircraft carriers with a 90 percent accuracy.[9]

All of the assessment systems we have described are extremely vulnerable to disruption or destruction in a nuclear war. The satellites can be attacked in space or effectively knocked out by attacking the handful of ground stations or data fusion centers that receive information from them. DSP ground stations in Australia and Denver could be attacked with conventional weapons or by sabotage, as they are housed in ordinary above-ground buildings. All together, there are only thirteen early warning sites to detect missiles, and these are fragile metal structures. The Navy's FOSICs in London and Rota are "soft," as is NSA headquarters at Fort Meade, Maryland.

Reconnaissance aircraft are more likely to survive than satellite ground stations. But using aircraft poses a huge problem for assessment, because potentially conflicting reports from dozens of aircraft and hundreds or thousands of ground observers must be coordinated. Eventually, all of these reports could be checked against each other with confirmations from other sources. But this process would take so long that it would do little to help a national leader who must immediately make critical "launch or wait" decisions in the midst of what might be a limited nuclear war.

Many assessment systems are vulnerable to jamming and other electronic countermeasures; in addition, other subtle, unintended effects could induce major failure. Jamming can be done using either intentional or unintentional electronic emissions that interfere with radio control transmissions from an earth station to a satellite, or from the satellite back to earth. Such transmissions could not only block the frequencies on which the sensor operated; they could also cause the satellite to shift orbit, make it shut itself off, or even cause it to send false or "doctored" information back to its ground station. Ma-

9. See "Soviets Resume Nuclear-Powered Ocean Surveillance Satellite," *Soviet Aerospace*, May 5, 1980, pp. 1–2.

nipulation of the transmitted data by an enemy is not as far-fetched
as it first sounds. Coded electronic transmissions known as telemetry
are used to control satellite operation from the ground. For the past
ten years both the United States and the Soviet Union have placed
enormous resources into telemetry intelligence, or TELINT, because
of its value in monitoring enemy missile flight characteristics.[10] It is
hard to believe that with the knowledge of enemy telemetry, and the
community of specialists telemetry has spawned, some attention has
not been given to intrusion into enemy satellite control for spoofing
or other exotic purposes.

Another problem that affects wartime assessment is the absence
of realistic testing of satellites and other ground stations. It could
produce subtle and unexpected results in an actual war. During the
1970s the light from the explosion of a natural gas line in the Soviet
Union temporarily blinded some American satellites. There were even
reports that this explosion was intentionally set to test American reactions, although they were never substantiated. One could imagine,
however, a limited nuclear attack on the Soviet Union setting off
natural gas, oil refinery, or other explosions. The explosions might
only blind the American satellites, but they might produce a mistaken
image of massive Soviet retaliation. The possibilities are numerous
for such subtle interactions between different parts of the forces, and
they grow more numerous as the systems become more complex.

Much attention has been given to the vulnerability of the individual sensors, such as earth-viewing satellites, radars, and reconnaissance aircraft. However, the problem of vulnerability may be even
more severe in the coordination and correlation of the data collected
by these sensors. The sensors used in tactical warning and damage
assessment collect evidence of electromagnetic or nuclear radiation.
The sensors do not count casualties, nor do they certify that military
targets have been destroyed. Exactly how estimates of damage to military, urban, and other targets are determined is a very complicated
business involving communications systems, computers, and math-

10. "Soviet Union Test Fires New Missile and Encodes Information from It," *New York Times*, February 16, 1980, p. 4.

ematical models. All of these must be coordinated for a reasonably accurate assessment of damage to be made. Raw data from observations of airplanes and satellites is transmitted to ground stations, where it is correlated and synthesized with other information, on meteorology for example. It is then processed and put into a format that is meaningful to people. Because of the great quantity of information and the very limited time available to make retaliation decisions, data is fed into on-line mathematical computer models whose outputs estimate civil and military damage.

The president of the United States may personally receive authentication of nuclear attack by observing light flashes and weapon explosion noises, but to make calculated decisions quickly about what to do next he will rely on computer estimates of civil and military damage. Nuclear damage modeling is considered one of the most difficult and arcane parts of military operations research, because of the many unstable factors that must be included and the difficulty of getting estimates on such variable phenomena. Radioactive fallout damage is determined by wind conditions over the United States and the Soviet Union, so this factor is extremely uncertain. Wind patterns must themselves be forecast to develop these estimates, and this requires the use of numerical weather prediction models that are themselves very large computer codes. Because of the uncertainties involved, statistical samplings of many different weather patterns are averaged for use in damage estimation models.

Presently, a mathematical model known as SIDAC (for Single Integrated Damage Assessment Capability) is used to process all damage assessment–related data. The SIDAC model is a computer program stored at the National Military Command Center in the Pentagon and at the hardened underground Alternate National Military Command Center.[11] From the data it would receive from satellites, ground stations, and other sources, it would arrive at estimates of population damage. The IONDS, DSP, reconnaissance aircraft, ground-based satellite stations, satellite communication links, and as-

11. United States, Joint Chiefs of Staff, *Catalog of War Gaming and Military Simulation Models*, Studies Analysis and Gaming Agency, 1977, pp. 217, 218.

sociated computers would all depend on SIDAC, or its successor, for
assessment of damage done to the United States. We will not go into
the details of SIDAC. However, there are reasons to believe that it is
exactly this type of coordinating device that could be the weakest link
in the wartime assessment system. The only serious outside review of
mathematical modeling in the defense community concluded that
the field was rife with abuses and that its standards were low or non-
existent.[12] All the same, throughout the wartime assessment system
mathematical models are used at critical points as coordinating mechanisms.

For any central coordinating mechanism to work, whether it is
a computer model or a human mind, there must be communications
from the outside world to the mechanism. This sounds so obvious
that we take it for granted. However, in a nuclear conflict electronic
communications could be substantially impaired, even if they are not
directly attacked. Nuclear explosions produce many side effects other
than blast and fire, the most important of which is electromagnetic
pulse (EMP). A nuclear burst over the United States would produce
an electromagnetic pulse that could cause widespread damage or disruption to electronic communications equipment, commercial power
and telephone lines, and especially to digital computers. There is
great disagreement in the technical community about the effects of
EMP, which demonstrates how little understanding there is about
large nuclear explosions.[13] At one extreme, some fear that a single
burst could knock out the power grid and all unprotected circuits.
This would leave the United States literally in the dark about what
was happening to it. Alternatively, some engineers feel the EMP
threat has been exaggerated and would produce few detrimental effects.

The wartime assessment system is also vulnerable to its own
complexity. A large number of things have to work properly for the
system to function. Most of these things are mundane pieces of equip-

12. Garry D. Brewer and Martin Shubik, *The War Game.*
13. "Nuclear Pulse I, II, and III," *Science,* May 29, 1981, pp. 1009–12; June 5,
1981, pp. 1116–19; and June 12, 1981, pp. 1248–51.

ment like power supplies, printers, and air conditioners. While attention naturally focuses on the highly visible and expensive components of the assessment system, it is the far larger number of ordinary components that could cause nightmares. A speck of dust might jam a printer because of a defective but still working air conditioner, causing a collapse of a whole segment of the assessment system. In the mid-1960s a Minuteman missile fired from its silo failed to take off because a speck of dust drifted into one of the electromechanical firing circuits. The piece of dust originated when the "dust protector" that covers the top of all missile silos was removed. Since then there have been only two additional tests of Minuteman missiles from operational, rather than test, silos. In both tests the missiles failed to launch.

Another example of the effect of complexity is that the NORAD warning center as of 1982 had yet to build a reliable emergency power supply.[14] Since the present NORAD facility was built in 1965 eighteen years have gone by, and still there is no reliable backup power system. Emergency power systems are not an exotic technology, as any ham radio operator can attest. The NORAD requirements are more stringent than those of a ham station. Even a weakening of electrical power causes an automatic shutdown of its computers, and getting a computer restarted can be difficult. Yet if one had to select the *single* most important center for either warning or assessment of Soviet nuclear attack, it would be NORAD. With all of the billions planned for satellites and high-energy laser weapons, the simple problem of a NORAD power supply somehow just slipped through the cracks, in the same way that the Pinto's defective gas tank slipped through all of the checks at the Ford Motor Company. This is not meant as a criticism of either NORAD or Ford, but only as a lesson in how any large organization functions.

That centralized assessment systems will not function properly in the midst of battle will hardly be news to any military commander or any student of military history. Military organizations historically have dealt with the chaos of the wartime information regime not by

14. "Fears of NORAD Blackout Chill Panel," *Baltimore Sun*, May 21, 1981, p. 8; "U.S. Warning System Called Unreliable," *Washington Post*, May 21, 1981, p. 28.

overpowering confusion through hardened communications, but by tailoring their structure to the decentralized character of war. Of course, this leads to less than optimal performance in battle when compared to a force directed by a central planner, but such a comparison begs the question of how a central direction mechanism could ever be devised. At Pearl Harbor, for example, the Japanese decided against regrouping their bombers for an immediate reattack of the American fleet because they feared opposition from ground-based aircraft.[15] Most American planes had been destroyed on the ground, a fact unknown to the Japanese until afterward when they carefully studied the intelligence photographs taken during the initial strike. During the battle, it was not possible for them to gather information systematically on damaged and surviving American aircraft. Communication among the attacking Japanese planes was available, but such communication did not permit each plane to transmit its local assessment of destroyed American aircraft to a central commander. Each Japanese pilot could choose to reattack particular ground targets, based on his own evaluation of their vulnerability and on operating constraints such as fuel status, visibility, and remaining ammunition. Information on each of these factors was available only to the pilot, and consequently the assessment of the immediate situation was left to him alone.

This example points to two responses to the problem of wartime assessment. First, in the absence of an integrated assessment a *devolution* occurs in which the assessment function devolves to local commanders. At Pearl Harbor the information acquired in battle by attacking pilots was of a fundamentally different sort than that of the central planners who designed the overall attack. No matter how accurate the planners' intelligence information was on American ships in port, number and location of aircraft, and air defense batteries, they could not impose direct control over the attack because they lacked information on the immediate battle situation of the moment. Each Japanese pilot had unique information on time and place that could not be easily communicated for centralized decision making.

15. United States Strategic Bombing Survey (Pacific), *Interrogations of Japanese Officials*, Naval Analysis Division, vol. 1, no. 113, p. 124.

The second response to the problem, also illustrated at Pearl Harbor, is the use of what can be termed "preplan attacks." Preplan attacks describe who does what against whom; they are formulated in their entirety *prior* to wartime operations. In battle, the forces attempt to carry out their preplanned assignments, but without direct control or communication from a central planning unit. Japanese aircraft squadrons were provided with a direction of attack on Pearl Harbor, but they were not guided to attacking particular American aircraft on the ground. No information on damage, retargeting opportunities, or opposing strength was given to the pilots during the course of the attack either from Tokyo or from the aircraft carriers in the Pacific.

An analogy with the preplan attack is found in the theory of maritime navigation. Dead reckoning is a way to determine the position of a ship without the aid of celestial observations. Its position is deduced from the record of the course already sailed, the distance made, and the estimated wind and current drift. The decision is made unaided by outside information and based only on data available prior to the start of operations. To one extent or another this is a common procedure for decision making used anytime that there is a substantial information blackout or a severe degradation in the quality of the arriving information. Most wars in history were run by national leaders using the principle of dead reckoning, with the course making from one battle to the next.

A crucial feature of preplan attacks is that they economize on communicated information in the course of battle. The more a military force deviates from preplan attacks toward integrated, or centrally controlled, attacks, the greater its dependence on communications networks and information-processing technology. Their job is to coordinate local assessments into an overall assessment capable of yielding centralized strategies, but this is very hard to do in wartime. Consequently, relying on preplan attacks, such as the Japanese did at Pearl Harbor, removes a large information-processing burden from the command system. Theoretically there may be a sacrifice in military effectiveness in a preplan attack as opposed to a plan that controls units both prior to and during battle. But the additional effectiveness of the latter plan is often impossible to attain in a world where the processing and communication of information are neither perfect nor cost-free.

Besides devolution of assessment to local commanders and pre-plan attacks, there are many other responses military organizations use to manage their forces in battle. However, we have raised the issue in order to point out the differences between wartime and peacetime assessment and to note the features of a nuclear exchange that are likely to reinforce these differences. If the direction of this comparison is correct, it suggests an even greater reliance on assessment by local commanders in nuclear war and also helps to explain why American war plans like the SIOP are organized as preplan attacks.

The unprecedented destructive power of nuclear explosions makes communications and command systems vulnerable to disruption as never before. As the prospect of communication and information processing failures increases, so does the likelihood that assessment will devolve downward in a military organization as a matter of necessity. This downward thrust of assessment has always been a feature of battle, but in nuclear war it is likely to be even more pronounced. In addition, we have no experience of what such a war would be like. Even if fully centralized assessment could be counted on, it is not clear that a central command unit would be able to make good choices because it has no experience about what constitutes a good, or even a feasible, choice in the first place. Typically, senior military commanders learn battle skills by repeated testing of their decisions in exercises or actual combat. With nuclear weapons there have been no such tests, and nuclear conflict is so different from high explosive wars that central command units cannot be relied upon by local commanders as they have been in historical battles of the past. One could expect great internal searching within the organization for instructions following the shock of nuclear attack, and an inability of central commanders to specify these insructions because they possess no experience about what to do. This, along with communication failures, will enhance the need for local assessment.

The great reliance in peacetime on net-assessment evaluations of conflict can create an expectation among war planners that comparable information will be available in wartime. They may assume nothing more than that the military organization following an attack will be connected, so that the different parts of it can communicate with one another. Or they may make more sophisticated assumptions, such as that very complex calculations can be undertaken after repeated nuclear attacks. They may draw up war plans that are more appropriate to a peacetime information regime in which integrated knowledge is communicated to a single mind. The many refinements that have been made to American declaratory strategy for nuclear war seem to have this feature, especially when compared to strategies of the 1950s. Then plans were organized as a single preplan attack that consisted of launching the entire nuclear arsenal against the Soviet Union in one massive salvo. This idea was even codified in the term SIOP, the *single* integrated operational plan.

Beginning in the 1960s more options were added to the SIOP, and in the mid-1970s wholesale revisions were incorporated to permit limited nuclear war, controlled responses, "building block" options, regional nuclear options, and a menu of other alternatives. All these options have distracted our attention from a far more serious problem. They all require detailed assessments about what is occurring in a battle, and they require complex coordination strategies for American nuclear forces. Most of the added alternatives to the SIOP amount to specifications of which weapons are to be fired, and which withheld. For these specifications to be feasible a communications network must survive to transmit messages, as must a damage assessment system that tells what is happening to whom. The damage assessment information itself must be a concentrated summary of many local assessments, to allow centralized choices to be made about which SIOP option to use. Here a peacetime assumption of the availability of integrated knowledge for assessment is imposed on a plan that must operate in war.

INFORMATIONALLY DECENTRALIZED NUCLEAR WARS

If there is a strong likelihood that knowledge in nuclear war will be decentralized, it is natural to ask what difference this might make.

The answer is that it makes a great deal of difference, largely because we have based American nuclear theory so fundamentally on having centralized knowledge of damage inflicted and received and on knowing the relative numbers of surviving warheads available to each nation. The idea of stability in nuclear war, that an initial attack will not lead to a quantum jump to all-out escalation, depends on the ability of each side to calculate what it can do and what can be done to it. The ability to ascertain reasonably valid estimates of damage and surviving force status is a cornerstone of politically directed nuclear attacks.

In many past campaigns, the outcome has been powerfully affected by imperfect estimates of damage and available forces. The Japanese, for instance, believed that the kamikaze attacks of 1944 and 1945 inflicted irreparable damage on the American fleet. Intelligence reports in Tokyo presented the "success rate" of these attacks as the percentage of kamikazes that hit and damaged American ships, but they failed to report that most of the struck vessels were small and replaceable.[16] Not a single American aircraft carrier was sunk by kamikaze attack. On the strength of this "success" the Japanese ignored the advice of their technicians who urged that kamikaze aircraft carry a larger explosive charge. If this had occurred, and the kamikaze program had been expanded, there is good reason to believe that the war would have lasted considerably longer.[17] Imperfect damage assessment prevented the most effective use of highly limited Japanese aircraft resources and significantly affected the outcome of battle.

The Japanese kamikaze example is not an isolated case; this phenomenon occurs frequently. At the battle of Jutland in 1916, Admiral Jellicoe of the Royal Navy had little clear idea of the disposition of German vessels or of the hits taken by his own fleet. He was able to see only flashes of light and splashes of water from bursting shells, without knowledge of the damage being caused. The German aerial bombing of Rotterdam in 1940 was initially thought to have inflicted

16. This example is noted in Charles Sorrels, "Some Further Implications of the Japanese Surrender in 1945," in Hudson Institute, "Communication and Bargaining Study Final Report," Croton-on-Hudson, N.Y., January 1970, pp. 99–100.

17. Ibid.

over one hundred thousand civilian fatalities, when in fact only about nine hundred Dutch citizens were killed.[18] And later, in the city bombings of Germany, notorious overestimates of the damage inflicted on the Nazi war industry were made. These examples all show how governments misdirected their war resources because of grossly mistaken figures, whether overestimates or underestimates. Given this experience it is surprising how little attention has been devoted to the subject of imperfect assessment in nuclear war.

As noted, many additions to American nuclear doctrine since the 1960s require greater control, precision, and selectivity in the application of force. A prerequisite for this control is knowledge of battle outcomes that can be concentrated in a single mind, or at least in a single committee or office with easy communications among its members. If this communicated knowledge does not exist or is greatly distorted, then the centralized decision makers would have little basis on which to make choices. While the necessary information could probably be gathered eventually, there is unlikely to be much time for data gathering in the course of an attack.

To understand how dependent American nuclear theory is on this kind of information, we need to have a way of characterizing who has knowledge about whom in the course of a war. We can do this very crudely with a scoring matrix for damage assessment and surviving forces, as in figure 4.2. The spaces in the matrix indicate whether concentrated damage assessment information is available to the leaderships of the United States and Soviet Union. An array of ones and zeroes are used to signify whether or not such information exists.

It would be no exaggeration to say that one matrix has dominated nearly all U.S. thinking. This analysis of nuclear strategy, which is found in academic articles and government reports is shown in figure 4.3. Here, leaders would be in possession of perfect information on damage inflicted and sustained, for both the United States and the

18. Louis J. Snyder, ed., *Masterpieces of War Reporting* (New York: Julian Messner, 1962), p. 49; Stanford Research Institute, "World War II German Fire Document Translations," Report MU 5865, Menlo Park, Calif., 1968, p. A-8.

Fig. 4.2. Assessment matrix

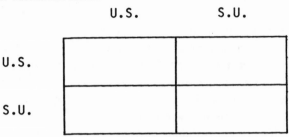

Fig. 4.3. Assessment with perfect information

Soviet Union. The United States would know how many of its missiles, planes, and submarines had been destroyed and would know how many the Soviet Union possessed even after repeated strikes. Similar information would be available on population casualties. Sensors, ground stations, communication systems, and computers would all continue to perform their jobs *during* the war.

Scenarios illustrating a nuclear campaign waged with such perfect information are not hard to find, and an influential one was offered by Paul Nitze in 1976 to advocate his conception of crisis stability.[19] Nitze's scenario is a poignant example of how often the

19. Paul Nitze, "Assuring Strategic Stability in an Era of Detente," *Foreign Affairs* 54 (January 1976):207–232. Our analysis also depends on Garry D. Brewer and Bruce G. Blair, "War Games and National Security with a Grain of SALT," *The Bulletin of the Atomic Scientists* (June 1979):18–26.

nuclear strategies that are advocated depend on damage assessments, communicated information, and burdensome amounts of computation without realizing it. The core idea in the Nitze analysis is that the relative throw-weight available to the United States and the Soviet Union following a series of strikes on military targets will determine which side is "superior."[20] Throw-weight is the tonnage of payload (warheads, decoys, etc.) that a nuclear force can deliver against enemy targets, and it is a common measure of the size of a nuclear force.

A Soviet first strike against American military targets is the opening move of the Nitze scenario. It destroys enough American missiles and bombers that the ratio of throw-weight available to each side shifts in favor of the Soviets. The numerical ratios are less important for our purposes than is the knowledge presumed available to American leaders; consequently we need not reproduce Nitze's figures. Not only do American authorities know how many missiles and bombers have been destroyed, but they also know which ones, for American targeting plans are optimized as the next step in Nitze's scenario. This requires knowledge about the survival and targeting of each American warhead. Soviet leaders are somehow presumed to know this information as well. American leaders then order a retaliatory strike against Soviet military targets to make the throw-weight ratio more favorable to the United States again. This attack is launched and monitored using a damage assessment system that has already been subjected to thousands of nuclear bursts. Yet the information is passed from sensor to computer to mathematical model, using the facilities described earlier, and it is presented to American leaders so that they may examine the resulting throw-weights available after this, the second salvo of the war.

The Soviet damage assessment system, which has itself absorbed several thousand nuclear explosions, then appraises the situation in both countries. Soviet computers optimize surviving forces against undestroyed American targets and recompute the relative throw-weight balance. According to Nitze, if the throw-weight balance at this point in the war is favorable to the Soviets (a conclusion he advances), then

20. Nitze, "Assuring Stability," p. 227.

Moscow "wins." His rationale is that a continued sequence of strikes would only drive the throw-weight ratio more in favor of the Soviets. If the United States chose to attack Soviet cities then Moscow could retaliate in kind, making this choice irrational. Implicit in the Nitze analysis, however, is the idea that repeated strikes would shift the throw-weight balance, and that such shifts would be observable by American and Soviet leaders. It is a view of war remarkably similar to that found in peacetime net assessments. Unfortunately, the information regime in wartime is unlikely to even come close to the requirements of the Nitze scenario, which depends on enormous amounts of communicated information and computation.

At first glance the constraints on information processing suggested by the vulnerability of wartime assessment systems would appear to influence the outcome of the exchanges only marginally. Destruction of the computer needed for optimizing targeting plans might degrade the retaliatory strike, but it need not prevent it altogether. The president might be denied information about some damage to the United States, but he also might receive enough information about other phases of the conflict to justify sound decisions. Seen this way the flow of the war might proceed through repeated strikes according to some sort of dead reckoning. Perfectly functioning assessment systems might not be essential, but merely desirable.

The difficulty with such a conclusion is that it treats the destruction of an assessment mechanism in the same way as the destruction of a weapon. But an assessment system conveys information, and information is not a physical "thing" like bombers or missiles. Destroying enemy weapons produces clear consequences, while destroying the means of assessment produces highly uncertain results. A nation's behavior will be shaped not by the forces it has relative to the enemy, but by the forces it *thinks* it has. If Soviet submarine commanders, for example, are cut off from higher commands it is doubtful that any limitation in U.S. strikes can impress them.

Any time a breakdown in communication channels is severe enough that individual commanders are essentially operating on their own with little knowledge of the overall strategic situation the powerful effect of information, or its absence, emerges. The tightly integrated nuclear command system will break up into separated islands of forces, each isolated from the other because of the inherent vulnerabilities in the assessment and communications systems that tie them together in peacetime. There will not be *one* assessment, in which the president looks over the situation and decides whether to retaliate, but *several*, each performed independently by isolated forces cut off from one another. Assessment then devolves downward in the command organization and decentralizes to the local commanders in charge of the separated islands.

A very simple example, involving only five military command centers and one political command center that controls the other centers, can illustrate this logic and some of its conclusions. For purposes of exposition, we could think of four of the military command posts as the four American commands that control nuclear weapons, namely the Pacific Command (PAC), Atlantic Command (LANT), Strategic Air Command (SAC), and the European Command (EUR). Each of these commands includes command, control, and communication facilities along with its nuclear and other military forces. The political command, called the National Command Authorities (NCA), includes the president and his military advisers, the JCS. In addition, an IONDS command post is included, which represents a satellite-based damage assessment system that reports to all other command centers.

This system is schematically represented in figure 4.4. The lines connecting the various command centers stand for communications. A line drawn between two centers indicates two-way communications are possible, perhaps over numerous channels. For ease of presentation the Soviet command system has not been represented, although including it would not add conceptual difficulties.

This command system cannot be characterized with the four-cell scoring matrix of figure 4.2 because the latter lumped a nation's entire assessment into a single cell. Either it functioned perfectly in its assessment of the United States or the Soviet Union, or it failed completely. But between these two extremes are likely to lie the most interesting and provocative possibilities, since assessment need not perform perfectly for it to "work" in the sense of giving commanders

Fig. 4.4. A stylized command system

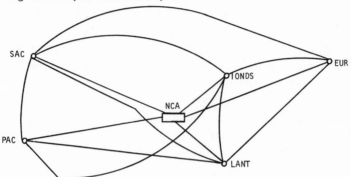

Fig. 4.5. Assessment matrix for stylized command system

	SAC	PAC	NCA	LANT	EUR	IONDS
SAC	1	1	1	1	1	1
PAC	1	1	1	1	0	1
NCA	1	1.	1	1	1	1
LANT	1	1	1	1	1	1
EUR	1	0	1	1	1	1
IONDS	1	1	1	1	1	1

a relatively faithful picture of the strategic situation. Alternatively, the assessment system need not fail entirely in order to produce catastrophe. A middle ground offers the most fruitful area for analysis.

By extending the scoring matrix of figure 4.2 we can characterize the information conditions when a nation's assessment system is represented in a more disaggregated way. Such a matrix is shown for the command system of figure 4.4 in figure 4.5. A one in a cell signifies a direct communications link between two centers, and a zero signifies the absence of such a connection. The only zero in this particular structure is between EUR and PAC, but this does not signify an inability to communicate, because these centers can be linked by intermediate centers. For example, PAC and EUR could communicate by sending messages through the NCA center, or through SAC or LANT. As a practical economic matter it is prohibitively expensive to link each command center independently to every other.

Now we can describe how an attack could dramatically transform the assessment not at the margin, but at its core. A Soviet attack, if sufficiently large, would mean changing the ones in figure 4.5 to zeroes. If the command centers themselves were destroyed, zeroes would be placed on the diagonal cell where the same center's vertical and horizontal coordinates intersect. This represents the Soviets knocking out command posts directly. Failures in communication among posts because of blast damage to equipment, EMP, jamming, or for any of the reasons already discussed would mean shifting of the off-diagonal ones to zeroes.

One thing that emerges even in this extraordinarily simplified model of a command system is the vast number of outcomes that could result from an attack. Even if it is supposed that all surviving centers use backup emergency communications that are able to reach all other posts, it turns out that there are 279 different configurations of surviving command systems.[21] Compare this to the standard analysis of six weapons when attacked, where there are but seven possibilities (either 0, 1, 2, 3, 4, 5, or 6 weapons survive). The reason for the geometric increase in alternatives for the command system is that the linkage of the centers drives up the totals. Four surviving posts might exist as two pairs (3 alternatives), a triplet and a single (4 alternatives), as a pair and two singles (6 alternatives), as four separated single units (1 alternative), or as a fully connected network of four posts (1 alternative).

If a faithful representation of either the American or Soviet command system were depicted, the largest computer on earth could not systematically analyze all of the possible alternatives. The practical effect of so many possibilities is that war planners do not, indeed

---

21. Computing formulas have been developed to ascertain the total number of alternatives. See Paul Bracken, "The Crude Analysis of Command Structure Design," Yale University, 1982.

cannot, look at very many contingencies that involve disruption or degradation of the command system, and by implication the assessment system. War plans have a strong bias in favor of guaranteeing retaliation, perhaps considering a handful of different ways to do this, and rely on little or no detailed contingency analysis for how command disruptions affect the detailed operation of the force. Only the simplest general procedures have been developed to handle the multitude of cases, such as ordering an isolated entity to search for contact with higher authorities.

The lack of detailed contingency plans to deal with disruptions in large complex systems often comes as a surprise to people. But the reason for a lack of planning gets back to the inability to anticipate the astronomical number of things that can go wrong in an emergency in which several parts of the system are acting up. The single-cause accident usually can be guarded against. However, a company like AT&T, for example, does not maintain contingency emergency plans for a major telephone outage because the planning for it would be too expensive. Instead, it relies on local assessments and measures to rectify whatever problems arise.[22]

A dependence on decentralized local assessment would surely characterize a command system that had just sustained a nuclear attack. The ramifications of this are that each isolated command post in a conflict would have to factor in the behavior of surviving commanders with whom he cannot communicate. Let us suppose a nuclear attack on the system of figure 4.4 was met by a limited American counterstrike, which ultimately led to the system of survivors shown in figure 4.6. The American command system must now be thought of as three separate players who are not in communication with one another. Player I is the NCA, which is linked to SAC and LANT. Player II is PAC, and player III is EUR. Supposing that the IONDS assessment system was even able to provide information on damage inflicted on the United States, but not on the rest of the world; how would the political commander, the NCA, assess the overall strategic situation?

22. "The Great New York Telephone Fire," *Spectrum*, June 1975, p. 34.

Fig. 4.6. Stylized command system following nuclear attack

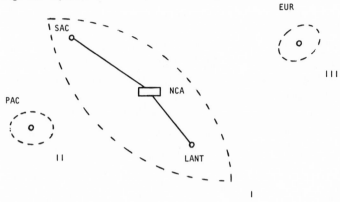

One thought that might occur to the NCA, or be suggested by his military advisers, is that the situation is unstable. It is unstable because, regardless of the damage sustained by the United States, the NCA has to consider the possibility that player III, the European commander, will lose control over the situation, and that nuclear weapons will be launched at the Soviet Union from his command. The NCA does not know the status of European nuclear weapons or their targeting; indeed, many weapons may have been wiped out in Soviet attacks about which he knows little or nothing. If the NCA wants to terminate the war, he can signal this to the Soviet Union by withholding follow-on attacks carried out by SAC or LANT. But if he believes that the EUR commander is likely to lose control, for example because the European force is especially accident-prone or inherently uncontrollable, then the NCA must put himself in the Soviet position of seeing follow-on strikes launched from Europe, and perhaps also from the other isolated player, the Pacific commander, as well. The damaged Soviet assessment system would not see such follow-on attacks as a signal for war termination, to say the least. The Soviet command system, if it had gotten this far, might be capable of issuing only one final order: fire everything in the house.

The logic of decentralized assessment leads to an unpleasant conclusion in this example. The NCA himself may want to terminate the war, but large amounts of isolated megatonnage outside of his control continue to salvo against the Soviet Union. The rational decision for the NCA then is to order SAC and LANT to fire also, on the grounds that the Soviets will inevitably empty their remaining arsenal if attacked by the isolated forces in Europe or the Pacific. Given all the alternatives it seems best to destroy as much of the inevitable Soviet return strike as possible.

The strategic situation seen from the EUR or PAC commander is somewhat different. Each commander's virtual isolation could be interpreted by them either as a mere communication breakdown, as the consequence of a limited Soviet-American exchange, or as an all-out attack in which no one was left alive to authorize them to fire. The interpretation selected would depend on their last information received, their individual personalities, and how vulnerable their weapons were to Soviet attack. If they controlled a protected force, they might not be as prone to use it before it was destroyed. They would also be influenced by whatever scraps of information they could obtain about the overall situation. If it appeared that Soviet attacks were continuing on the American homeland, there would be considerable pressure to fire promptly on the chance that some damage to the United States could be prevented.

It is clear, then, that a degradation in the assessment process will produce changes that can totally change the nature of the problem. Disruption of command systems does not necessarily lead to marginal losses in effectiveness; it can lead to a radical transformation of the controllability of a war. In an informationally decentralized nuclear war, authority too will be decentralized. The course of action that will be taken will depend on behavioral details of the isolated players, their weapons, alert status prior to attack, and many other microscopic features of the tactical wars being fought. Here, an assessment must take account of the joint action of all of the separate actors when they are not informed about the strategic state of the world or each others' preferences. Only through analysis of the assessment information available in this disconnected environment can a realistic sense of the controllability of nuclear exchanges be had.

5 The Special Problems of War in Europe

Many of the problems inherent in nuclear crises solely restricted to intercontinental range arms have their counterparts in the European theater. The nature and utility of warning information must be considered, for example, and due thought must be given to war plans. But a nuclear war in Europe is different in truly fundamental ways. First, in Europe there are thousands of nuclear weapons integrated into conventional ground forces, and this situation radically transforms the command and control problem. Second, because of the coalition nature of both NATO and the Warsaw Treaty Organization, it is possible that Italy or Turkey could explode nuclear weapons on Soviet soil. Third, the scale of the battlefield in both space and time is shrunk from intercontinental ranges, compressing decision times into minutes and making the very distinction between strategic and theater conflict meaningless.

The flight time of a Pershing 2 missile from a West German base to any of the Soviet High Command posts around Moscow is about twelve minutes. Such brief flight times effectively fuse strategic and theater war into a seamless twelve-minute campaign. Other NATO aircraft are also within range of Russia's cities. The geographic asymmetry of the European situation provides the linkage for escalating theater to a strategic war. Washington and New York are safe from theater nuclear destruction, but Moscow and Leningrad are not. It is hard to imagine that the Soviet Union would accept an artificial distinction between strategic and theater war if its High Command in Moscow were attacked by NATO nuclear weapons.

The unique character of theater nuclear war demands a separate treatment of it that identifies its most distinctive features. In this chapter we examine the special problems of European security, looking particularly at the decisions and organizing principles central to theater warfare. Of course, more general considerations of warning, assessment, planning, and command and control are not absent in a theater conflict. All of them are very much in evidence. But a unique set of problems arises because of such factors as the decentralized coalition control of nuclear weapons and the Soviet command's much-reduced reaction time (shrunk from thirty to twelve minutes).

The perspective on NATO taken in this chapter may need some further clarification at the outset. Broadly speaking, we are mainly interested in the relationship of strategy to actual force structures. We will not analyze peacetime nuclear politics and logrolling, factor inputs of materiel and manpower, or the technical characteristics of new missile systems. All of these are important in their own right, and all have received a great deal of attention.[1] What has been lacking, however, is an analysis of the complicated relationship between NATO's strategy and the force structure that has been evolving for the past three decades. It is this relationship that will be the greatest determinant of what happens in a future European crisis, and this mechanism also that will enforce the remarkable deterrent which NATO has built to protect itself from attack.

An example can illustrate our approach. Most standard discussions of NATO strategy give central emphasis to theater nuclear weapons as a mechanism for retaliation against invasion. The threat of this retaliation and its credibility are widely studied to determine whether or not NATO would actually use nuclear weapons to counter it. This formulation of the NATO strategy problem, however, is so barren of detail that it is of little help in determining which decisions the NATO leaders actually would confront. NATO decision makers will not be faced with *one* choice on nuclear usage, but with *many*. The NATO force structure makes this certain, because it is made up of so many parts that interact in a nonsimple way.

---

1. For example, see Richard E. Neustadt, *Alliance Politics* (New York: Columbia University Press, 1970); and John M. Collins and Anthony H. Cordesman, *Imbalance of Power: Shifting U.S.-Soviet Military Strengths* (San Rafael, Calif.: Presidio Press, 1978).

Decisions will have to be made about a host of problems: whether to evacuate urban populations; whether to release nuclear weapons to the operational control of Turkey and Greece; whether to implement the massive demolition and flooding plans that exist; whether to disperse nuclear artillery rounds on German soil; whether to airlift well over three hundred thousand American military dependents back to safety in the United States. Taken alone, each of these is a hard choice. When they are taken together in all of their interrelatedness, they change what is most often perceived to be the key NATO strategic question, nuclear usage, into a far more complex, unstructured, and uncertain one. Determining options and the consequences of decisions in this framework is not at all clear. What is clear, however, is that it is likely to be considerably different, from the simple matter of using or not using nuclear weapons. By treating European security problems in the more complicated framework, some initial steps toward more realistic problem analysis can be taken.

This chapter begins with a description of the difficulty of even defining a theater nuclear war. Then the nuclear systems are described, and force structure features (that is, the formal and informal lines of authority and communication among the different administrative offices and levels of the military command) are highlighted. Another fundamental aspect of force structure, the flow of information through the lines of authority and communication, is analyzed, and European attitudes toward nuclear war are examined.[2] We show how information flows are intimately related to command and control of European nuclear forces, to the linkage between theater and strategic warfare, to war termination, and most important, to the enforcement mechanisms that implement the NATO deterrent strategy.

BACKGROUND ON EUROPEAN NUCLEAR FORCES

The variety of theater nuclear weapons in Europe is so great, and the force structures in which they are embedded are so different from intercontinental nuclear forces, that to get a clear understanding we

2. These complementary aspects of structure are used in Alfred O. Chandler, *Strategy and Structure* (Cambridge: MIT Press, 1962).

first need some basic information about them. The very first item needing clarification is the definition of theater nuclear war itself. The term has no standardized meaning; there are not even accepted defining criteria for it. Not only is there a lack of agreement among specialists about what ranges qualify to be termed "theater," but there is no agreement that range is itself a defining criteria.

This definitional impasse involves more than semantics. Theater nuclears do exist, and they have come to take a middle position in the hierarchy of conflict, between conventional high-explosive wars and intercontinental nuclear exchanges. For better or worse, this conceptualization shapes the definition of theater nuclear forces held by American political leaders. In 1975, for example, Secretary of Defense Schlesinger articulated the widely accepted idea that if NATO's conventional armies were unable to withstand Soviet attack, "NATO political leaders may choose to accept the risks of first [nuclear] use."[3] It is clear from many other comments that the secretary embraced a three-pronged concept of NATO strategy: conventional nonnuclear, theater nuclear, and strategic nuclear forces. This strategy relies on conventional forces to repel a Soviet conventional attack; if this were to fail, use of theater nuclear forces would be warranted. If the Soviets were to retaliate with their own theater nuclear forces, then U.S. intercontinental nuclear weapons would be called upon.

This conceptualization does not actually define a theater nuclear war. But it suggests a functional definition of theater nuclear war as a buffer between conventional warfare and all-out intercontinental nuclear exchange. Leaders in the United States have come to think about these weapons in terms of their function rather than technical definition. European conceptualizations appear to be different, as we shall see later, and this difference confounds the problem of conceptualizing theater nuclear war.

Figure 5.1 shows how theater nuclears would function in two conceptions of war. The first diagram depicts a simpler alternative conception of a theater nuclear war. This conception of political

3. As quoted in "U.S. Backs Tactical Atom Arms against a Soviet Push in Europe," *New York Times*, May 30, 1975, p. 1.

Fig. 5.1 The intermediate role of theater nuclear war

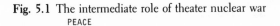

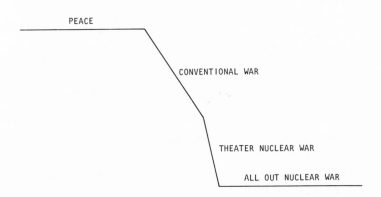

strategy was popular in the 1950s, but was officially abandoned by the United States in 1962 when means for greater political control of nuclear forces were formulated. In this conception, there is an abrupt transition from peace to all-out nuclear war, that is, massive intercontinental exchanges involving extensive destruction of urban and industrial areas. Conventional and theater nuclear forces are exercised as well, but mainly in conjunction with the intercontinental attack rather than as a buffer or escalation-control device. This conception of theater nuclear forces is still favored in Europe.

The lower diagram in figure 5.1 illustrates the intermediary role of theater nuclear weapons. Conventional forces would be used first to repel attack, resort to theater nuclears would follow a failure to resist with conventional means, and intercontinental attack would backstop theater nuclear usage. Thus three layers of military defense would be provided.

I must emphasize that this conceptualization is not a description of the actual course of a conflict nor does it detail the structural capability to carry out its three-layered distinction of conflict. It is intended only as a highly simplified conceptual model of current American thought on theater nuclear war.[4] These conceptual models, however simplified, play a powerful role in framing how leaders think about this kind of conflict, nonetheless, because their simplicity offers one way to cope with the enormous complexity of the European defense question. There is always the problem, however, of whether the right simplifying ideas are contained in the conceptual models, and whether the same models are shared by both allies and adversaries. Most important, we must ask if there is a match between the simplifying strategy and the force structure needed to carry it out. A lack of connection between strategy and structure, we will see, has characterized American thinking on NATO strategy.

For all its defects, our functional definition of theater nuclear war as intermediate between conventional and intercontinental war does specify what theater nuclear weapons are. They are simply those nuclear weapons that are intended for other than intercontinental attack. But this definition is still fuzzy, vague about its inclusion of allied and opponent nuclears, and, most important, indifferent to the really hard questions of theater warfare. It slides over the fact that this "intermediate" nuclear conflict will appear to the Europeans, including Europeans in Russia, to be strategic in the fullest sense of the word. And it focuses on certain obvious questions suggested by the diagrams in figure 5.1, such as when nuclears would be used and when full intercontinental attack would be initiated. These are simple decisions, in the sense that they do not involve fitting together all the pieces of the defense picture. Indeed, this formulation suggests a clar-

---

4. A good review of various conceptualizations of theater nuclear forces can be found in Harold A. Feiveson, "The Dilemma of Theater Nuclear Weapons," *World Politics* 23 (January 1981): 282–98.

ity and definition to the nuclear decision that is unlikely to exist in real life.

That it leaves so much to be desired is testament to two things. First, the definition reflects an ambiguity about the wartime purpose of these forces. The very absence of a shared sense of objectives and concept of use has important deterrent implications. Second, decisions about deployments must be made, and have been made, even though definitional problems remain. In the practical world, the mere lack of an unambiguous set of objectives is hardly an obstacle to the acquisition and deployment of thousands of nuclear weapons. Defense organizations have a way of running themselves even without clear and consistent guidance. Choices have to be made, and they *are* made. A failure to define unambiguous centralized direction for a defense system means only that direction is supplied from decentralized, or bureaucratic, sources.

A good way of understanding the European nuclear situation, then, is to turn from important, but still inadequate, conceptualizations of function to the question of process. This is an onerous task. With so many different kinds of nuclears dispersed among so many different nations, it is difficult to find patterns and categories that meaningfully simplify the problem of how to think about nuclear war in Europe. Alluring, oversimplified conceptual models, such as that theater nuclears are for conflicts intermediate between conventional and strategic wars, offer an easy way out. This path is attractive, but the model that is produced is wildly invalid. National security planning has often fallen into this trap. But what is really necessary is to ground a conceptual model in the world of actual force structures, of which the weapons themselves are one important part.

Theater Nuclear Weapons

We can get a sense of the heterogeneity of NATO's theater nuclear forces just from listing the systems that NATO has fielded. Nuclear mines, artillery, surface-to-surface and surface-to-air missiles, air-delivered bombs and rockets, and naval weapons have been in use for well over two decades.[5] It is widely reported that some six thousand nuclear warheads are deployed in Europe as of the early 1980s, and this number excludes tactical nuclear weapons that are currently held in reserve in the United States and would be sent to Europe in a crisis.[6]

Table 5.1 shows one estimate of the breakdown in types of nuclear warheads deployed by NATO in the early 1980s. Warheads, not delivery vehicles, are presented in this table. This estimate is approximate, but it illustrates the broad characteristics of the NATO warhead stockpile.

The most striking feature of this breakdown is the extent to which all services, and nearly all branches of services, have been nuclear-

Table 5.1. U.S. and NATO Theater Nuclear Warheads in Europe

	Number	Percentage of Total
Atomic Demolition Munitions (ADMs)	300	5
Artillery Rounds	1,400	23
Surface-to-Surface Missiles	1,990	33
Bombs and Missiles for Aircraft	1,719	28
Surface-to-Air Missiles	350	5
Antisubmarine Weapons for Aircraft	380	6
	6,089	100

Sources: Adapted from J. J. Martin, "Trends and Asymmetries in the Theater Nuclear Balance," Science Applications, Inc., November 1981, pp. 26–41; and Jeffrey Record, "U.S. Tactical Nuclear Weapons in Europe: 7,000 Warheads in Search of a Rationale," Arms Control Today 4 (April 1974): 4.

5. A detailed catalog of NATO and Warsaw Pact nuclear weapons may be found in R. T. Pretty, ed., Jane's Weapon Systems (London: Jane's Yearbooks, 1976).

6. See source for table 5.1.

ized. Only the U.S. Army infantry and armor do not possess nuclears, assuming, that is, that the nuclear land mines known as atomic demolition munitions (ADMs) are not counted as infantry weapons.[7] The philosophy that modern combat necessarily involves joint land, sea, and air operations has been carried into the nuclear age by arming each of the services with atomic weapons. The large number of warheads that are being used on World War II–era weapons is also remarkable. Although it has become a cliche to speak of the revolution in military affairs caused by nuclear weapons, the fact of the matter is that air-delivered ordnance and artillery were among the most basic casualty-inflicting mechanisms of World War II and more than 50 percent of NATO nuclear warheads are for just these delivery systems. Nuclear weapons may be revolutionary in a *technological* sense, but as far as the *organization* of military forces is concerned, they have produced less momentous consequences. Military forces in Europe are not organized on a radically different basis from their World War II counterparts, despite being equipped with nuclear arms. The U.S. Army did experiment with a radically different organization, known as the Pentomic Division, beginning in 1956. It was designed as a more decentralized and dispersed ground combat force. Decentralization was suited to the disrupted communications environment of the nuclear battlefield, and physical dispersion of troops offered a less lucrative target for enemy nuclear weapons. However, under the shift to a conventional emphasis for the defense of Europe during the Kennedy administration the Pentomic division structure was abandoned in favor of a more traditional form. The period 1956–61 represents the only real attempt by any army in the world to restructure itself for the nuclear battlefield.[8] Soviet forces are similarly organized along traditional lines. All of this strongly suggests that force structure is a relatively enduring feature of military organizations, and that its effects can be greater and more long-lasting than those of technology.

7. U.S. Army infantry units were at one time provided with a nuclear recoilless rifle, the Davy Crockett. It was ordered withdrawn in 1967. *New York Times*, March 25, 1967, p. 10.

8. Russell F. Weigley, *History of the United States Army* (New York: Macmillan, 1967), pp. 537–38.

Armies have not been built *around* nuclear arms; instead, nuclear arms have been built *into* traditional military organizations. This is the main way theater nuclear forces differ from strategic forces.

The integration of World War II–style forces with sophisticated warning and intelligence systems creates additional tensions. With the strategic nuclear forces, new institutions were designed based on the technological characteristics of the weapons. The whole system of checks and balances, vertical integration of warning with the offensive forces, and reliance on near real-time fusion centers was thought through by building organizations around the unique features of nuclear weapons. The organizations took into account their destructiveness, short flight times, and the implications of potential nuclear accidents. In Europe, however, information-processing and intelligence systems that produce "pictures" of the ground battlefield are overlaid onto classical military force structures. Although these sophisticated automated systems may represent the next evolution in military organization, an attempt to use them to manage every threat on the European nuclear battlefield raises deeply troubling questions about effectiveness and safety in a confused and chaotic environment.

In Europe, nuclear weapons are also dispersed among the different force structures of the nations in the NATO coalition. The nature of this dispersion of weapons is a highly complicated subject that has not yet been fully analyzed. We will give only an overview here. Broadly speaking, all nuclear weapons committed to NATO are American-owned, with the exception of the independent nuclear force of Britain. France has its own independent nuclear force, but as France left the military structure of NATO in 1965 French weapons are not generally counted in NATO totals. American-owned warheads are provided for allied delivery vehicles under a series of *bilateral* treaties and agreements between the United States and the various host nations. The weapons are governed not by a multilateral NATO instrument, but instead by individual arrangements made between various countries and the United States.[9] The exact nature of these

9. See Irving Heymont, "The NATO Nuclear Bilateral Forces," *Orbis* 9 (Winter 1966): 1025–41.

agreements is kept highly secret, as indeed are the deployments of American-owned nuclear warheads on foreign soil. Nonetheless, by compiling information on the delivery vehicles for nuclear warheads (which are owned by host nations), we can come up with a picture of the national distribution of NATO's nuclear assets. Figure 5.2 shows an estimate of this distribution.

The procedure by which the United States maintains physical control of the warheads in the host nations is the so-called dual-key control mechanism. Not really a key at all (although it once was), it is the simple procedure of maintaining the warheads under U.S. custodial control. One key is the warhead, and the other the foreign-owned delivery vehicle. When weapon is matched to delivery vehicle and the system is launched, or fired, it is as if both keys were turned together.[10] About half of the six thousand weapons in NATO are

Fig. 5.2. Nuclear-capable weapons systems in the possession of NATO European nations

	BRITAIN	NETHER-LANDS	BELGIUM	W. GERMANY	TURKEY	GREECE	ITALY
MINES (ADMs)				X	X	X	X
ARTILLERY	X	X	X	X	X	X	X
LANCE	X	X	X	X			X
HONEST JOHN	X	X		X	X	X	
NIKE HERCULES		X	X	X	X	X	X
PERSHING I				X			
FIGHTER-BOMBERS	X	X	X	X	X	X	X

Sources: M. Leitenberg, "Background Materials in Tactical Nuclear Weapons Primarily in the European Context," in Stockholm International Peace Research Institute, ed., *Tactical Nuclear Weapons: European Perspectives* (London: Taylor & Francis, 1978) pp. 109–36; International Institute for Strategic Studies, *The Military Balance 1980–81* (London: The International Institute for Strategic Studies, 1980).

10. "Europe Now Shuns Its Nuclear Trigger," *New York Times*, November 1, 1979, p. A3.

under dual-key control.[11] American warheads deployed for use by American troops on European soil do not have this control feature, and neither does the independent British nuclear force.

The distribution of weapons shown in figure 5.2 only begins to suggest the complications that arise from dual-key nuclears. For example, ownership of a delivery vehicle does not necessarily imply that the nuclear warheads to be used with it are stored on the host nation's territory. It might turn out that Dutch artillery units would receive their warheads from American custodial units on German soil. Alternatively, it is possible that American artillery rounds could be stored in Belgium or Britain, to be flown into Germany for matching with Dutch artillery weapons during a crisis.[12] Each country in the NATO coalition has its own unique needs and problems, although in some cases geographic factors would undoubtedly influence deployments. For example, Turkey and Greece are so remote from the central front in Europe that it is unlikely that warheads would be dispatched to them from this area.

The most important observation to be made about figure 5.2 is that this great diversity of theater nuclear weapons is controlled by seven national command organizations, representing six different languages. Although joint planning can ameliorate some problems of coordination, political realities inevitably will influence the extent to which coordination can occur. Each national military organization is under separate national control. Turkish forces serve under Turkish command, not under any direct NATO command.

We saw earlier how standard military organizations have not been restructured for theater nuclear warfare. Neither have Europe's national military forces, which have remained organizationally unchanged by the addition of nuclear arms. Nuclear arms have been overlaid onto the conventional forces of the independent military establishments of countries participating in NATO. Thus, there are no special NATO fighter squadrons or artillery battalions simultaneously composed of Italians, Greeks, and Belgians. Common sense

11. Ibid.
12. The examples are hypothetical. Reports suggest that nuclear artillery rounds are stored in the Netherlands, "Dutch Feeling Is Strongly Antinuclear," *Baltimore Sun*, March 20, 1981, p. 13.

suggests why it would be extremely difficult to bring about this kind of organization for NATO. Language barriers, questions of national sovereignty, control, and responsibility, and cost sharing are among the many factors that immediately come to mind. NATO's dual-key nuclear weapons are integrated into national military commands for reasons of organizational necessity.

After this brief examination of the background of theater nuclear forces, let us take a closer look at the weapons themselves and the force structures in which they are embedded.

NUCLEAR MINES. Nuclear land mines, often called atomic demolition munitions (ADMs), have been fielded by the United States at least since 1960.[13] They are stored primarily in West Germany, Turkey, Greece, and Italy and are intended to destroy bridges and tunnels and to create delaying obstacles in mountain passes.[14] They are useful in mountainous terrain and natural invasion corridors, and would have special suitability for blocking or delaying invasion in the Anatolian region of eastern Turkey, along the Greco-Bulgarian border, and in northeastern Italy.

ADMs are used by specially trained teams of five or six men. The teams do not appear to be integrated into standard infantry or artillery units but instead report along special lines directly to army and corps commanders.[15]

There are conflicting reports about Soviet possession of ADMs, but nothing is known for certain about how they are used if they do indeed exist. They may play an important role for behind-the-line forces or for sabotage by military or nonmilitary agents. A small, portable ADM has been developed, and U.S. Special Forces units reportedly have missions involving placing portable ADMs at enemy airfields, command posts, and logistic centers in the event of war.[16]

13. Leitenberg, "Background Materials," p. 127.
14. See sources for figure 5.2.
15. U.S. Congress, Senate, Committee on Foreign Relations, *U.S. Security Issues in Europe: Burden Sharing and Offset, MBFR and Nuclear Weapons*, 93d Cong., 1st sess., 1973, p. 15.
16. William M. Arkin, "Nuclear Weapons in Europe," Institute for Policy Studies, Washington, D.C., pp. 11–12.

Soviet KGB and special forces also are rumored to be armed with compact ADMs for a similar purpose. If such tactics were to be employed, it would seem necessary to turn control of the ADMs over to the units prior to actual hostilities to permit time to penetrate to their targets. This, of course, raises troubling problems of command and control.

ARTILLERY. For years rumors of the existence of Soviet nuclear artillery were in circulation, but in 1977 they were confirmed by U.S. Army intelligence.[17] Very little additional information is known about Soviet nuclear activities in this area, however. The United States, in contrast, has had nuclear artillery deployed in Europe since 1953.[18] That both nations now seem to have these systems raises the possibility that in a future war in Europe extensive nuclear firepower would be deployed low enough in the military organization to support the ground-gaining arms of the armor and mechanized infantry. This would be true battlefield nuclear war.

The maximum range of American nuclear artillery is about eleven miles, and that of the Soviets between eleven and eighteen miles, depending on the weapon.[19] The yield of the American warheads is estimated at two kilotons.[20] Little is known about Soviet yields.

American artillery units are organized for support of both division and corps operations. Nuclear rounds have been developed for the weapons basic to these units, the 155-millimeter and 8-inch howitzers. This means that nuclear artillery strikes would involve two separate channels of command. Coordination would take place through

17. U.S. Department of the Army, Office of the Assistant Chief of Staff for Intelligence, *Understanding Soviet Military Developments*, Pub. AST-11005-100-77 (1977), p. 71. This document also implies the development of nuclear mortar rounds for use by the Soviet infantry. See also Robert Kennedy, "Soviet Theater Nuclear Forces," *Air Force*, March 1981, p. 78.

18. "U.S. Atomic Cannons Arrive in Bremerhaven," *New York Times*, October 9, 1953, p. 8.

19. Kennedy, "Soviet Forces," p. 79; and Department of the Army, "Understanding Soviet Developments," p. 71.

20. International Institute for Strategic Studies, *The Military Balance 1980–1981* (London: International Institute for Strategic Studies, 1980), p. 92.

the fire control centers of the standard Army division. The purpose of this fire, like all artillery fire, would be to support the ground-gaining arms, isolate the battlefield, and provide depth to the combat. These tasks would be assigned in different degrees to division, corps, or special artillery groups. Although for Soviet artillery the assignment would be different, the basic task structure would be along the same lines. At least two command structures, division and army, and probably more, would have to be coordinated.

We should note that the main emphasis in American artillery since World War II has been the development of quick-reacting, decentralized fire control.[21] Thus, all artillery in U.S. armored and mechanzed divisions is entirely self-propelled, allowing it to move as rapidly as the combat arms it supports. In the 1970s, the Soviets also began to emphasize this same trend.[22] Overlaying nuclear capability onto this trend suggests that a strong decentralizing force will be at work in a battlefield nuclear war, because the artillery units will have been trained to be self-contained, independent, and reliant on their own capabilities.

TACTICAL MISSILES. Tactical nuclear surface-to-surface missiles are intended to support division-level operations. Missiles with maximum ranges of less than about 115 miles would fall into this class. The United States has fielded, and given to its NATO allies, the Lance and Honest John. They have ranges of sixty-eight and twenty-three miles, respectively.[23] The yield of the Honest John is estimated to be twenty kilotons.[24] The Lance possesses a variable yield selection of between one and one hundred kilotons.[25]

The Soviets have fielded a family of tactical nuclear missiles that have become known as Frogs (for Free Rocket Over Ground). The latest Frog variant has a range of thirty-seven miles and a yield in the

21. U.S. Department of the Army, *Operations*, Field Manual 100-5 (1976), p. 2–14.

22. Ibid.

23. *Jane's 1976*, pp. 41 and 440.

24. Leitenberg, "Background Materials," p. 111.

25. Ibid.

one-kiloton range.[26] A replacement for the Frog, the SS-21, was fielded in 1979, but only to divisions stationed within the Soviet Union.

The Soviets have fully integrated the Frog into their divisional force structure, as figure 5.3 shows. A Frog battalion is a standard

Fig. 5.3. A Soviet motorized rifle division

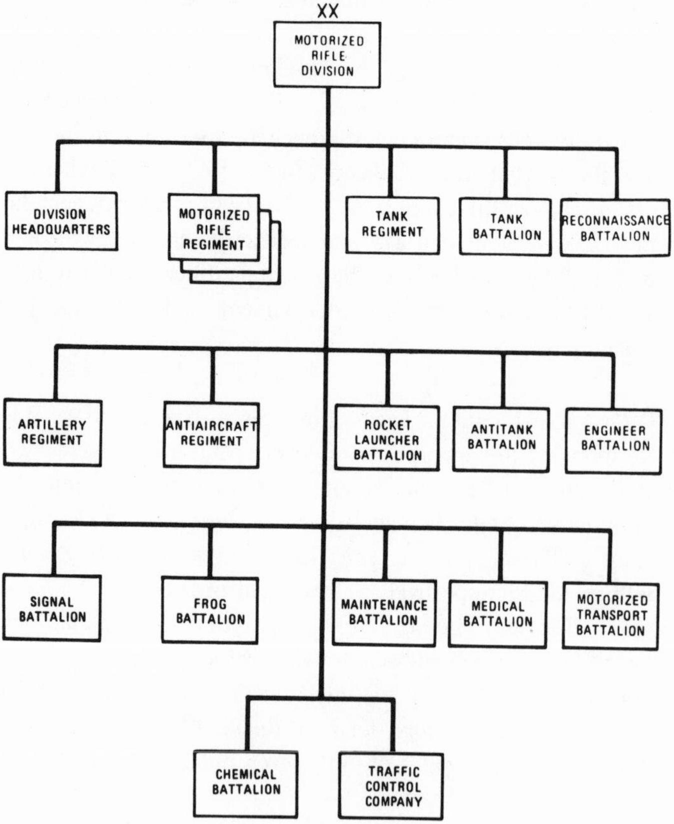

Source: Department of the Army, "Understanding Soviet Developments" (1977), p. 15.

26. *Jane's 1976*, p. 442.

part of their division. This is another instance in which theater nuclear arms have been overlaid onto existing conventional force structures. In this particular case, the Frog series of rockets has been in use since the 1950s as just another form of divisional artillery. The Frog is capable of carrying either conventional, chemical, or nuclear warheads. However, its poor accuracy indicates that it would have little effect with a conventional warhead. Of course, there would be no way for a defender to know the warhead type prior to detonation.

During the 1979–80 invasion of Afghanistan, Soviet motorized-rifle divisions carried Frogs with them, provoking the kind of speculation that could be expected on a much larger scale if Soviet forces went on alert in Europe.[27] Since the Frog is part of the motorized-rifle division, its movement into Afghanistan was interpreted by some as simply the implementation of standard operating procedures associated with any division movement. Alternatively, others have read it as a threat to use chemical attacks in Afghanistan, where other movement of chemical decontaminating equipment was also detected.[28] Although the threat of nuclear use in Afghanistan is certianly remote, any operations in Europe would immediately raise this question. The Soviets might even manipulate this dilemma of interpretation to frighten or intimidate their foes.

BATTLEFIELD SUPPORT MISSILES. Designed to assist at the corps level of command or, in the case of the Soviets, the equivalent army level of command, battlefield support missiles include missiles with ranges of less than about 575 miles. The only NATO missile in this category is the Pershing I, with a range of about 450 miles.[29]

For the Soviets, their Scud series of missiles fills this role. They are integrated into the army level of command, as shown in figure 5.4. Here again, these surface-to-surface missiles take their place along with pontoon bridge and artillery regiments in a traditional conven-

27. "Soviets Rotating Forces in Afghanistan," *Washington Post*, January 19, 1980, p. A9.
28. Ibid.
29. Leitenberg, "Background Materials," p. 112.

Fig. 5.4. A Soviet army

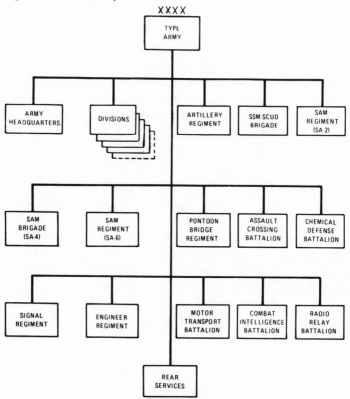

Source: Department of the Army, "Understanding Soviet Developments" (1977), p. 12.

tional force structure not terribly different from the ones that over-powered Germany in World War II. Scuds have a range of about 185 miles.[30]

Soviet armies are grouped into frontal units that are comparable to U.S. army groups, that is, consisting of up to fifteen or twenty divisions. This Soviet command grouping also has its own theater nuclear weapon, independent of the nuclear weapons in the Scuds

30. *Military Balance 1980–1981*, p. 89.

assigned to its armies. This is the SS-12 Scaleboard, with a maximum range of about 560 miles. If located in Poland, it could reach nearly all targets in West Germany and the Benelux nations. It reportedly carries a one-megaton yield warhead.[31] The Scaleboard is now being replaced by the SS-22, with a range of 620 miles, and the army-level Scuds are being replaced by a longer-range SS-23.[32]

The Scud/SS-23 and Scaleboard/SS-22 are of especial interest because they are the longest-range, and most destructive, nuclear weapons integrated into the Red Army organization. All of the longer-range surface-to-surface missiles are controlled by the Soviet Strategic Rocket Forces (SRF), which is the rough counterpart of the American Strategic Air Command. The Soviet Army and the Strategic Rocket Forces are radically different organizations. The Soviet Army is basically a conventional army, whose organization developed in centuries of trial-and-error military evolution. Like other conventional armies, it is trained to do many different things. By contrast, the SRF is completely organized around the technological revolution inherent in nuclear weapons.

Some evidence suggests that the development of the Scaleboard and SS-22 missiles was an attempt to lengthen the range of Red Army nuclear firepower so that the army would not have to resort to weapons of the Strategic Rocket Forces.[33] It is not clear whether this represents the outcome of some bureaucratic dispute between the two organizations or signifies a Soviet attempt to decouple theater and strategic forces.

NAVAL THEATER NUCLEAR SYSTEMS. Both the United States and the Soviet Union deploy a wide diversity of theater nuclear weapons at sea. The heterogeneity within this class of weapons alone is enough to make wartime interactions extremely difficult to predict, or even to conceptualize, during peacetime. American nuclear forces

31. *Jane's 1976*, p. 46.
32. Kennedy, "Soviet Forces," p. 79.
33. John Erickson, "Soviet Theater-Warfare Capability: Doctrines, Deployments, and Capabilities," in Lawrence L. Whetten, ed., *The Future of Soviet Military Power* (New York: Crane, Russak, 1976), p. 121.

are centered on the carrier task force, whereas the Soviets emphasize cruise and surface-to-surface missiles. Although extensive attacks against the American carriers with the Soviet nuclears is probably to be expected, the nuclear weapons of both sides could also easily be targeted against critical land targets, such as ports, bases, troop concentrations, and logistic centers. The command of these forces would be through naval lines of authority and communication.

The United States maintains about five carriers in the European area, but in crisis or war these would be reinforced considerably. Since the early 1950s, the U.S. Navy has been given a major role in nuclear delivery, based on the nuclear torpedoes and antisubmarine rockets and the aircraft aboard these carriers.[34] This subject has received little public attention, and few details are available on the numbers of aircraft involved, the number of missions possible, or the yields of nuclear munitions carried. As with many U.S. Army systems, carrier aircraft could serve in a dual role, delivering either nuclear or conventional warheads.

Soviet naval theater nuclear weapons consist of surface-to-surface and cruise missiles. Their Shaddock cruise missile has a range of about 115 miles and is deployed on both submarines and guided missile cruisers.[35] Other missiles include the Serb and Sawfly, with ranges of 700 and 1,800 miles, respectively.[36]

The standard Soviet Navy force structure that would control these nuclear weapons would be complemented by a complex satellite-based ocean surveillance system.[37] Presumably, RORSAT and EOR-SAT satellites would transmit target location data on the U.S. fleets back to ground stations in the Soviet Union, where it would be used to direct sea- and ground-based nuclear air attacks against the U.S. carriers. American carrier-based forces would be under considerable pressure to neutralize elements of the Soviet fleet along with the land-based aircraft that support them. The pattern that seems to be emerg-

34. Leitenberg, "Background Materials," p. 120.
35. *Jane's 1976*, p. 50. There is also a land-based Army version of the Shaddock.
36. Ibid., p. 186.
37. Michael McGuire, "Soviet Naval Programs," in Paul J. Murphy, ed., *Naval Power in Soviet Policy* (Washington, D.C.: Government Printing Office, 1978), p. 89.

ing is similar to that of many World War II naval battles, but with the incorporation of nuclear arms and more sophisticated sensor systems into the forces. Of course, these technical developments change the nature of war at sea considerably from World War II, but the force structures themselves are an extension of those developed to wage classical naval campaigns.

AIR DEFENSE FORCES. The air defense units of the Soviet Union are divided between those intended for defense of inland targets and those deployed forward with army and air force units to assist in combined arms operations. The former are controlled by a specially dedicated command, the National Air Defense Forces, which controls radars, fighter-interceptors, an extensive warning-communication network, and nearly ten thousand surface-to-air missiles (SAMs).[38] Command of these assets, which are geographically dispersed from the German border all the way to China, is exercised through a central control facility in Moscow.[39] Although the SAMs in this system do not appear to have nuclear warheads, they would be intimately involved in a European nuclear war because they would be used to destroy incoming NATO aircraft, which in all probability would be armed with nuclear bombs and rockets. The Moscow command center that directs air defense against theater attack is the same one that directs defense against intercontinental range attacks. Its destruction in a theater war would simultaneously strip away protection from strategic attack by American bombers and cruise missiles. Here is a critcal example of the way force structure can couple theater and strategic war. By having force structures with overlapping theater-strategic and conventional-nuclear missions, a nation reduces the likelihood that a clean distinction between the different kinds of war can be maintained.

NATO's air defense forces consist of a network of early warning radars and weapons deployed from northern Norway through central

38. U.S. Department of the Air Force, *Soviet Aerospace Handbook* (Washington, D.C.: Government Printing Office, 1978), p. 65.

39. Philip A. Peterson, *Soviet Air Power and the Pursuit of New Military Options* (Washington, D.C.: Government Printing Office, 1979), p. 35.

Europe and eastward into Turkey. One of the primary armaments of this system is the Nike Hercules, which can be armed with either a conventional or nuclear warhead. Its nuclear yield is about one kiloton, which it can deliver over a slant range of eighty-four miles.[40] Although ostensibly under the control of dedicated air defense organizations, the Nike missile is a U.S. Army system and it is widely reported that its main role in battle would be in surface-to-surface bombardment for destruction of enemy troop or armor concentrations.[41] This points up the fact that standard organization charts cannot be completely relied upon to understand European nuclear force structure, or indeed any kind of military force structure. In virtually any organization, there are informal lines of authority and communications that will greatly influence its actual behavior. These informal lines are the least susceptible to centralized political control, because informal communications and procedures tend to be worked out in the lower levels of the organization. They are likely to be completely overlooked when the question of what constitutes an important strategic factor for senior decision makers is discussed.

AIR FORCES. NATO air forces are equipped for dual capability, nuclear or conventional, and one of the most critical military decisions in any crisis will be the determination of arming capability for these aircraft. This is an extremely complicated decision because of the many internal and external uncertainties that must be balanced. But it is an inherently difficult decision even in the presence of complete certainty and cost-free information. Among the critical uncertainties are weather conditions, fuel availability, enemy deployments, and enemy warhead load (nuclear or conventional). Beyond this, there is the question of what missions NATO aircraft will be assigned to. They could be used for gaining air superiority over the battlefield, close support of ground forces, deep strike of enemy air bases, or battlefield interdiction. The decision facing NATO air force com-

40. Leitenberg, "Background Materials," p. 111.
41. Robert Shreffler, "The New Nuclear Force," in Stockholm International Peace Research Institute, *Tactical Nuclear Weapons: European Perspectives* (London: Taylor & Francis, 1978), pp. 309–12.

manders will be to allocate targeting assignments to these aircraft, and this will entail selecting the type of warhead to be carried. Only if the decision is delegated to trained air force personnel who have familiarity with all of the subtleties and complexities present can it be made rationally.

I have provided this sketch of the decision problem facing NATO air forces in order to set the context of how aircraft are likely to be used in a conflict and how they are likely to be deployed in peacetime to prepare for this assignment. It is misleading in the extreme simply to compare NATO air forces in numerical terms to Warsaw Pact air forces. The mere fact that NATO is reported to have fourteen-hundred front-line aircraft and the Warsaw Pact three thousand tells us nothing about the dynamics of combat or the controllability of war.[42] It not only fails to consider the organizations that allocate and control these forces, but it sweeps away the basic decision problem for which these air forces were built in the first place.

Principal NATO nuclear-capable aircraft include the F-4, FB-111, and F-104. The FB-111 has a combat radius of about 1,150 miles, and it could strike targets throughout Eastern Europe and western Russia (including Moscow and Leningrad) with nuclear weapons.[43] There were 170 FB-111s in Europe in 1980, most of which were based in Great Britain. The British maintain their own Vulcan and Buccaneer nuclear bombers, which can be staged in either Britain, Cyprus, or Turkey and have ranges of 2,300 and 1,150 miles, respectively. These ranges would permit striking virtually all important targets in western Russia.[44] For the most part, the yields of the nuclear weapons carried by these aircraft are large, in the range of hundreds of kilotons or even a megaton.[45]

The organization of NATO's nuclear-capable air forces is determined by the standard air force structures that control them. This organization is necessary in order to decide rationally on aircraft al-

42. Kennedy, "Soviet Forces," p. 80.
43. Ibid., p. 80.
44. Ibid.; and Bill Gunston, *Bombers of the West* (New York: Scribner's, 1973), p. 77.
45. Leitenberg, "Background Materials," p. 119.

location and armament type so that decisions can be made that will optimize the effectiveness of the limited number of aircraft.

There is one important exception to this organization. The NATO quick reaction alert (QRA) force of aircraft and Pershing missiles is under control of the Supreme Allied Commander Europe (SACEUR), the highest-ranking military officer in NATO. QRA aircraft are kept on a very high alert, even in peacetime, and are thought to be armed with their nuclear weapons on board.[46] The purpose of the QRA is to deter a Soviet surprise attack by maintaining a fully ready nuclear strike force instantly available for retaliation. As the QRA aircraft are on continuous alert, and hence exposed to attack, they would have to be dispatched to their targets *before* any incoming Soviet missiles or aircraft attacked them. Under conditions of political tension the QRA aircraft are kept on even greater levels of alert, with some aircraft maintained on runway alert ready to launch on a moment's notice. Although the QRA is a "theater" nuclear force, it could strike most of the urban areas west of the Ural Mountains, including Moscow, with megaton-class weapons.

Soviet air forces are also fully capable of delivering nuclear weapons, and many of the same basic decisions would confront their commanders, except that they would likely be on the offensive. Their MiG 23 and 27 fighters have ranges of about six hundred miles, which would permit them to cover most targets on the continent. Furthermore, many analysts believe the Soviets are in the process of developing a deep strike orientation to their air force, which could bring extensive combat to the Benelux nations and Britain soon after the onset of war (effectively ten to fifteen minutes).[47] Again, one of the most fundamental problems for NATO will be the intense uncertainty as to whether an incoming strike is conventional or nuclear. Therefore it is vitally necessary to have a procedure for establishing rules of engagement for the integration of European nuclear weapons with the NATO political structure.

46. Ibid., p. 43. A permissive action link (PAL) device is required to be unlocked before the weapons could be employed.
47. See Peterson, *Soviet Airpower*, pp. 5–11.

The operations of Soviet air forces stationed in forward areas are under the control of frontal and army commanders. This subordination of the air force to the ground force commander is quite different than in NATO, where army commanders typically "nominate" targets to air force controllers. The ultimate targeting decision in NATO is left to the independent air force, whereas for Soviet air forces it is the ground commander who makes this decision.

Soviet Naval Aviation also contributes considerable nuclear air-striking power against both land and sea targets. Their Backfire bombers, deployed in peacetime near Murmansk, on the Baltic, and in the Crimea, have a range of some 5,700 to 6,900 miles. Thus Backfires could reach (unrefueled) past the Azores in the Atlantic, cover the entire Persian Gulf, and easily operate against virtually all targets in Europe.[48] In theory they would have surveillance problems in their ability to find the American carriers. However, the relative success shown by the backward Argentine Air Force in finding British surface ships in the 1982 Falklands War indicates that this problem may have been exaggerated. The Soviets would also rely on their RORSAT and EORSAT ocean reconnaissance systems, which apparently have a direct link-up with Soviet Navy vessels. Communication between the surface ships and the Backfires could then cue the bombers to their targets. Also not to be dismissed is the Soviet intelligence establishment's ability to locate targets through the nether world of COMINT, SIGINT, and human agents.

The surging of Backfires from the Baltic area and the Crimea would certainly be an ominous indication that an attack was imminent on NATO, or that high-level psychological warfare was being waged. It would of necessity trigger many NATO countermeasures aimed at protecting the U.S. carrier fleets in the Atlantic and Mediterranean. It would, for example, raise demands that the Soviet ocean reconnaissance satellites be instantly destroyed or at least blinded, because they were being used to direct strikes against the American carriers. In broader terms, the real significance of this kind of inter-

48. Paul Murphy, "Soviet Naval Aviation: Its Development, Capabilities, and Limitations" in Murphy, *Naval Power in Soviet Policy*, pp. 185–94.

action is that long-distance nuclear forces have been placed under the direct control of traditional military organizations, in this case the Soviet Naval Aviation, that have roles and missions whose importance is provincially seen to be at least as great as their political bargaining or signaling value.

MEDIUM AND INTERMEDIATE RANGE BALLISTIC AND CRUISE MISSILES. Medium and intermediate range ballistic missiles (M/IRBMs) are classified as having ranges between 690 and 1,726 and 1,726 and 3,450 miles, respectively. At present, NATO does not field any M/IRBMs, although agreements have been reached to deploy a cruise missile and long-range Pershing 2 missile beginning in 1983. In the past, however, NATO fielded a variety of these systems. In the early 1960s, for example, there were seven IRBM bases, four in Britain, two in Italy, and one in Turkey, armed with megaton-class Thor and Jupiter missiles. In addition, Mace and Matador cruise missiles with ranges in excess of six hundred miles were deployed in West Germany. All of these systems were withdrawn in the 1960s, largely because of their vulnerability. If they were not used immediately, they risked being destroyed.

Although plans are uncertain because of popular political opposition in Europe, it has been agreed to place 108 Pershing 2 launchers in West Germany. Stationed there, they could reach targets as far as Moscow with a flight time of twelve minutes. Accompanying the Pershing would be the ground-launched cruise missile (GLCM). GLCMs are descendants of the old Matador and Mace cruise missiles, but with a terrain contour-mapping navigation system that makes them among the most accurate nuclear delivery vehicles. They are scheduled for initial deployment in 1983, but there are some doubts that they will ever be placed in Belgium, the Netherlands, Italy, West Germany, and Britain. Pershing 2 is to be a U.S. Army weapon and GLCM is to be a U.S. Air Force weapon, although both will be closely integrated with the American SIOP.

The Soviets have continued to rely on M/IRBMs built in the 1950s. The SS-4 MRBM has a range of about 1,120 miles and is based in the Soviet Union to cover targets in Western Europe and

China.[49] It is estimated to have a one-megaton warhead, as is the longer-range SS-5 IRBM; thus, it would have a devastating effect if fired into urban Western Europe.[50] Both the SS-4 and SS-5 were developed with the idea of holding Western Europe hostage to Soviet nuclear bombardment, as a counterdeterrent to the superiority of the U.S. Strategic Air Command in the 1950s and 1960s.

The SS-20 IRBM, with a range of 3,100 miles, is the ostensible replacement for the SS-4s and SS-5s.[51] It is mobile and carries three MIRV warheads, making the threat to Western Europe in target coverage terms even greater than it was in the 1960s. About seven hundred SS-4s and SS-5s were aimed at Europe then, and the prospect for the 1980s is that a much larger number of IRBM warheads, perhaps on the order of two thousand, would give less than ten minutes' warning of attack. Soviet M/IRBMs are under the control of the Strategic Rocket Forces.

OTHER LONG-RANGE THEATER NUCLEAR FORCES. In addition to the weapons already described there are long-range systems that are often referred to as theater weapons. The distinction between the terms "theater" and "strategic" in this case has only a tenuous connection with reality, and they amount to little more than convenient semantic classifications. Long-range theater weapons are described here both for completeness' sake, and because some command and control distinctions are worth noting.

The United States has assigned around fifty Poseidon missiles aboard American SSBNs to SACEUR.[52] Precisely what this means is not clear, but presumably it would imply that SACEUR, who is always an American general, has operational control over the missiles once they are released by the president. Authority would pass to SACEUR instead of to the U.S. Navy, which ordinarily controls them. The range of the Poseidon missile is sufficient to reach most

49. *Jane's 1976*, p. 15.
50. Ibid.
51. *Military Balance 1980–1981*, p. 89.
52. Robert Metzger and Paul Doty, "Arms Control Enters the Gray Area," *International Security* 3 (Winter 1978/1979): 32.

targets in the Soviet Union. They are almost surely intended to fire against airfields and M/IRBMs in the western Soviet Union, which are physically adjacent to ICBM fields. In such a "theater" nuclear war Moscow would somehow have to determine that incoming Poseidon missiles were launched from officially authorized SACEUR-controlled stocks, rather than from the U.S.'s central strategic submarine force.

In addition to the American SLBMs allocated to SACEUR, the United Kingdom possesses four SSBNs carrying 192 nuclear warheads.[53] Authority to launch this force rests with the British prime minister, and operational control goes to the chief of staff of the British Navy.[54] However, in the event that a nuclear attack destroys the responsible authorities capable of giving such an order, it has been reported that British submarine commanders retain authority to launch their missiles on their own.[55]

France also possesses nuclear weapons that could become involved in a war in Europe. France maintains Mirage aircraft and five SSBNs armed with eighty missiles that are capable of striking targets in the Soviet Union. France has been described as the wild card in the European nuclear situation, because its behavior could so easily trigger escalation. French strategists have argued that this is precisely the rationale behind the French nuclear force: to enforce deterrence by guaranteeing that a Soviet attack would lead to major nuclear exchanges.

Finally, some have suggested the use of American strategic weapons in a theater role. An attack on Soviet divisions in Eastern Europe or the western Soviet Union, with land-based Minuteman missiles launched from the United States, for example, would represent a theater use of these weapons. It has been argued that such an attack would intentionally blur the distinction between theater and strategic conflict, while at the same time retaining American authority over the weapons in question. Such ideas have been termed "limited nu-

53. Ibid., p. 30.
54. Lawrence Freedman, *Britain and Nuclear Weapons* (London: Royal Institute of International Affairs, 1980), p. xiii.
55. Ibid.

clear options," and their incorporation into the SIOP in the mid-1970s was an attempt to strengthen the coupling between theater and strategic forces. Of course, the line of authority for such an attack would pass through the Strategic Air Command.

The number and diversity of organizations that control European nuclear forces creates many special problems. Three observations can be made about the importance of such a highly differentiated command structure to theater war. First, there is no centralized organization in control of all theater nuclear forces. This is true of strategic forces to a degree, but theater forces in particular are dispersed over many different commands and subcommands. Nuclear artillery, battlefield support missiles, and naval weapons are all controlled by different organizations. It is not so much the large variety of theater nuclear weapons that is important as it is the large number of different organizations and lines of authority that have responsibility for determining how these weapons are used. Army divisions, aircraft carrier groups, fighter squadrons, commando teams, and air defense units all have their own nuclear weapons. The coordination necessary for a centrally directed, and politically controlled, conflict is made difficult by the large number of different organizations whose actions must be coordinated. Moreover, each of these organizations is designed and trained to complete its own peculiar mission. The training, indoctrination, and "corporate culture" of each of them will powerfully affect their actions in time of war.

Second, the geographic confinement of Europe means that choices will have to be made not in the thirty-minute flight time of an intercontinental missile, but in the roughly ten minutes that it takes a Scaleboard, Lance, or Shaddock to reach its target. It seems intuitively plausible that reduction in decision time by a factor of three increases the difficulties of political management in wartime by far more than this factor. The number of interrelated choices involving the many organizations that control nuclear weapons further complicates the difficulty of management. Below some threshold it is better to speak not of decision time but of reaction time. With ten minutes' reaction time, there would be a strong bias in favor of decentralized decision making and the use of preplanned procedures.

The compression of decision time also makes it exceedingly difficult to separate a theater from a strategic campaign. Western European capitals and Moscow could be destroyed with only a few minutes' warning. This would not necessarily happen by long-range attack; it could happen because of tactical spillover of artillery firefights or a wayward fighter aircraft. In these instances there would effectively be zero warning.

Last, added to the above factors is the fact that the national commands do not even share a common language, let alone a set of common political goals. Coordination problems will arise from having nuclear-armed fighter bombers of nine nations, from firing nuclear artillery on allied territory, and simply from trying to manage the inventory of nuclear weapons once they are dispersed to national control.

EUROPEAN ATTITUDES AND NUCLEAR WAR

The bewildering complexity of theater nuclear forces stands in contrast to the simple deterrence strategies that govern their use. This is more than coincidental, for they are deeply related. NATO leaders over the past thirty years have not been fools; they have possessed a keen sense of the consequences for Europe if a war should ever erupt there. And although they have not attempted to comprehend fully the operational direction of theater nuclear war, they have generally acquiesced to, or even encouraged, the deployment of a diverse array of nuclear warheads in Europe. At the same time they have developed relatively simple theories about deterrence, conventional war, and coupling. For all of this simplification, however, there has been little or no demand for simplifying the forces into either an exclusively centralized second-strike deterrent or a coherent warfighting force. The reason for this is intimately related to European attitudes toward nuclear war.

When NATO was formed in 1948 it was assumed as a matter of course that resort to atomic weaponry would be essential if the West were to offset the Soviet superiority in conventional armies. At this time, most of Western Europe was both willing and eager to accept the American lead in military matters. The destruction and demoralization of World War II had drained too much spirit for a dynamic European leadership to reassert itself in strategic affairs.

In the United States, also, the overriding concern in 1948 was the development of a strategy to forestall Soviet conquest of Europe. Yet even with this objective there were important undercurrents that are largely forgotten today and that bear upon the current state of atomic defense. For instance, in one of the earliest articles concerning nuclear defense in Europe, which appeared in the *Saturday Evening Post* of October 15, 1949, General Omar N. Bradley, then chairman of the Joint Chiefs of Staff, commented on the view that Europe could be defended solely with atomic weapons:

> This train of thought represents so much compound folly that it is hard to answer it patiently. . . . It foolishly assumes that the atom bomb is omnipotent. It fails to explain how, if some millions of invader troops moved into Western Europe and were living off the country, we could use the bomb against them without killing ten friends for every enemy foe.

General Bradley's recognition that nuclear defense could entail the destruction of Western Europe was the first surfacing of an intractable dilemma that lasts to this day. Surprisingly, it took a few years for the Europeans themselves to realize the full implications of atomic defense. Opinion polls taken in Germany in the early 1950s indicated that the public believed Soviet aggression was deterred by fear of America's industrial mobilization capability, not by its atomic arsenal.[56] This belief was to change as the new Eisenhower administration emphasized the strategy of massive retaliation. Europeans were to become much more cognizant of nuclear weapons and their destructive capabilities.

In addition to the massive retaliation strategy, another factor that focused European attention on nuclear issues was the rapid devel-

56. Hans Speier, *German Rearmament and Atomic War* (Evanston, Ill.: Row, Peterson & Co., 1957), pp. 112–13, 132–40.

opment of battlefield nuclear weapons by the U.S. Army. Although nuclear bombs had accompanied SAC bomber deployments to Great Britain in the late 1940s, there was a great deal of secrecy over such weapon movements. Tactical nuclear weaponry for ground warfare, on the other hand, was intentionally publicized as a visible commitment to European defense. Just as in the 1930s the French government decided to release films of the Maginot Line for deterrent effect, so was there a great deal of television, newspaper, and magazine publicity surrounding the development of U.S. Army nuclear weapons.

The first Army weapon landed on the European continent was the 280-millimeter Long Tom atomic cannon, which reached Bremenhaven in October 1953. It was a cumbersome weapon whose symbolic value far exceeded its military capability. It was tested in 1952 in Nevada in fully operational mode, i.e., with an atomic charge and with troops observing the shot.[57] A great deal of publicity surrounded it, and President Eisenhower ordered it sent to Korea as an obvious nuclear threat to force the North Koreans to terminate the war there.[58] Its deployment to Europe in 1953 was followed in 1954 by shipments of Honest John and Nike missiles. All were intended to bolster the confidence of the Europeans and to serve notice on the Russians of the consequences of attack. In the heady days of near-complete American superiority over the Soviets, and in an era when Europe had not recovered enough self-confidence to question American actions, the momentum behind nuclearization of the battlefield seemed to make sense.

The realization in Europe of the actual consequences of using these weapons was not long in coming after this publicity. In December 1954, the NATO Council announced that it was basing all of its future planning on the assumption that atomic weapons would be used in any war. Such a public declaration naturally stimulated considerable newspaper and magazine coverage in Germany. It was almost inevitable that the popular press would emphasize the sensa-

57. "Cannon Fires Atomic Shell," *New York Times*, May 26, 1953, p. 1.
58. Weigley, *United States Army*, p. 536.

tional and catastrophic effects of nuclear weapon use, and that is exactly what happened.[59]

Sensational press coverage about nuclear destruction in Germany continued in early 1955 and set the stage for elite and popular reaction to a major military exercise held in June, known as Carte Blanche. This exercise was designed to test the NATO Council's 1954 decision on early use of nuclear weapons. It was held with more than three thousand NATO aircraft and, because of space constraints, was run in a north-south rather than an east-west direction. It took place in France and the Low Countries and in the region from Hamburg to Munich in West Germany. Three hundred and thirty-five simulated atomic weapons were "dropped" on more than a hundred targets during the exercise. These resulted in an estimated 1.7 million Germans "killed" and 3.5 million "wounded." Casualties from fallout were not computed. Thus, in a span of nine days of simulated war, three times as many civilian casualties were inflicted on Germany as in the entire six years of World War II. Press and public reacted with total shock. People inside and outside the German government believed that NATO was intent upon blowing up the Federal Republic.

Since 1955, it has been exceedingly difficult to arouse any serious West German political interest in detailed nuclear warfighting schemes, largely because of the images of nuclear war formed by exercises like Carte Blanche. Such exercises seem to have convinced Bonn that nuclear issues were not a fit topic for open public debate. After Carte Blanche, discussions were confined to generalities as a matter of course.[60]

When discussions of military policy cannot be kept to such generalities, a political storm often breaks out. In October 1962, for example, the Hamburg magazine *Der Spiegel* published the results of the Fallex 62 exercise run by the German defense ministry. An estimated 10 to 15 million people were "killed" in these war games,

---

59. Gordon A. Craig, "NATO and the New German Army," in William W. Kaufmann, ed., *Military Policy and National Security* (Princeton: Princeton University Press, 1956), pp. 220–27.

60. Stanford Research Institute, *An Assessment of European Attitudes on Tactical Nuclear Force Modernization* (Menlo Park, Calif.: Stanford Research Institute, 1977), p. 37.

even though targeting plans were selected for "purely military" purposes. Civilian destruction at these levels is virtually impossible to explain in terms of rational foreign policy objectives. And this possibility of massive destruction, so astutely observed by General Bradley in 1949, has continued to this day to be one of the strongest forces shaping NATO military and strategic policy.

Over the years official American policy has aimed at lessening the collateral consequences of war in Europe. American nuclear weapons have been made more accurate, constraints on targeting have been developed, and warhead yields have been reduced in selected cases. Yet these changes have been marginal. The basic problem of controlling unwanted civil-sector damage is made nearly impossible because of the concentration of roughly fourteen thousand tactical nuclear weapons, ten thousand artillery pieces, four thousand combat aircraft, and more than seventy divisions in one of the most urbanized areas on earth. In the event of war a substantial percentage of these forces would be targeted on West Germany, a nation the size of Oregon, with a population density more than twice as great as the northeastern United States. The geographic confinement in Central Europe means that if any significant proportion of the conventional, nuclear, and chemical firepower deployed there were actually used, the resulting destruction to the civilian sector would be extraordinarily high. Indeed, it would likely be much higher than indicated in such highly controlled simulations of war as Carte Blanche or Fallex 62, because such exercises have tended to emphasize the minimization of civil-sector destruction.[61] The official Fallex 62 war games with their estimate of 10 to 15 million West Germans killed could be a serious underestimate of the consequences of an actual war.

The methods used to determine collateral civilian damage in simulations of nuclear war are fully centralized computing schemes, but, we pointed out in discussion of assessment in nuclear war, there is little realistic prospect of such centralized control in actual conflict. Collateral damage will be caused by military forces that are not fully

61. Some of this material is drawn from Paul Bracken, "On Theater Warfare," Hudson Institute, HI-3036-P, July 1979.

coordinated by a central programming unit. It will happen because the assumptions of instantaneous error-free transmission of information are untenable.

European reaction to what they see as the suicidal nature of such a war has had direct effect on NATO's approach to security. Norway and Denmark have refused permission for any nuclear weapons to be deployed on their soil,[62] and West Germany has demanded a strategy of forward defense, whereby any military operations would be conducted immediately on the border, and has opposed waging a defense in depth.[63] A defense in depth with tactical nuclear weapons would only extend the area of devastation.

But the most important consequence of the view that a war in Europe is suicidal has been the deterrence strategy, which is the real foundation stone of NATO's plans and forces. It is here where the truly strategic, rather than theater, character of a war from the European perspective shows itself. Although Americans may have a strong interest in limited nuclear warfighting, most Europeans find little reason to believe that this kind of war would not destroy the very prize being defended. For this reason, they have been more interested in deterring, rather than in fighting, a war.

In their view, theater nuclear weapons in Europe are a mechanism for ensuring that a conflict would go nuclear, rather than for destroying enemy forces. Weapon requirements are therefore quite different than those needed for a second-strike deterrent. If it is desirable to ensure that a nuclear war is triggered, a fully controllable, invulnerable force may be positively *undesirable*, because employment of such a force would depend on a rational decision to execute the threat. In the face of the suicidal consequences of a war in Europe, it is easy to see why a rational political leader would never take steps leading to devastation. What is needed instead of a rational procedure

62. Nils Orvik and Niels J. Haagerup, *The Scandinavian Members of NATO*, Adelphi Paper No. 23 (London: The International Institute for Strategic Studies, 1965), p. 4.

63. Federal Republic of Germany, Federal Minister of Defense, *The Security of the Federal Republic of Germany and the Development of the Armed Forces* (Bonn: 1976), p. 25.

for going to war is a posture that is so complex that war could be triggered in any of a number of different ways without rational control. Although the European deterrence strategy is uncomplicated, the force structure needed to enforce it is necessarily extremely complex. The almost overwhelming complexity of theater nuclear weapons and command organizations in which they are embedded describes a force structure that exactly fits the NATO strategy of suicidal deterrence.

The fit between the European strategy of deterrence and the theater nuclear force structure actually built is seldom recognized by Americans. Complaints of a lack of serious thought behind the development of the tactical nuclear forces pervade the American political science literature. These views fail to see that theater nuclear war in the European perspective is not intended to be an intermediate sub-strategic war, as Americans envision it, and it is not designed to gain battlefield advantage through attrition of enemy forces. It is intended to enforce deterrence by necessitating that any war be nuclear. What some observers see as a disorderly and thoughtless development of highly differentiated nuclear forces is in fact precisely the kind of force structure needed for a deterrence strategy whose implementation would be suicidal. Although debates among nuclear specialists have broken out over the years about the need for conventional forces, tactical nuclear warfighting postures, and other alternative foundations for NATO security, what has been ignored is that command structure in this particular case is deeply related to political strategy. The NATO strategy of relying on nuclear weapons is politically and militarily credible because the governing command structure is so unstable and accident-prone that national leaders would exercise little practical control over it in wartime. What other command mechanism could possibly be built to invoke a nuclear conflict that, for all practical purposes, is tantamount to a regional doomsday machine?

ENFORCING NATO'S DETERRENT STRATEGY

NATO forces are structured to circumvent the classic problem of a deterrent strategy: that to actually implement a threat once deterrence has failed is often counterproductive. Because of the absolutely fundamental importance for deterrence of being able to go into a suicidal nuclear war, it is important to explore some of the ways that this threat could be carried out. Broadly speaking, three factors make the NATO threat believable: decentralized and delegated control of nuclear weapons once they are put on alert, the ambiguity of command authority over the employment of nuclear weapons, and the complexity of wartime and crisis management. Although these three factors help enforce the nuclear deterrent threat, they are certainly not without major risks and problems. It is the very manipulation of risk that gives credibility to the NATO posture, however, even if it ultimately contributes to a loss of political control.

The decentralization of NATO's control over nuclear weapons is a function of the degree of alert that has been ordered. In peacetime, most of NATO's six thousand nuclear warheads are kept in protected storage igloos, known as "special ammunition sites."[64] It is estimated that more than one hundred special ammunition sites exist in NATO.[65] Although these sites are protected by guards, they are not hardened in any military sense of the term. They could be destroyed by conventional, nuclear, or chemical attack and there is consequently a strong incentive to disperse the warheads from them in time of crisis.

Not all of NATO's nuclear weapons are kept in storage sites. As discussed earlier, the QRA aircraft and some Pershing missiles are kept on alert at all times. The number of QRAs on alert is classified, but whatever the number it is certain to increase in periods of tension.[66] Furthermore, an undisclosed number of surface-to-air missiles, artillery rounds, and other nuclear weapons can be kept on alert status, and apparently are.

The alerting procedure for NATO is complicated, but in concept it amounts to a large-scale dispersal from the storage sites in time of crisis. Some six thousand weapons are turned over to the military forces that control the delivery vehicles for them. Figure 5.5 illustrates the concept. Here we have made the plausible assumption that War-

64. Leitenberg, "Background Materials," pp. 16, 34.
65. Ibid.
66. Ibid., p. 36.

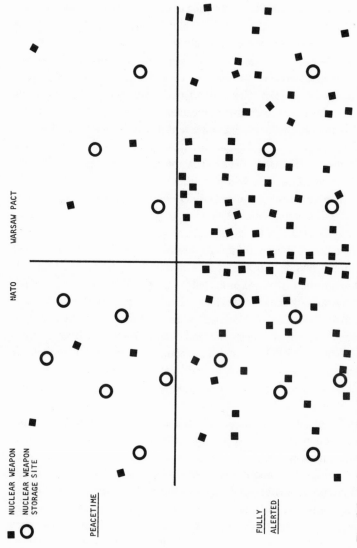

Fig. 5.5. A theater nuclear force alert

saw Pact forces follow a similar dispersal procedure, although they have fewer storage sites.

Technically, NATO could decide to disperse only some of its nuclear weapons from their storage sites. Some might be kept in order to field a more controllable force, for example. Weapons that are exceedingly difficult to control, or those that are especially provocative such as nuclear artillery, might be kept in their storage sites. However, there are major risks associated with this decision. Since NATO storage site locations can be assumed to be well known to the Warsaw Pact, leaving nuclear weapons in their storage igloos might encourage preemptive attack.

A NATO decision not to go on full alert in the face of Soviet preparatory moves might then turn a crisis into the Soviets' golden opportunity to disarm NATO. If the Soviets made a preemptive attack on NATO when it was in a status of only partial dispersal of its nuclear weapons, NATO would find it practically impossible to organize a counterattack. For this reason there are likely to be strong pressures within NATO for a general release of weapons to NATO military forces assigned the task of using these weapons. Without such a release, the military would be unable to carry out its assignments and might not even be able to mount a credible deterrent to attack.

Once NATO were to go on alert, as indicated in figure 5.5, its nuclear forces would be geographically dispersed. Its six thousand warheads would be spread from the North Sea to the plateaus of eastern Turkey. At this point, if fighting were to break out we must assume that operational control of these weapons would devolve to the highly differentiated commands that maintain physical control over them. For example, it is unlikely that centralized control over self-propelled artillery could be achieved, because these forces depend on movement and concealment for their survival. Since NATO's nuclear weapons are integrated into conventional forces, each force would have its own peculiar operating constraints. In an actual battle, even one initially restricted to conventional weapons, the fact that nuclear weapons were deployed with these units would substantially increase the likelihood that some of these thousands of weapons would be fired.

As a practical matter, we must seriously discount the prospect that centralized political command could intervene in a large conventional war to maintain detailed control over nuclear weapons. Political leaders would have little ability to respond in the very short decision times that characterize modern combat, and, even if there were sufficient time, these leaders would lack detailed information on local conditions and knowledge of how to operate combined arms forces. Decisions of this sort cannot even be made at a high level inside the military command structure; they must be delegated lower in the hierarchy to division and brigade level. The development of nuclear weapons has done nothing to change this organizational feature of conventional forces, and we should be skeptical of purported technological solutions to problems that have deep organizational roots.

Specifically, the electronic locks that are on these weapons, known as permissive action links (PALs), do nothing to alleviate the organizational and environmental pressures to decentralize and delegate control of most theater nuclear weapons.[67] While it may be technologically possible to lock weapons against unauthorized use, this is hardly the issue in a European crisis. The same effect as an unbreakable lock would come from removal of the weapons from Europe altogether. For, if weapons were sent into battle while political authorities retained control of the codes needed to unlock them, there could be no guarantee, not even a likelihood, that all of the codes could be matched with their respective weapons in the confusion of a conventional or perhaps a chemical-nuclear war. The political command, or any centralized depository for the codes, could be attacked, thereby paralyzing the military's ability to strike back. Practically speaking, a strong pressure exists to release any needed codes at the same time that the weapons are dispersed from their storage sites. In peacetime planning this pressure can be ignored, and elaborate enforcement can be devised to keep the tactical nuclear weapons locked until they are just about to be fired. But even a moderately intense military crisis in Europe will expose the vulnerability of such procedural schemes. Sending thousands of locked weapons into the fog of

67. PALs are described in ibid., pp. 41–42.

war flies in the face of every known military tradition. The peacetime controls for preventing unauthorized use of nuclear weapons would then be swept away as irrelevant to the new condition of a real possibility of war. Then, in order to field a viable force, either ad hoc controls would be devised or previously established verbal understandings would be employed. This is not to say that PALs are useless. PALs do successfully prevent the unauthorized use of a nuclear weapon in peacetime by an aberrant member of the military, and thus they are an important part of the command system. Furthermore, they prevent any terrorist who might somehow seize a NATO weapon from actually using it.

PALs are analogous to the peacetime checks and balances that prevent accidental nuclear war. They were neither designed nor intended as a means of providing centralized political control in battle. Although we know little about Soviet alerting practices for their theater nuclear weapons, the organizational and environmental variables facing them would be similar. One U.S. Army intelligence publication says of Soviet theater forces that "once authority to use nuclear weapons has been obtained, they will be controlled by front and army commands."[68] And once command is delegated to the front and army level it is not hard to imagine a further decentralization to even lower levels in the hierarchy.

Once NATO and the Warsaw Pact have distributed tactical nuclear weapons to their front-line units, there would be two armies in densely populated Europe, each poised to jump the other. Remaining longer-range nuclear forces, such as the FB-111 and Vulcan aircraft, Pershing, Poseidons, and SS-4s, SS-5s, and SS-20s, would all have to be readied for use because of the possibility of instantaneous ignition of war. The nuclear weapons would be controlled by eight NATO nations alone, and within each command, warheads would be enmeshed deep in the conventional force structures. If violence were to break out at this point, it would be hard to conclude otherwise than that decentralized control over nuclear weapons would be the dominant command mechanism.

68. U.S. Army, *Understanding Soviet Developments*, p. 25.

The second major factor that enforces the NATO threat to employ nuclear weapons is the ambiguity surrounding the authority to use them. The dual-key bilateral nuclears stand out here. The intense uncertainty and lack of clarity that surrounds command mechanisms of the non-American members of NATO make it virtually impossible to discount the chances of retaliation, once NATO has gone on alert.

An ambiguity in command means that opaque, multiple, or possibly even competing lines of authority are perceived by the military organization responsible for physical possession of the nuclear weapons. An organizational redundancy exists in which several different interpretations of the command authority are simultaneously held. Even an individual group may hold more than one view about precisely who can order the use of nuclear weapons. Ambiguity of authority is a common phenomenon in many military organizations. It especially shows up in highly stressful situations in which secrecy or political sensitivity have prevented the practiced development of standard operating procedures. Palace revolts, coups, impeachments, and civil wars all generate an uneasiness in command organizations because there is no predicting how authority will be perceived by the diverse military units involved in the stressful events.

Although to date there have been no instances of nuclear weapons being fired because of an ambiguity of command, there have been cases of what could at least be called uneasiness about an indistinctness in command relationships. During the revolt of the French generals against President de Gaulle in 1960, Paris ordered one of its previously scheduled nuclear tests to be conducted several days ahead of plan so that the warhead would not fall into the hands of the generals.[69] More recently, in 1974 when Turkey invaded Cyprus, there was considerable concern in the United States about the American nuclear weapons stored in Turkey and Greece. There were deep splits in both governments about national policies. The situation reached the point where U.S. Marines with the 6th Fleet in the Mediterranean were alerted and prepared for a helicopter assault of the nuclear weapon

69. Donald G. Brennan, "The Risks of Spreading Weapons: A Historical Case," *Arms Control and Disarmament* I (1968): 86.

storage sites in Turkey in order to maintain U.S. possession.[70] During this crisis the nuclear warheads kept on alert aboard the QRA aircraft of the Greek and Turkish air forces were removed from the planes because of American fears that stability of command could not be maintained.[71] The vital security of the Greek and Turkish states was not at risk over the Cyprus dispute. But since security would be at risk in a NATO crisis, we must expect even greater pressure on the respective commands to take preemptive action.

One of the greatest sources of ambiguity about the authority over nuclear weapons are the binational understandings and agreements established between the United States and the various nations that have American nuclear weapons. These are kept highly secret, but these are indications of ambiguity, vagueness, and probable reliance on verbal understandings among the binational military units involved. The American defense pact signed with Turkey in 1980, for example, runs to one hundred pages, of which only six pages were submitted to the Turkish National Assembly.[72] In the United States, this particular agreement was treated as an executive agreement, partly to circumvent congressional scrutiny and approval.

A particularly interesting example of ambiguity over the use of foreign bases for nuclear attack arose in Greece in 1980. Here the issue was not Greek use of American nuclear arms, but rather American use of Greek bases to launch nuclear strikes. There is evidence that the Greek government, in the form of its foreign ministry, refused to yield this privilege. Despite this, the Greek defense ministry proceeded to sign an agreement with the United States anyway.[73] In a crisis, it is quite possible that major reassessments about the exact nature of the relationship would be called for. And, although all nuclear weapons stationed in Greece are technically under the control

70. "Cyprus Stirred U.S. to Protect Atom Arms," *New York Times*, September 9, 1974, p. 10; "Cooling Off the Nukes," *Newsweek*, August 12, 1974, p. 17.

71. "U.S. Weighs Status of Nuclear Warheads in Greece," *New York Times*, September 11, 1974, p. 12.

72. "America's Sticky Turkish Delight," *New Statesman*, June 20, 1980, p. 921.

73. "Doing a Turkey in Greece," *New Statesman*, October 31, 1980, p. 10; "The U.S., Greece and A-Arms," *New York Times*, February 27, 1981, p. A27.

of American units, the United States could do very little to protect these weapons against a determined attack. An attack might be motivated by internal splits in the host government, fears that nuclear weapons might be launched from their territory, fears that they might *not* be launched, or some other combination of events.

We should be skeptical about the ability of any bilateral understanding signed in peacetime to anticipate the stresses of a nuclear crisis. No matter how secret the details of authority over weapon use, the consultation procedures, and the collateral damage guidelines, such agreements always raise more questions than they settle. One of the only ways to establish any sort of agreement is to rely on vague and ambiguous terms. Clarity and openness in such agreements are desirable in principle, but it is hard to imagine how any two governments could sit down together in an official meeting to map out the precise details of nuclear usage. Could European governments be compelled to specify exactly how many civilians they would be willing to "lose" just to fix the collateral damage guidelines for nuclear use on their own soil? For the Western democracies that dominate NATO, this would be simply unthinkable. Even if it were done, the details would still be meaningless, given the uncertainties of war and the impact of Soviet counteractions.

The ambiguity over command of nuclear weapons may actually contribute to the credibility of the NATO deterrent, since it makes it all but impossible to predict the outcome of a crisis that involves the alerting of military forces. Ambiguity may enforce alliance cohesion, for the odd reason that any one of a number of countries could trigger the war, dragging the other coalition members with them into World War III. This may make it effectively impossible for the states of NATO, or the Warsaw Pact, to surrender or capitulate individually.

The third and final factor that enforces NATO's nuclear threat is the complexity of crisis and wartime management. Here complexity refers to the number of weapons, organizations, and decisions that would have to be coordinated for war. Beyond a certain point, such complexity could swamp NATO's decision-making capacity, thereby yielding wartime command to the decentralizing forces described earlier. This observation relates directly to the nuclear usage question

often advanced as the cornerstone of NATO security. Although nuclear weapons are indisputably the physical foundation of NATO
deterrence, the decision surrounding their use will not be a single,
well-defined one, but rather will involve many interrelated choices.
With increased complexity there is more likelihood that the nuclear
threat will be carried out.

A sense of the complexity can be best gained by example. One
particular choice would be whether to release nuclear land mines in
order to block mountain passes, valleys, and other invasion corridors.
This decision cannot be made in isolation from other choices. Nuclear mines are intended for use on NATO territory, but NATO
would need to give atomic arms to those nations most in need of
them. This likely means West Germany, Italy, Greece, and Turkey.
But a decision to disperse nuclear mines would immediately raise the
issue of a general nuclear weapon dispersal, because of the weapons'
great vulnerability to preemptive attack if they remain in centralized
storage. If NATO were to decide on a general dispersal, the troops in
rear areas would have to be moved forward, refugee movements would
have to be controlled, and orders would have to be issued from political to military commanders about exactly what they are to do in
the event of war. This last requirement in turn would create the need
for coordination of coalition objectives among NATO political leaders.

The seemingly simple decision to authorize use of nuclear land
mines, then, would be but the first link in a chain reaction of other
decisions that would be difficult to decouple from one another. If
these decisions could be decoupled, NATO would be in a better
position to bargain with the Warsaw Pact by taking a series of individual coercive actions that would escalate the crisis in a controlled
way. After it issued mines to the troops, it could systematically release
artillery weapons, tactical missiles, and other weapons in an effort to
convince the Warsaw Pact that NATO was willing to stand fast against
any threat. Carried into wartime, this line of thought follows the
American view of theater nuclear weapons as a layer of forces intermediate between conventional and strategic conflict.

But, for better or worse, the decisions needed to implement this

American version of nuclear strategy are *not* decoupled from one another, and a decision to take the first step toward war might well produce a cascading sequence of interactions among the many parts of the NATO force structure. Complexity of decision making contributes to deterrence because it raises the risk that the military aspects of a crisis would get out of political control. Once nuclear weapon dispersal has occurred, the forces of decentralization and delegation and the ambiguity of command authority make nuclear usage so unpredictable as to create a threat that no attacker can discount. Force structure complexity achieves the goal of deterrence in a way that is fundamentally different from the three-stage American concept. So many redundant triggers to nuclear war exist that, as a practical matter, the deterrence certainly ought to be credible regardless of whatever political breakdowns, stresses, and errors work against it.

Yet a deterrent strategy based on the likelihood that wartime complexities will swamp decision-making capacity and control, leading to escalation and enforcement of the nuclear threat, creates problems even if it is credible. Thomas Schelling and Herman Kahn long ago noticed that NATO strategy is greatly dependent on "the threat that leaves something to chance" and a fear of "rocking the boat" for its credibility.[74] As observations about political bargaining in a crisis their arguments seem persuasive. But perhaps we still have a gnawing feeling that in a really intense crisis West Germany is going to be enormously reluctant to endorse a decision that turns over nuclear weapons to the Turkish Air Force as a way of enforcing a threat that leaves something to chance. Doesn't such a strategy risk coming apart at the seams just when it is called upon to do its job? The often-asked question as to whether nuclear war in Europe can be limited hides a more important and realistic question. Can a nuclear *alert* in Europe be controlled? If it cannot, then political leaders may be so terrified of the consequences that they will refuse to take even the most precautionary measures in a crisis. Put as starkly as possible, if their

74. Thomas C. Schelling, *The Strategy of Conflict* (London: Oxford University Press, 1960), pp. 187–203; Herman Kahn, *On Escalation* (Baltimore: Penguin, 1965), pp. 63–66. See also Thomas C. Schelling, "Nuclear Strategy in Europe," *World Politics* 14 (April 1962): 421–32.

choice is to be red or dead, they will invariably choose the former, as it lacks the permanency of the latter.

Let us look at one such choice and the implications that would flow from it. Suppose the German government agrees to the dispersal of nuclear artillery rounds from storage igloos. By so doing, it has abdicated responsibility over its own destiny. Because artillery weapons are intrinsically short-range, reliance on them could lead to a nuclear war being fought only in the forward area of NATO, that is, a conflict restricted to West Germany. Even if the conflict were terminated on terms acceptable to NATO, the extensive use of nuclear artillery could devastate much of West Germany. The specter of Soviet-American nuclear artillery duals across the urban corridors of Germany or of atomic firefights through Hamburg and the Ruhr valley would put enormous pressure on Bonn to proceed cautiously on the decision to disperse these weapons.[75] Any decision would likely be made in the midst of domestic chaos because of NATO military preparations and movements, and because of massive refugee traffic (about which almost no forethought has been given).[76] Moreover, the Soviet emphasis on nuclear preemption would be on everyone's mind. If one had to pick the one single event that might just act as trigger, it would be the dispersal of NATO nuclear warheads from their storage facilities. For all of these reasons, internal fights within NATO would be likely to break out over this decision. The political fighting might lead to outright disruption of the alerting process to forestall Soviet retaliation. As the Anglo-French Alliance of 1940 became unglued, this is precisely what happened.[77]

Another choice that would surely disrupt NATO cohesion would be whether or not to authorize use of nuclear land mines in the

75. See Paul Bracken, "Collateral Damage and Theater Warfare," *Survival* 22 (November–December 1980): 203–07.

76. Ibid.

77. In June 1940 French military units physically blocked a British bomber force from using an airfield in Marseilles as it was about to launch an attack on Italy. British officers on the scene requested permission from Prime Minister Winston Churchill to clear the runway with machinegun fire. This permission was refused and the air strike never took place. Noel Barber, *The Week France Fell* (New York: Stein & Day, 1976), pp. 93–95.

mountain passes connecting Anatolian Turkey with the Soviet Union. In the 1960s the Turks requested a special arrangement for predelegated control of these devices so that they could be used quickly.[78] In the event that the mines were needed, other NATO members would then be confronted with the decision to turn over nuclear weapons to Turkey, and it would almost surely be seen as a first step in a general release of all nuclear munitions. Especially if a crisis were slowly building up in Europe, NATO members would be reluctant indeed to exacerbate tensions by such actions. Would Germany, Denmark, and the Netherlands really be willing to initiate nuclear war in order to defend Turkey? Any nuclear release might be seen as producing a catalytic effect that might induce the Warsaw Pact to disperse its own nuclear weapons.

Northern European NATO members are especially likely to have major concerns over the Turkish, Italian, and Greek fighter bombers armed with nuclear weapons. If the Soviets were on full alert with dispersed warheads, a single Turkish pilot could trigger World War III, as could a Soviet naval officer in charge of a Shaddock cruise missile. A chain reaction of nuclear salvos could spill over political boundaries in a matter of minutes, because of the ten-minute flight time that is required for Scaleboards to reach Germany and the Low Countries from Eastern Europe. Or a Soviet missile frigate within range of Naples might decide that it was about to receive an incoming nuclear attack. Scenarios like these could become overwhelmingly realistic possibilities in a crisis, and they might create strong incentives for accommodation.

Another defect of the strategy described in this chapter is that it is impossible to discuss it in public. What government can possibly announce that its security is dependent on turning nuclear weapons over to a battalion commander who just might pull the trigger even if he were not authorized to do so? Even governmental and academic studies have difficulty comprehending the extraordinary nature of this strategy. As a result, their attention has been devoted mainly to the

78. "Turkey Requests Leeway in Using Atom Land Mines," *New York Times*, April 6, 1967, p. 1.

understandable issues suggested by the abstract theories of limited war. Unfortunately, the force structure that has actually been built is totally unrelated to these particular strategies. It is far better suited to a strategy of deterrence by massive duplication of a nuclear hair trigger. One of the reasons for the intensity of the current debate in Europe about nuclear armaments is that the authorities really don't have any good answers to give to the critics. The nuclear freeze movement and other groups are asking questions for which no one has an answer, and they are consequently making many officials extremely uneasy.

Finally, and this should be obvious by now, if a war occurs it is likely to be intrinsically uncontrollable because the NATO command system has not been designed to provide such control. A policy of centralized warfighting control would present NATO members with a rational path for going to war. But the potential devastation of a European conflict would keep political leaders from ever voluntarily taking this path.

Although a few analyses of strategic war termination have been written, to my knowledge none has ever dealt with war termination in Europe. The lack of attention given to this subject is stunning. Some fundamental questions badly need to be asked. Regardless of how easy or hard it would be to disperse NATO's arsenal of theater nuclear weapons from their storage sites, once war breaks out it is going to be extraordinarily difficult to get them back under lock and key again.

The survivability of many of these weapons depends on mobility and concealment. Consequently, they are carried by mobile armies, ships at sea, and dispersed aircraft. The inventory control problems of such a force are immense, especially in an environment where communications are disrupted and coherent political authority may not exist. In the event of conflict, possession of nuclears might become one of the few symbols of authority, and military commanders might be reluctant indeed to return them to centralized, and vulnerable, storage.

A nuclear cease-fire would be precarious in the extreme. Any national force, even any sub-national group, that felt the terms of the cease-fire were not totally equitable could restart the war in spectacular manner. Opportunities to take care of long-standing grievances—such as the Cyprus dispute or the Armenian problem—could prove so attractive as to be irresistible. It would be all but impossible to determine culpability in these chaotic conditions, as it is virtually impossible to distinguish the source of nuclear weapon bursts. Therefore, how to get thousands of unused tactical nuclear weapons back under central control is one of the most important questions facing NATO if there is to be even a rudimentary political direction given to a conflict.

6   Command and Control

Command and control as we define it here amounts to a system that brings the individual pieces of a defense system together into a coherent overall structure. Warning, plans, assessment systems, and theater forces are integrated by means of command and control. This chapter describes the evolution of the command system from the 1940s to the present and then explores its tendencies toward stability in crisis.

By taking what may be called a life-cycle approach to the American command system, we can see certain parallels between it and other large, complex organizations. The birth of the new organization is often accompanied by highly responsive and direct contact. Later, in the developmental period, fundamental coordination problems caused by its increased complexity and scale of operations are worked out. For the American command the late 1950s were such a period, and at this time the military may have absorbed more technological change in a shorter time than any other organization in history.

Next, the system entered a transitional phase of development. U.S. policy makers realized that the continuance of patterns established in the early development period of the late 1950s would only lead to a dangerously inflexible force. With great difficulty, changes were enforced onto the command that permitted more detailed involvement in alerting and wartime operations by political leaders. Finally, a mature command organization followed, which has been strongly influenced by a number of adverse trends over which planners have had little control.

THE AMERICAN COMMAND STRUCTURE

The dawn of the nuclear age in 1945 did not create any great difficulties for command and control. The small number of nuclear weapons in the immediate postwar era, literally only a handful, made the nuclear force easy to manage. The strict secrecy that had surrounded the Manhattan Project and the universal perception that atomic weapons were different from all others led to tight centralized control of the existing weapons.

The weapons consisted of the fissile material and the nonnuclear explosive components. The military was not allowed to have physical possession of either. The Atomic Energy Act of 1946 created the Atomic Energy Commission, and set up a coordinating link between the AEC and the military, the Division of Military Applications, within AEC. All atomic weapons and related components were under the immediate control of AEC civilian guards. Only upon direct presidential orders would these weapons be turned over to the military for matching with delivery vehicles. For this reason, President Truman had fully centralized, and almost personal, control over America's nuclear force at this time.

The deficiencies of this arrangement became more and more obvious as the Cold War began and it appeared atomic weapons might have to be used on short notice to defend Europe. The Czechoslovakian and Berlin crises reinforced this perception, and some nonnuclear bomb components began to be given to various military units sometime in the late 1940s. Still, arguments persisted in the executive branch that turning over the complete weapons to the military would be too dangerous, that some kind of accidental use might occur. The military, on the other hand, argued that it could not carry out its mandated assignments unless it had prompt access to these weapons.

As often happens with such debates an outside event determined the outcome. The outbreak of the Korean War in 1950 led to a searching reappraisal of security policy and by 1951 actual nuclear weapons were transferred to U.S. Navy aircraft carriers.[1] Other trans-

1. Norman Polmar, *Strategic Weapons* (New York: Crane, Russak, 1975), p. 19.

fers of completed weapons to overseas bases occurred at this time as well.

An intriguing study could be made of the actions and preparations involving nuclear weapons that followed the Chinese intervention in Korea in November 1950. It is known that no nuclear weapons were in Korea or even in the Far East at the time of the invasion. Had tactical nuclear weapons of anything like the number and diversity later deployed in Europe been available to the Eighth Army in Korea in late November 1950, it is not hard to imagine that some might have been used against the invading Chinese forces. Especially given President Truman's remarks in his November 30, 1950 press conference (see chapter 3), it seems clear that the American government was in a state of shock, feeling its forces might be physically driven from the Korean peninsula following the invasion by three hundred thousand Chinese Communist forces. Although there have been many studies of why the United States did not use nuclear weapons in Korea, they have overlooked what might have been a determining factor, the fact that none were there to use in the first dark days after the invasion.

By September 1952 an agreement giving a greater number of complete weapons to the military was reached.[2] It also permitted overseas basing and control of weapons. Within the United States weapons still had to be stored at AEC-controlled storage sites. In the event the weapons were needed, the Strategic Air Command was to send transport planes and trucks to these storage sites, and there the weapons would be transferred to military control for matching with intercontinental bombers. Even in 1954 this release procedure haunted SAC commanders, who needed to know the detailed pickup schedules for internal planning purposes.[3] To them, this cumbersome procedure

2. M. Leitenberg, "Background Materials in Tactical Nuclear Weapons Primarily in the European Context," in Stockholm International Peace Research Institute, ed., *Tactical Nuclear Weapons: European Perspectives* (London: Taylor & Francis, 1978), p. 13.

3. See the declassified report contained in D. A. Rosenberg, "A Smoking Radiating Ruin at the End of Two Hours," *International Security* 6 (Winter 1981/82): 19.

was one more obstacle against going to war soon enough to destroy Soviet bombers on the ground.

By all accounts AEC control of weapons in the United States was a complete fiction by 1952 or 1953. Any request by the military would have been met with immediate AEC agreement. Therefore, AEC control became an unnecessary layer of bureaucracy that could potentially disrupt the smooth movement of the nation's growing war machine. By 1956 the entire nuclear stockpile had been turned over to the military.

There was an interesting parallel to these events in the Soviet Union. Apparently not until the 1960s was the Soviet military allowed custody of nuclear warheads. Previously the weapons were kept not by any civilian groups as in the United States, but by special KGB units.[4] In both nations the immediate reaction to the development of nuclear weapons was the conviction that they were so fundamentally different and destructive that only a command mechanism outside of the ordinary military control structure would be safe enough for them. The result was a high degree of central control of these weapons both in the United States and the Soviet Union.

However, in both nations this political control eroded. The pressure for prompt nuclear use drove the United States to gradually abandon an exclusively civilian command mechanism in favor of more direct military control. Similarly, in the Soviet Union after the fall of Khrushchev in 1964 the military gained greater control over nuclear weapons as well.

EARLY DEVELOPMENT, 1955–60

The period between 1955 and 1960 was critical in the development of modern nuclear forces. Prior to it, there were so few nuclear weapons that command and control posed few problems. The advent of a Soviet nuclear capability in bombers and missiles, however, changed the operating environment considerably. Now not only did the United States need to plan for a Soviet attack; it was necessary to develop forces that could go to war on a moment's notice.

4. See John Barron, *KGB* (New York: Reader's Digest, 1974), p. 13.

The American nuclear strategy of the day, which corresponded to the political doctrine of massive retaliation, called for unconstrained all-out attacks. Within this strategy there may have been room for some sort of small reserve force, but holding this force back would be done in anticipation of post-strike intelligence information, so that well-targeted follow-on strikes could be launched.

This strategy required three things of the command structure. First, a large nuclear force was needed, preferably one that could pack a devastating shock into its first salvo. The SAC bombers with their large-yield warheads met this need. The stated intent of this force was to turn the Soviet Union into a smoking, radiating ruin in a few hours' time.

Second, an excellent warning system was needed. The greatest failure for this nuclear strategy would have arisen either from a Soviet surprise attack that crippled SAC on the ground or from an unexpected attack that did not allow SAC to destroy the time-urgent Bravo targets, such as long-range air armies, medium-range missiles, and submarines in port. Consequently, the American command structure emphasized warning, both tactical (as with the DEW Line, the Pinetree Line, and BMEWS) and strategic (as with listening posts and aerial reconnaissance overflights). The warning system had to deliver advance information on early preparations for war so that SAC could strike at the earliest moment in order to blunt a Soviet attack on Europe and limit damage to the American homeland.

The strategy's dual emphasis on tactical and strategic warning was not inconsistent. The ideal war for the command structure of this era was a war in which rising political tensions would lead to Soviet mobilization in Europe. Strategic warning would be picked up through overseas listening posts and spy aircraft; and, just as the Soviets were set to launch a ground invasion, or just after they had begun a ground invasion, SAC would be "released" to unwind its war plan. It was a preemptive, *not* a preventive, war. However, the historic difficulty of interpreting strategic warning in a timely fashion and the physical vulnerability of SAC to surprise attack meant that tactical warning would also serve as an important hedge against something going wrong. Regardless of the reasons, which might be misread COMINT or a terrified president who refused to take action, SAC did not want to be paralyzed on the ground. The DEW, Pinetree, BMEWS, and SOSUS all enhanced the ability of the United States to launch its massive strike even under conditions of strategic surprise.

Finally, the strategy called for a streamlined command structure, so that there would be no hitch in the orders given by the president to go to war. The diffuse and ad hoc way that President Roosevelt controlled the joint chiefs was effective in World War II, but something more concrete and practiced had to be developed for controlling a nuclear force. As a consequence, in 1958 Congress passed the National Security Reorganization Act. The effect of this act was to remove the military departments and service chiefs from the chain of command authority. Since 1958 the unified and specified commanders of the United States have reported directly to the secretary of defense, and the secretary of defense has reported to the president. The secretaries of the Army, Navy, and Air Force are no longer in the chain of command. A whole layer of intermediate bureaucracy was thereby removed from the command of nuclear forces. This action followed on the heels of the removal of AEC civilians from physical control of the nuclear weapons themselves. By the late 1950s nuclear weapons had been fully turned over to the military, and clear, direct command channels had been established between the unified and specified commanders of nuclear forces and the president.

In this command structure, the role of the president was to give a simple order of Go or No Go. The literature on nuclear war today, both classified and unclassified, still uses the 1950s jargon, speaking of "getting the nuclear release," (that is, getting a presidential authorization to carry out a war plan). In the 1950s, "release" was an apt metaphor. It implied a binary condition of go or no go, and it conveyed an image of a massive nuclear force that, when fully alerted, was restrained only by one thin rope held by one man. Once the president released the cord, the force would go into a spasm attack against the Soviet Union.

The president was critical to the command mechanism, as he alone could give the release. Consequently, his security, survival, and, if necessary, replacement were all considered very carefully. In 1957 a secret fund was established by Congress to pay for the protection of the presidency in emergency conditions.[5] The main purpose of the fund was to underwrite a network of Presidental Emergency Sites outside of Washington where the president could be taken and protected in a nuclear crisis. Several of these sites had already been constructed, and President Eisenhower actually tested one facility, at Raven Rock Mountain near Camp David, for three days in 1955.[6] A special AT&T communications center was also built inside Short Hill Mountain, Virginia, to provide communications for the emergency sites.[7]

In addition to ensuring the safety and security of the president, plans were taken to replace him if necessary. During the Eisenhower administration the practice of keeping a Black Bag, or Football as it is called, began. The Black Bag is nothing but a locked briefcase containing the codes the president would send the military in order to release the force. The Black Bag is kept near the president at all times in order to ensure that a prompt release could be obtained in an emergency, even if the president was traveling outside Washington. In the Eisenhower years Vice President Nixon was also given a Black Bag, so that if something happened to the president no time would be lost or disruptions would occur in getting the presidential release.[8]

Besides understanding these features of the U.S. command structure in the late 1950s, we should also understand the things that were *not* required. Communications, warning, and command posts were needed, but they did not have to be survivable against Soviet attack. Once the release from the president was given and communicated to the nuclear forces, and once the forces had been sent into action, the entire command and control system was superfluous. While timely

5. Bill Gulley, *Breaking Cover* (New York: Warner Books, 1980), p. 43.
6. Robert Walters, "Going Underground," *Inquiry*, February 1981, p. 13.
7. Ibid., p. 15.
8. William M. Manchester, *The Death of a President* (New York: Harper & Row, 1967), p. 230.

warning was needed, survivable warning was not, because its only function would have been served once it had given indication of attack.

A hardened command system wasn't required and a hardened command system wasn't built. Only rudimentary protective measures were taken. There was reluctance to admit openly that the command system had no function but to launch SAC once and for all, but the operative system that was built did just this. When SAC built its new underground command post at Offutt Air Force Base in Nebraska in 1957, it was only about thirty feet underground. Even a small, inaccurate Soviet nuclear weapon could have destroyed it. Yet to this day the official history of the Strategic Air Command continues the myth that the United States possessed a hardened, survivable command system in the 1950s.[9]

Neither were the Big L warning and control systems described in chapter 2 survivable against nuclear attack. Some analysts had argued against this design on the grounds that a limited nuclear exchange might be conceivable and that such an exchange would require a surviving command structure to terminate the war before it reached apocalyptic levels of destruction. One internal Rand Corporation report on the subject in 1960, for example, lamented that "since present plans do not envision adequate protection for the Big L systems it is relevant to ask whether it might not be better to abandon all attempts at protection and simply accept the fact that the systems will be disabled by the first wave of the enemy bombs."[10] The BMEWS radars in Canada, Greenland, and England were all large, above-ground metal structures. The most important BMEWS site in Greenland was supplied with electric power from oil-fired generators that were aboard a ship in a nearby harbor, with the electric lines carried on above-ground poles to the radar site. Even a conventional attack would have knocked out BMEWS.

9. See Office of the Historian, Strategic Air Command, *Development of Strategic Air Command, 1946–1976* (Offutt Air Force Base, Nebr.: Strategic Air Command, 1976), pp. 58–59.
10. J. B. Carne, "Protecting Big L Systems—Should We Do More or Are We Doing Too Much?," Rand Corp., D-7279, March 1960, p. 3.

The planning for a new NORAD facility brought to a head the dispute about whether to build hardened command posts, and the Air Force eventually won the argument against truly hardening the sites. Until 1965, the NORAD command center was located in above-ground cinder block buildings in Colorado Springs. The communication between NORAD and BMEWS and SAC was nearly all over AT&T telephone lines, which obviously were not designed for withstanding nuclear attack. However, in the late 1950s it was decided to move the NORAD command post to a more secure location, as its existing facility could have been neutralized so easily by sabotage. At the time, a few hand grenades could have blacked out the nation's entire warning system. When proposals appeared to build NORAD headquarters in a hardened site, SAC actually opposed the plan, calling it a superfluous waste of resources. The most important function of NORAD and its many warning sensors was, in the view of the SAC, to be blown up, for this would provide unambiguous warning of attack.[11]

When the plans to move NORAD inside Cheyenne Mountain were made, the proposed site was still *not* hardened against dedicated attack, and this gave rise to a bureaucratic battle between the Air Force and Rand Corporation civilian planners.[12] To the civilians, a truly hardened NORAD would be the first of a whole network of hardened command posts for SAC, other military commanders, and, most important, for the president. The civilians wanted hardened sites in order to be able to wage limited nuclear war with protected leadership and control.[13] It would be essential to have a headquarters that could provide orders and conduct assessments in wartime, for this strategy to make sense. They argued that NORAD should be built deeply *beneath*, not *inside*, Cheyenne Mountain. They were overruled, and although NORAD was made harder than before, it was not built to withstand a

11. Interview with former Rand project leader on the NORAD design problem.
12. Ibid.
13. See Herman Kahn, "Why Go Deep Underground?" in *Proceedings of the Second Protective Construction Symposium* (Santa Monica, Calif.: Rand Corp, 1959), pp. 5–37; also J. B. Carne, "Communications Vulnerability," in the same volume, pp. 69–74.

direct nuclear attack. The exact hardness of NORAD is probably somewhere between 500 and 1,000 psi. The Rand civilians in 1959 argued for a deep 10,000-psi structure. With Soviet tests in 1961 of fifty-eight megatons, it was clear that NORAD was not survivable when it was finished in 1965, especially if one considers the vulnerability of the communciations connecting it to the outside world. Plans advanced to move SAC headquarters to a hardened site were also scrapped and SAC stayed in its unhardened 1957 facilities.

The theory behind the "soft" design for command and control was that the purpose of all of these systems was to get warning in order to launch a nuclear attack. In the 1950s, there were no plans to fight a limited or controlled nuclear war. War plans were posited on a single massive salvo of weapons. The assumption in the United States was that the military command posts had no function after they launched their missiles.

We can conclude from this that in the developmental years of the 1950s there was a match between all of the pieces going into the command structure. This is not to say that the particular strategy would have "worked," in the sense of avoiding surprise and success-fully preempting the Soviet Union early in a war; this will never be known. Nor can we say that the strategy would actually have been selected by the president. The president could have attempted to switch strategies at the last minute, however difficult this would have been because of command structure constraints. We can say, nonetheless, that at this time a congruence existed between strategy and command structure.

TRANSITIONAL PHASE, 1961–67

In the early 1960s major structural changes were made in the Amer-ican command system, mainly directed toward permitting greater po-litical intervention in the alerting and firing processes. After the in-flexible control of the 1950s, this marked a change in command structure that has set the pattern for nearly all later developments. In the early 1960s there was a searching reappraisal of first how to es-tablish command over these lethal weapons and then how to integrate the rapidly expanding number of technologically sophisticated systems of warning, intelligence, and control with the nuclear forces in a coherent manner.

These changes were justified by two new requirements: the need to apply force in limited amounts and the need to involve political leaders in whatever application of force was to occur. A new emphasis on *limitation* in attack, whether in the avoidance of cities or the sparing of enemy command and control centers, demanded something far different from the older concept of a highly effective warning system wired to a massive nuclear strike force. It first required survivable nuclear forces—forces that could not be destroyed in a disarming attack, no matter how large. Forces had to be survivable independent of any strategic or tactical warning in order to enable the political leadership to maintain control of events. Otherwise, control might revert to each side's warning and alerting systems, as had happened in World War I. For forces to be survivable did not necessarily mean that a nation would have to forgo the option of first use of nuclear weapons. It only meant that the nation would no longer be dependent on a de facto strategy of launch on tactical or strategic warning with all of the threat of loss of control that this strategy implied.

A second feature of flexible response, as these revisions were called, was that a surviving national command authority (NCA) would make decisions *during* a war. In the 1950s the only function of the president had been to give a release to go to war. But flexible response called for the president (or his successor) to make decisions during the war. Also, it was the president who would negotiate with Moscow to terminate the war. (Nobody seems to have thought much about war termination in the 1950s.)

Third, flexible response required survivable communication between the NCA and the nuclear forces. Equally important, it meant that communications between the leaders of each side during the war were essential. These communications need not be restricted to verbal exchanges; reliance could also be placed on "signaling" communications such as going on alert or use of attacks to convey "messages." Naturally, the communications requirement reinforced the necessity of political involvement in the alerting and operations of the forces.

Finally, flexible response meant that *prewar* involvement of political leaders in war planning had to increase. Certain needs had to be reflected in the prepackaged plans drawn up by the military, such as to avoid destruction of enemy political command centers at the outset of conflict. Instead of war planning that was "bottom up," that is, which came from the military organizations and their intelligence branches, planning had to be "top down," coming from a political leadership equipped with a loyal, competent staff to assure that plans reflected the political strategy.

The above requirements for flexible response sound like a tall order, especially when viewed in the light of what today is considered the movement in the 1960s toward "mutual assured destruction." Certain grotesque caricatures of both American plans and the command structure built to carry out these plans have been put forth, especially by critics of what is termed MAD (for mutual assured destruction). They are a serious, and potentially dangerous, misreading of what America's nuclear arsenal was designed for. Some fundamental and extremely difficult problems were thought through during the 1960s, with the overall intent of establishing political control over the process of nuclear war. To be sure, the command system that was built did not meet all of the theoretical requirements demanded of it, yet most of the changes made in command structure in the early 1960s have been accepted either consciously or unconsciously over the following two decades. In this period the foundations of the system we have today were established.

The main problem in 1961 was not so much to conceptualize and design a new command and control system for flexible response as it was to take the very large and expensive existing command system that it had inherited and turn it around to support the new requirements. In 1961, the Big L, SOSUS, Pinetree, BMEWs, and other massive systems were already completed or were well along in construction. Moreover, the decision to use the Bell Telephone network for strategic military communications had long since been made. The cost of discarding the command and control system inherited from the 1950s in favor of a totally new one would have been astronomical, and a new system would have taken years to construct.

Therefore, a decision was made to use the physical and technical apparatus inherited from the 1950s but to reorganize control policies for flexible response. In other words, major changes were made in tactics, procedures, and operating rules, but only minor changes were made in hardware. The whole endeavor was exceedingly subtle, and it ranks as one of the cleverest examples of managerial thinking in American national security policy.

The basic problem defined in the early 1960s was the need to centralize political control of the forces, while at the same time recognizing the inadequacies of this kind of control. From one perspective, the ideal command structure for the nuclear strategy of the early 1960s was that of the late 1940s and early 1950s, a diagram of which is shown in figure 6.1. Here, complete centralization of the nuclear

Fig. 6.1. A centralized command system

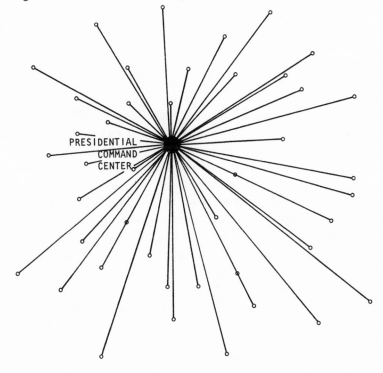

forces is represented by the linkage of all weapons, which are indicated by the outlying small circles in the figure, to the central presidential command post. Each weapon can be carefully controlled by the president and his military staff, and a war might see highly nuanced use of nuclear weapons for demonstration, signaling, and ordinary military attacks. President Truman in the early 1950s had a command system of roughly this kind, although at that time there was no tradition of the president telling military commanders how to use the weapons given to them. Control in this setup was as centralized as physically possible. Detailed management of the nuclear forces was maximized, and, in principle, the setup offered considerable possibility of engaging in elaborate wartime negotiating with the enemy.

However, the deficiencies of such a command system are quite obvious. The entire control system can be disabled by a *single* enemy nuclear weapon fired at the central presidential command center, and paralysis of the retaliatory force would result. Thus, this form of command system is just too vulnerable to attack to ever be a credible deterrent.

An additional failing of this type of structure is that it places too much detailed military control with the civilian leadership, a leadership that is likely to lack both the information-processing abilities and the management and technical background needed to perform this function. As the size of the nuclear force grows, as measured by the number of launchers or the number of warheads, the span of control of the central command grows exponentially large. For example, it might be difficult for a central presidential command center to manage a nuclear exchange involving a few hundred weapons, but to believe that an exchange with several thousand weapons could be managed in the same way strains credulity. The only way out of this problem is to organize the command organization away from fully centralized control, and the only real way to do this in a world where military organizations are responsible for security is to structure the nuclear command so that it meshes with the organizational structure of the military. Without such a command organization, the absence of hierarchy would lead to an information overload that would swamp the decision-making process.

For these reasons, and also because an expensive physical command and control system had already been started in the fifties, a more decentralized concept was chosen. This is illustrated in figure 6.2, which is not meant to faithfully depict an exact system but to illustrate the design philosophy. This particular diagram is of the National Military Command System (NMCS). Here, presidential control of the nuclear forces is exercised through a small number of primary command centers, and from there to secondary command

Fig. 6.2. A decentralized command system

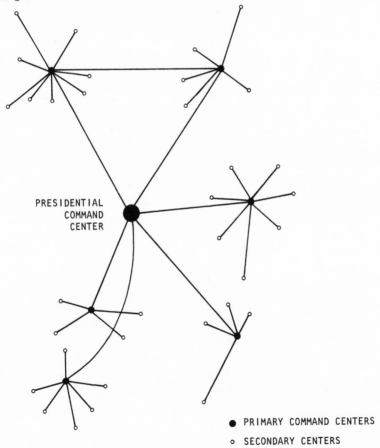

PRESIDENTIAL
COMMAND
CENTER

● PRIMARY COMMAND CENTERS
o SECONDARY CENTERS

centers or actual nuclear weapon units. The structure matched the hierarchical organization of the U.S. military, providing layers of administration for concentration of expertise. In particular it closely fit the military structure codified into law by the 1947 National Security Act and the 1958 National Security Reorganization Act.

The 1958 act had removed operational control of the field commanders from the military departments and service chiefs, streamlining control of the military. The key idea in the command revisions of 1961 and 1962 was that the nuclear-relevant unified and specified commands should act as the primary command centers illustrated in figure 6.2. They would exercise direct control over nuclear forces from their individual command centers and would report to the presidential command center through the joint chiefs, who would function as the president's military staff. Civilian control would be enforced through a direct link between the president and secretary of defense, who together were defined as the NCA, and the unified and specified commands. Presidential control of nuclear weapons was more decentralized than in the system in figure 6.1, but there was a greater centralization of authority over the combatant commands because more complex messages could be exchanged between them. The president would do more in this setup than simply release the military to go to all-out war.

The primary command centers of the unified and specified commanders occupied their own subordinate layer of control over the nuclear forces. The hierarchy was easy to design, as it derived almost directly from the National Security Act and its 1958 reorganization, which specified the chain of military command. The links in the chain of command authority each had their own command centers; these are the secondary centers shown in figure 6.2. Broadly speaking, command authority would flow from the unified and specified commanders to the numbered armies, navies, and air forces. Secondary command centers would then be the headquarters of these units. Figure 6.3 illustrates this flow of command authority. The secondary command posts could be on the ground, underground, at sea, or in the air. Only selected commands with nuclear weapons are shown in the figure.

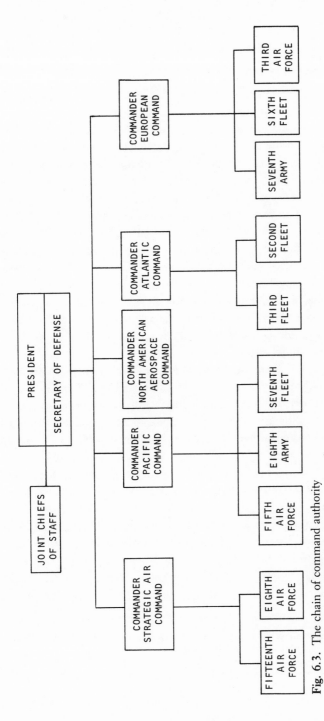

Fig. 6.3. The chain of command authority
NOTE: For space reasons not all units are shown.

The command and control system constructed in the early 1960s was built to match the decentralized structure displayed in figures 6.2 and 6.3. For example, the main SAC force-monitoring and flight-following control mechanism was a Big L system known as 465 L. Its design specifications called for "an effective alternate SAC Head-quarters and the capability of de-centralization to numbered AF [Air Force] level."[14] The alternate headquarters was intended as a means of protecting the main SAC headquarters from surprise attack. This points to the special way the entire command structure managed the problem of an attack directed against it. The fear since the late 1950s was that a Soviet ICBM attack directed against Washington could wipe out the command mechanism before it had time to send the codes needed to authorize retaliation to the forces. This was known as the decapitation attack. The new requirement for a president to make decisions *during* a war compounded this problem. How could the United States guarantee that an attack against the president during the war would not paralyze the U.S. forces that had been held back from the initial attack?

Because there are relatively few primary command posts in the decentralized structure of figure 6.2, these major centers could easily be destroyed by direct attack, thus isolating the retaliatory nuclear force from the orders needed to employ it. At first glance, the decentralized system of figure 6.2 seems only marginally more survivable to enemy attack than a fully centralized command system. Even in 1962, it would not have been an undue additional targeting burden on the Soviet nuclear forces to go after five or six additional aiming points.

This dilemma was resolved through the command procedure of the presidential center. Its function was not to act as *a trigger to launch nuclear weapons*, but as *a safety catch preventing other triggers from firing*. The primary command centers were to serve as the triggers, but their ability to fire would be restrained by the viable functioning,

---

14. System Program Office 465 L, "A Technical Review of the Implementation of Strategic Air Command Control System 465 L," SACCS Project Office, Offutt Air Force Base, Nebr., June 1965.

and the survival, of the presidential command center.[15] If the safety catch of this system were destroyed, direct operational control would devolve to the primary command centers—in effect, the unified and specified commands of the NMCS, according to the chain of command authority.

This analogy between the American command structure and a revolver can be extended still further. The safety catch vetoes other actions besides pulling the trigger. In a way, the alerting process itself serves as a graduated safety catch. When there is no declared alert a safety catch may be considered on, and other parts of the military system may be procedurally blocked from taking certain actions. In a revolver, the safety catch and triggering mechanism are never part of the same system, but are always organized independently. This has a correspondence too in the command system. The alerting mechanism is integrated with the nuclear forces through checks and balances in which the actions of one command permit other commands to take action. Furthermore, once a single safety catch is off, command of the revolver devolves to the trigger. In a nuclear environment, it might prove necessary to have this devolution flow to many different and redundant triggers in order to protect the command system against decapitation.

Such a devolution of command raises a hazy subject: Just who can pull the nuclear trigger? The American government has never offered official details on this subject, other than to assert that only the president is authorized to order the use of nuclear weapons. However, despite the absence of official comment to the contrary it seems clear that a literal interpretation of this statement is not possible. On a common-sense basis, it would make the entire U.S. arsenal vulnerable to paralysis when attacked by a handful of nuclear weapons. Since it is absolutely basic to the command restructuring of the early 1960s to provide a *set* of triggers controlled by a centralized safety catch, it may be useful to us to survey the unofficial reports on this

15. This description is also expounded in Thornton Read, *Command and Control* (Princeton: Center for International Studies, Princeton University, 1961). The collaborators of this particular report included those who later worked on the redesign of the American command system.

subject to see if they are consistent with the broad pattern of command and control described here.

Plans for emergency authorization, or predelegation, to use nuclear weapons in certain contingencies were reported in 1957 to the Joint Committee on Atomic Energy.[16] The basis for exercising such predelegated authority was to be presidential incapacitation or the breakdown in communication during an emergency. This implicitly restricted the authority to second-strike use only. Reportedly, written orders would be relied on, but verbal orders were also used in granting the authority.[17] In September 1957 a former commander of NORAD, General Earle E. Partridge stated in an interview that he had been given emergency authority to use certain nuclear weapons.[18] Apparently the reason behind these measures was the fear that there might be no president surviving to send out the necessary orders if the United States absorbed the first blow in a nuclear war.[19] In 1964, General Lauris Norstad, then a former commander of American forces in Europe, broadly hinted in an interview that he too was given such power by President Kennedy.[20]

In 1977 Daniel Ellsberg asserted that such predelegated authority had been given to the military by presidents Eisenhower, Kennedy, and Johnson.[21] Ellsberg was in an intimate position to know about these matters as he had been closely involved in the revision of war plans in the early 1960s as a consultant to the government. He stated that the authority had been given to the "six or seven three- and four-star generals"; these generals must have corresponded to the unified and specified commanders.[22] In an interview in 1980 Ellsberg supplied more details about this authority, reporting that in 1961 he had

16. "The Fear and the Facts," *Time*, September 25, 1964, p. 17.

17. Ibid.

18. This interview in reprinted in *U.S. News & World Report*, October 5, 1964, p. 49. See also "Just Who Can Push the Button?," *Philadelphia Inquirer*, August 19, 1981, p. 15.

19. *U.S. News & World Report*, October 5, 1964, p. 33.

20. Ibid., pp. 47–49.

21. "Ellsberg Says Army Held A-Bomb Power," *New York Times*, November 4, 1977, p. A9.

22. Ibid.

uncovered in the White House signed letters from the president to each of the unified and specified commanders who possessed nuclear weapons authorizing their use in certain emergency conditions.[23] The letters strongly implied that the conditions were retaliatory use in the event of a massive Soviet attack.

We are less interested in changes in the details of predelegated nuclear usage authority from one administration to the next than we are in the need for it in order to protect the command system from decapitation attacks. Perhaps the most articulate explanation of the reasoning behind predelegation was given by General Nathan F. Twining in 1966. General Twining was clearly in a position to speak with some authority, both as a four-star Air Force general and as a former chairman of the Joint Chiefs of Staff:

> How will the President, upon whose shoulders rests the ultimate decision, elect to exercise his ultimate authority over the control of rifle fire, mortar fire, fire from ships at sea, fire from aircraft, and nuclear fire power, *however delivered?*
>
> In terms of basic logic, it would appear that he has only three options:
>
> 1. The President can shut his eyes and hope that nothing will happen.
>
> 2. He can maintain personal (and detailed) control at all times, making no provision for national response in event of massive damage to the seat of government.
>
> 3. He can predelegate authority to be exercised under certain grave circumstances.
>
> With respect to the first option in terms of logic, no Chief Executive could be so derelict in his duty. With respect to the second, the Chief Executive would be inviting an enemy attack if the enemy knew that the United States would be paralyzed by the delivery of only one nuclear weapon on the seat of the government.
>
> On the basis of just plain common sense, therefore, it would appear that the third option—predelegation of authority to take military action in event of certain circumstances—can be the only valid solution

23. "Nuclear Armament, an Interview with Dr. Daniel Ellsberg," *Conservation Press*, 1980, p. 2.

to military fire control. This option might assume, of course, that so long as the President or his successor is alive and the government continues to function, that personal and detailed control would be maintained at White House level. But, if the nation were under attack, and there was no Washington, D.C., left, America could fight back rather than die with its own powerful force immobilized.[24]

Predelegation of authority for use of nuclear weapons from a president to a military commander naturally raises constitutional questions as well as concerns about how to integrate control mechanisms for nuclear weapons into a democratic form of government. The Constitution states that Congress is responsible for declaring war, and it would seem that a major, or even a minor, use of American nuclear weapons even in retaliation would be an act of war. But the founding fathers never had to contemplate the prospect of all-out wars waged in less than an hour, when there would be no time to clear things with the Congress. President Eisenhower for one was deeply troubled by the possibility in the nuclear age of having to override constitutional consideration in an emergency. In the 1950s, the problem was that once warning came in SAC might have to be launched on short notice, without time to gather the Congress together to vote a declaration of war even though the United States was technically landing the first blow in a preemptive attack.[25]

At a deeper level one must ask if democratic government could survive a nuclear war because of the need to violate grossly the Constitution in some attack situations, combined with the shock to democratic institutions of the resulting exchange. Although it is easiest to devise a scenario in which the president was forced into retaliating simply to save American lives, this is but one of many scenarios. What if a president, through ineptitude, shortsightedness, or a misplaced belief that war should be left to the generals, lost control of events to the dynamics of the alerting process? In the aftermath of a war started this way, with 100 million Americans killed for no real

24. Nathan F. Twining, *Neither Liberty Nor Safety* (New York: Holt, Rinehart & Winston, 1966), p. 243.
25. See Robert E. Ferrell, ed., *The Eisenhower Diaries* (New York: Norton, 1981), pp. 311–12.

reason, the democratic form of government might be swept away as were the monarchies of Central Europe in World War I.[26] How to design mechanisms to command these weapons was something that raised many questions in the early 1960s, when the matter was being thought through, but the questions only produced more questions, and gradually the questioning stopped.

Virtually every examination of these perplexing matters has concluded that only the president has the authority to order the use of nuclear weapons but that this power may be delegated without limit, according to his wishes.[27] The power to delegate arises from his function as commander in chief, and delegation is the rule rather than the exception in how he commands all executive departments. The answer is exactly as suggested by General Twining. The president alone can issue orders to a private in the Army to fire his rifle, but this power can be delegated downward through the long chain of command to the individual soldier. In principle, nuclear weapons are no different.

The Constitution and American law do provide for a succession to the presidency. In theory, the president may die or be incapacitated, but the presidency itself can never be destroyed. The chain of succession follows with the vice president, speaker of the House, president pro tempore of the Senate, and then through the cabinet secretaries in the order of their department's creation: State, Treasury, Defense, Justice, Interior, Agriculture, Commerce, Labor, Health and Human Services, Housing and Urban Development, Transportation, Energy, and Education. The difficulties of using this chain of succession for command authority in a nuclear war are obvious. All of these officials have their offices and residences in the Washington area. In a surprise attack, admittedly the worst, most stressful case, all of them might be killed. In the chaos, how could the military find

26. See Elisabeth Crawford, "Survival of Democratic Government in Thermonuclear War—An Overview," Hudson Institute, May 1964.

27. See U.S., Congressional Research Service, *Authority to Order the Use of Nuclear Weapons* (Washington: Government Printing Office, 1975); and U.S., Congress, House, Subcommittee on International Security and Scientific Affairs, *First Use of Nuclear Weapons: Preserving Responsible Control*, 94th Cong., 2d sess., 1976.

the secretary of housing and urban development and determine that all of those higher on the list were in fact dead? More important, what good would it do to turn over the world's most destructive military force to a man who did not know the slightest thing about it, or perhaps even about international affairs and national security in general? It might do more harm than good to have some of the cabinet secretaries who have held office during the past twenty years take over the nuclear arsenal from the military in such an emergency.

Even the vice president cannot always be counted on to understand the highly technical business of commanding the nuclear forces. Lyndon Johnson as vice president, for example, did not have a Black Bag assigned to him, but inherited President Kennedy's in Dallas at the time of the assassination in November 1963. But Johnson did not have the slightest idea of what was in the bag; he had never been briefed on its contents.[28]

In a true emergency in the early 1960s there just would not have been time to give an elaborate briefing about SIOP alternatives to a new president, because to do so would have risked isolating the forces from the authorization needed to use them.

In summary, it seems that the formal existence of predelegated authority to use nuclear weapons in certain emergency conditions protected the command system shown in figure 6.2 from decapitating attacks. The presidential center served as a safety catch, holding back the multiple nuclear triggers embodied in the primary commands, corresponding to the unified and specified commanders. A Soviet attack on the presidential command center would then be an attack on the safety catch of the entire command structure, and the Soviets would be destroying the one mechanism holding back all-out retaliation. To encourage the Soviets to play by these rules, no nuclear weapons were placed near American command centers in Washington, Nebraska, and Colorado. In this structure, a decapitation attack on Washington was countered by launching the full weight of the American arsenal.

There could be no guarantee that the Soviets would play by the

28. Manchester, *Death of a President*, p. 261.

rules of the game of limitation in nuclear war. However, if they did not, America's retaliatory strength would not lie paralyzed, waiting for political directives that could never be sent. In the literature of the day a Soviet attack on the presidential command center was taken as a clear message, a signal, that they had no interest in bargaining during the war, and this Soviet action was even described as their "anti-game" strategy.[29] The term was apropos.

Besides the triggers in the primary command centers, there were additional triggers in the secondary centers. Every unified and specified command established an alternate command post in case the main one was destroyed. SAC developed an airborne command post as an alternate that was difficult for the Soviets to target. Other commands did likewise. Because of its importance, however, the SAC airborne command post was kept in the air twenty-four hours a day throughout the year, and could, in certain circumstances, order the launch of the nuclear weapons under SAC's jurisdiction. Ever since February 3, 1961, this aircraft, code-named "Looking Glass," has been airborne without interruption.[30] Each Looking Glass aircraft flies an eight-hour shift and is replaced, before it lands, by an identical plane. It is usually manned by a two-star SAC general. Other unified and specified commanders maintain airborne command posts but keep them on the ground until a sufficiently high alert is declared or some other stimulus requires that they be launched. Recall that during the 1980 NORAD missile alert the airborne command post of the Pacific Command in Hawaii was actually sent airborne as a protective measure.

There are other systems that back up the fundamental mission of the airborne alternates. The Air Force, for example, has the Emergency Rocket Communication System (ERCS). Special radios fitted to selected Minuteman missiles beep a code to forces on the ground when launched. It seems safe to guess that the message sent from ERCS is simple and short: "Go." Besides ERCS, there is the Post-

29. See Thornton Read, "Limited Strategic War and Tactical Nuclear War," in Klauss Knorr and Thornton Read, ed., *Limited Strategic War* (New York: Frederick A. Praeger, 1962), pp. 105–07.

30. Office of the Historian, Strategic Air Command, *History of Strategic Air Command*, p. 93.

Attack Command and Control System (PACCS), a network of SAC airplanes that is also capable of launching the force in an emergency.

The number and exact nature of other secondary systems are kept highly secret, but their function and organization can be discerned from an extension of the safety catch and trigger analogy. In peacetime nonalert conditions it would be imprudent to have alternate airborne command posts of the primary commands flying around the country with a switch that could launch the nuclear forces. Similarly, the arming of secondary centers would be too dangerous in peacetime. It seems likely, then, that these alternate and secondary centers would take on the role of a trigger only upon destruction of the main primary command centers. Moreover, they would be tied directly into the warning and intelligence network so that they could get the latest information prior to attack. As the alert level increased the safety catches preventing them from firing would be removed. The function of these alternate and secondary commands, be they airborne or in some hidden location, would be to ensure that official predelegated orders would be issued even in the event of a massive attack against the command structure.

It is worth emphasizing that the commanders of the alternates and the secondary commands are lower in rank than those of the primary sites. Thus, the SAC Looking Glass aircraft is manned by a one- or two-star officer, whereas CINCSAC himself is a four-star officer. Consequently, a Soviet attack on the command structure would serve to greatly decentralize nuclear authority away from the White House to a score of one- and two-star officers of the unified and specified commands. It seems more than plausible that authority would devolve even further from here, cascading downward as the military feared that its retaliatory power would be paralyzed. European nuclear forces would be especially subject to deep downward devolution of authority, perhaps including delegation to the dual key nuclears of the allies. As an attack developed, authority would be diffused downward through the organization through a layer of top and middle management. Individual weapon crews would probably never know whether they were working from direct or predelegated presidential orders.

The restructuring of command in this transitional period of the 1960s entailed other changes that fit together into a relatively coherent whole. First, the forces were made more survivable, not only to allow for a protected second-strike capability but also to prevent the warning and alerting process from driving decisions on the use of vulnerable weapons. There was renewed emphasis on hardened missiles and hidden submarines as the backbone of the American strategic force. Bombers were viewed as less survivable and controllable than the new Minuteman missiles, which were then coming into the arsenal. Consequently, the entire force of B-47 bombers was phased out by 1966, a force which numbered 1,200 when the Kennedy administration took office in January 1961.[31] The remaining B-52s were maintained at a high state of readiness, with about 50 percent of them on runway alert.[32] Unlike the B-52, the B-47 was not easily operated on airborne alert, and it was considered less survivable because it had to be maintained on runway alert. During the 1962 Cuban missile crisis B-47s were dispersed to many civilian airfields, including Logan Field in Boston. Other B-52s, fully armed with nuclear weapons, were kept on airborne alert beginning in January 1961.[33] Airborne alerts were reduced in 1966 because of improvements in radar coverage of the Soviet Union, and they were eliminated altogether in 1968, after a B-52 loaded with H-bombs crashed in Greenland.[34] Along the same lines of reducing dependence on vulnerable bomber forces, the "soft" Jupiter and Thor missile squadrons in Britain, Italy, and Turkey were removed by 1963.[35]

The concept that all missiles need not be launched at the outset of conflict led to a redesign of the Minuteman control system. Originally, Minuteman was designed to fire only in blocks of fifty missiles

31. Polmar, *Strategic Weapons*, p. 54.

32. William W. Kaufmann, *The McNamara Strategy* (New York: Harper & Row, 1964), p. 217.

33. "U.S. Cutting Back A-Bomber Alerts," *New York Times*, May 7, 1966, p. 1.

34. "B-52 with H-Bombs Plunges into Ice in Greenland Bay," *New York Times*, January 23, 1968, p. 1.

35. There is some confusion about precise timing of this because of the Cuban missile crisis, see Barton J. Bernstein, "The Cuban Missile Crisis: Trading the Jupiters in Turkey?," *Political Science Quarterly* 95 (Spring 1980): 97–125.

at a time, a design that reflected the emphasis on early blunting attacks on the time-urgent Bravo targets. In 1961, Minuteman was provided with a selective launch capability.[36] Consequent with these changes, war plans were revised to include withholding some nuclear weapons from initial strikes, as detailed in chapter 3.

In the area of suvivable communications, methods had to be developed to connect the president with the unified and specified commanders. The growing number of U.S. nuclear weapons sent to Europe made this problem more complex. Emergency communications now had to be established with the British and French prime ministers to coordinate actions in Europe, which was considered the most likely site for the outbreak of World War III. Other Europeans would also have to be contacted in an emergency. Many of the weapons in Europe could strike Moscow, and so their employment had to be coordinated with the American SIOP in order for flexible response to have any meaning. Political control necessitated that the president be able to communicate with the British prime minister, the Canadian prime minister, and other NATO leaders to obtain permission to use nuclear weapons on or over their territories.

A communications system for the president would also have to work well enough that the American unified and specified commanders, not just the NATO political leaders, would be confident that it would neither collapse nor lose control after the first few nuclear shots were fired. This is an important point. The communications system would not only have to work in conflict, but American military commanders would have to be convinced ahead of time that it offered them a reasonable chance of survival. This was a sharp difference in design philosophy from the 1950s. If military commanders expected the system to break down, they would be highly likely to interpret any brief disruption in command as resulting from all-out attack, necessitating a response in kind. Political control would then be impossible.

The White House responded to the need for survivable presidential communications by deciding to exploit the most redundant,

---

36. Desmond Ball, *Politics and Force Levels* (Berkeley, Calif.: University of California Press, 1980), p. 194.

geographically dispersed communications system ever built: the
American common carrier network, and especially the Bell Telephone system. This philosophy was codified in an executive memorandum of August 1963, which created the National Communications System (NCS). The NCS technically consists only of U.S.
government communications assets, such as those operated by the
departments of Defense, State, Commerce, Treasury, and other agencies, but all of these tie into the Bell network or other common
carriers. Consequently, NCS integrates government communications
with the civilian system. The charter for the NCS, issued after the
Cuban crisis by the White House, made its priorities clear: "Initial
emphasis in developing the NCS will be on meeting the most critical
needs for communication in national security programs, particularly
to overseas areas."[37] The principal emphasis on overseas areas arose
from the Cuban missile crisis, when President Kennedy was unable
to notify South American leaders of his proposed actions because the
State Department communications system became overloaded.[38] Latin
American ambassadors were also unable to contact their governments
because of bottlenecks in communication between North and South
America. A repetition of this in a European crisis would have had
catastrophic consequences.

The exact details of how the president would communicate with
the nuclear command centers, and foreign allies, are naturally enough
shrouded in secrecy. In the late 1950s, AT&T proposed that its automatic switching centers be used for critical military communications.[39] The great redundancy of the Bell network would allow communication from almost any point in the United States to any other

37. U.S., President, Memorandum to Heads of Executive Departments, "Establishment of the National Communications System," August 21, 1963, p. 1.

38. Raymond Tate, "Worldwide C³I and Telecommunications," in *Seminar on
Command, Control, Communications, and Intelligence*, Harvard University, Spring
1980, p. 26.

39. A description of this design for military service can be found in J. B. Carne,
"A Critical Look at Automatic Switching and Restoration Schemes for Increasing the
Survival Capability of Military Communication Networks," Rand Corporation, D-
7283, March 1960. See also Paul Baran, *On Distributed Communications*, Vol. 1,
Introduction to Distributed Communication Networks; Vol. 9, Security, Secrecy, and
Tamper-Free Considerations; Vol. 11, Summary Overview (Santa Monica, Calif.:
Rand Corp., 1964).

point, even after major communication centers were destroyed by nuclear attack. By routing emergency messages over the automatic switching net, the system would automatically bypass any destroyed communications centers in cities or elsewhere, as the originating and intermediate switches searched for a route connecting the caller and the station sought. In effect, a "self-healing network" would result, as elements that had been destroyed would be replaced by alternate paths around the neutralized junction. Figure 6.4 shows such a distributed network. There are many paths connecting any two nodes, so that even if many nodes are destroyed there is reasonable probability that communications will be established. The idea could be extended to transatlantic communications in order to bring NATO leaders into the system, because of the interconnection of the American and European telephone systems via communication satellites and submarine cables. In conjunction with the government's less elaborate radio and telephone network, the entire system would offer a great amount of survivability for presidential and military communications. Although this design philosophy did have defects, one can only admire the cleverness of the overall approach.

The survival of the president is closely tied into a surviving communications system. Any president makes dozens of trips outside of Washington during his term, and he stays in touch with events through prior coordination with local AT&T offices. Many details of this emerged in 1963 because of the assassination of President Kennedy. For the trip to Dallas, advance teams set up special continuous telephone circuits between several locations in Dallas and Washington. In this way, the president would be as close as the nearest telephone to the National Military Command Center. Other circuits allowed the president to reach London or Paris on four minutes' notice, and undoubtedly he was within even easier reach of major American command centers if the need arose.[40] The beauty of this setup was that even if the president were out of Washington when a surprise attack occurred he could communicate with command posts. Enemy missiles that destroyed communication nodes would not block the linkage of the president to the military, because calls would be au-

40. Manchester, *Death of a President*, p. 62.

Fig. 6.4. A distributed communications system

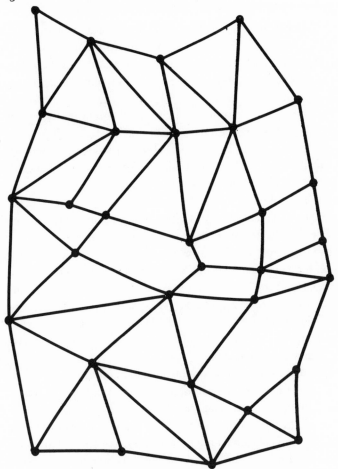

tomatically rerouted by the intermediate surviving switches. Redundancy, rather than hardening, was the tactic relied upon. It may seem odd that greater reliance was not placed on the monumental military communications system. However, 95 percent of all military communications were actually carried over common carriers like Bell, so it was easier to go directly over the commercial telephone system.

For suvival a president could hide anywhere in the country where there was a telephone—which is everywhere. Plans could be drawn up, say, to set up circuits between seventy-five geographically dispersed sites and the major command centers. Codes would then be required to guarantee that the caller was indeed the president. Such a plan would be economical because of the existence of the circuits and the relative ease of keeping a Black Bag of authentication codes near the president.

A Soviet attack of sufficient mass could trump the system described, though, by taking out so many intermediate switches as to drive the probability of connection between a hidden president and the military to zero. In fact, all evidence points to a Soviet targeting emphasis on Bell Telephone switching centers for just this reason. Soviet targeting also emphasizes the destruction of electric utility plants, apparently to cut off electricity to command and communication centers. The counter to this is the same as the counter to any Soviet command structure attack. An attack of this kind would effectively blow up the safety catch on the American arsenal and would result, in principle, in an immediate release of the full SIOP. This also explains why no hardening of SAC headquarters, NORAD, or some White House bunker is really essential. Attacks on these centers would be interpreted as command structure attacks, and control would revert to the default anti-game option.

The final element in revamping the communications during the transitional period was the establishment of the Washington-Moscow Direct Communications Link, or "Hot Line." It was set up in 1963 in response to the Cuban missile crisis, with one terminal in the NMCC in the Pentagon and the other in the Kremlin.[41] During the Cuban crisis Kennedy and Khrushchev had to communicate through roundabout channels, including midnight meetings by intermediaries in Washington restaurants. The Hot Line has proved its value repeatedly in the intervening years. Yet the fact that it was needed at all was an indication that the control of crises through informal sig-

41. W. P. Hooper, W. M. Rogers, and J. G. Whitman, Jr., "Earth Station for the U.S.-U.S.S.R. Direct Communications Link," in William G. Schmidt and Gilbert E. LaVean, eds., Communications Satellite Developments: Technology (Cambridge: MIT Press, 1974), p. 105.

naling, such as going on alert, was not as transparent a means of communication between the superpowers as originally thought. According to key participants in the Cuban crisis, signals and messages were often ambiguous or misunderstood when received. This wasn't supposed to happen, as the policy of elaborate wartime bargaining depended on reading signals clearly. The need for the Hot Line demonstrates how concepts that sound good in peacetime studies can lead to different and adverse results in practice.

The changes undertaken to transform the American command system in the early 1960s combined an understanding of the hierarchical organization of the military, the need for civilian inputs to war planning, and an appreciation of the architecture of the civilian and military communications systems. The transformation was managed without radical, or costly, physical restructuring of preexisting command and control systems.

Following the changes in U.S. command structure in the early 1960s there occurred a substantial buildup of Soviet strategic forces. In 1962, the American arsenal consisted of about 4,000 strategic warheads, compared to only 400 for the Soviets.[42] Of these 400 only about 40 were on ICBMs, and these were of dubious reliability. By 1966 they had deployed over 250 ICBMs, and by 1974 the total was 1,570.[43] In addition, the Soviets added 44 modern nuclear weapon–firing submarines over this same period.[44] As a result, the maturing American nuclear forces no longer held unilateral sway over their environment. In a near-war crisis in the early 1960s, America effectively monopolized the negotiating environment, and thus it had considerable latitude.

This is not to say that if there had been a nuclear war in the early 1960s it would have remained limited to countermilitary targets. Uncontrollable escalation, or presidential selection of fundamentally different strategies, could have occurred for many reasons. Nonetheless, the command changes that had been undertaken, assisted by

---

42. Based on author's calculations from data in Polmar, *Strategic Weapons*, p. 46.
43. Ball, *Force Levels*, p. 58; and Polmar, *Strategic Weapons*, p. 82.
44. Ibid., p. 86.

America's nuclear superiority, were in conformity with the strategy of flexible response. This is no small accomplishment, because nuclear superiority alone, without the changes in command structure, would have probably meant that any nuclear exchange would have been unlimited in scope.

THE MATURE COMMAND STRUCTURE, 1968 ONWARD

The American command structure of the late 1950s developed into a system with greater political control during the early 1960s. There were many problems in doing this, including major defects in implementing the programs that supported the policy of flexible response. The cleverness of the policy does stand out, however, as did that displayed in so many other governmental policies of the early to mid-1960s.

Yet, like the latter policies, the thinking behind command restructuring, however clever, was incapable of making the world fit the mold demanded of it. Gradual, evolutionary changes led to a mature American command structure that appears unable to control the nuclear forces. Because the system is mature, it is therefore extremely difficult to change in other than marginal ways. Its failure to provide a convincing mechanism for controlling the forces applies across a range of states of conflict. This means much more than an inability to wage a controlled nuclear war. The question "Can nuclear war be controlled?" is but one of many that must be asked. This extreme question ignores the system's potentially more significant deficiencies, such as whether nuclear forces can even be alerted safely, or whether the system is inherently vulnerable to surprise attack even when strategic and tactical warning is readily detected by its intelligence component.

Let us now look at the factors that have shaped the mature command system as it evolved from the late 1960s to the present:

1. Environmental changes, especially the expanding Soviet threat
2. Vertical integration of warning and intelligence systems with the nuclear forces

3. Structural complexity

4. Erosion of the common carrier communications network

5. Greater than anticipated vulnerability of the system's pieces to blast, radiation, EMP, and shock

Environmental Changes

One possible reason why the command restructuring of the early 1960s was effective was that Soviet nuclear forces could mount an all-out attack of no more than one hundred to three hundred nuclear weapons against the United States. At the time, the Soviets were constrained not by warhead shortages, but rather by the absence of reliable delivery vehicles capable of reaching the United States. When the records of the period are declassified, they will show that the Soviet Long Range Air Armies, their Badger and Bison aircraft, had extraordinary difficulties operating at long ranges. The Soviet ICBM force of the time was minute, with estimates ranging from forty to seventy-five ICBMs in 1962. These ICBMs were extremely unreliable, and something like half might have blown up on their launching pads.

Too much can be made of the numerical superiority of the United States. Although it existed, and in some sense the United States might have "won" a nuclear war in the early 1960s, the consequences for the West would still have been catastrophic. If even fifteen or twenty Soviet ICBMs reached their mark in the United States, fatalities could have reached the tens of millions. In Europe, West Germany would have been completely devastated, beyond anything ever seen in history, and the major cities of Western civilization, London, Paris, and Rome, would have very likely been wiped out. If this is victory, then the dimensions of national security clearly need reexamination.

Yet the "small" Soviet nuclear force of this period turned into the "large" force of today. Along the way, missiles were placed in underground hardened silos, theater nuclear weapons were built up, and a modern SSBN force was constructed. From the one to three hundred nuclear warheads threatening the United States in the early

1960s, there are in 1983 some eighty-five hundred warheads. The difficulty of destroying such a force in a way that limits damage to the United States has increased by much more than a factor of forty. For all practical purposes, when viewed in terms of thousands of one-on-one duels, as one warhead impacts on a missile silo, it is impossible. The sheer size of both arsenals drives each side to search for other weak links, and these more and more appear to be the command structures that control the forces, because of the management difficulties that arose from the expansion of nuclear forces. Now these management structures themselves offer the prime targets for an attack that has any chance of avoiding annihilation.

Vertical Integration

The trend toward vertical integration of warning and intelligence systems with the nuclear forces began in the late 1950s, and was described in chapter 2. Throughout the 1960s and 1970s, data from spy satellites, submarine and aircraft probes, communications and signals intelligence, and human agents were coordinated via interconnected data fusion centers. Information was passed from warning and intelligence sensor to force commander, permitting instantaneous status reports. There were always human intermediaries in this process, as experience indicated that human intervention was necessary to make the system run smoothly.

Each increment to the vertically integrated warning and force system gave advantage. Warning time of attack was increased; the safety of the bomber force and the navy's antisubmarine force was improved; and NATO theater nuclear forces were better able to exploit information collected by intelligence. The procedures and communication lines that permitted vertical integration had to be developed by trial and error over many years. The need for compartmentalization and the requirement to work within the checks and balances of the alerting process made the task even more difficult.

The system that resulted from these changes must surely be the most technologically elaborate organization ever constructed by man. But did it make any overall improvement in the responsiveness of the forces to changes in enemy activities? In its individual increments, improvements certainly occurred, yet its aggregate effect was to produce a total system that was tightly coupled and highly interdependent, one in which a small stimulus reverberated worldwide. This system tied together the strategic, theater, and conventional forces into a synergistic whole. But it produced such strong internal overcompensation dynamics that layers of checks and balances, "fail-safe" procedures, and human interventions were necessary to dampen them. On the one hand, the instability of intense alerts could reinforce the tendency to attack. On the other, it could compel prudent leaders to order de-alerts to avoid provocations or to keep from losing control of events. The unilateral standing down from high alert would not necessarily lessen the danger of war, however. It might lower the chance of an accidental war happening because of instability of command, but it might also encourage an enemy attack. Both pressures on decision making exist in a crisis.

Structural Complexity

The clear pyramidal chain of command displayed in figure 6.3 may have started out as a pyramid in concept, but twenty years of integrating a complex warning and intelligence system into this organization have produced something very different. Tight coupling of nuclear forces has occurred because there are many organizational units that are not shown in figure 6.3, and these units are linked with parts of the organization well outside of the pyramidal authority lines indicated on the figure. Over the last two decades, scores of slanted and horizontal lines have come to interconnect the commands and numbered armies, air forces, and fleets in a way that violates a smooth flow of authority. Sometimes the lines supply intelligence information; other times they have to do with authority and coordination. The result is a structurally complex command system that diverges from the classical military hierarchy inherited from centuries of development. The people in the command are organized according to precise hierarchy. However, the total organization includes authority and communications lines that bypass the clear lines of that hierarchy.

Because of this structural complexity, there were breakdowns in command and control by the late 1960s, when its full impact began to be felt. In January 1968, the U.S.S. *Pueblo* was captured by the North Koreans in international waters, where it was operating on a mission for NSA collecting signals intelligence about North Korean military activity. It is widely believed that communications failures led to the capture, both because warning messages that trouble might occur were ignored and because no combat forces were readily available to fight off the North Koreans. But given the organizational structure of the command system of the *Pueblo*, the communications foul-ups come as no surprise. The *Pueblo* reported to the commander of naval forces, Japan, *not* to the Seventh Fleet as would be suggested by figure 6.3 for a vessel operating in the Korean area.[45] The commander of naval forces, Japan, was an administrative headquarters whose responsibilities were logistical. The Seventh Fleet was an operational force. The *Pueblo* was assigned to the commander of naval forces, Japan, apparently as a security cover. Effective control lay with NSA and coordinating committees in the Office of the Secretary of Defense. Unfortunately, coordination with the only military forces capable of protecting the *Pueblo*, the Seventh Fleet, was not fully worked out because of the difficulty of crossing organizational lines of authority due to the highly secret nature of the *Pueblo*'s mission.

The *Pueblo* crisis was presaged a year earlier when the U.S.S. *Liberty*, operating in the eastern Mediterranean during the 1967 Middle East war, was sent six urgent messages to move away from the battle area. Two messages somehow went to the Philippines, one to Greece, one to Germany, and one was completely lost. The effects of compartmentalization of information showed up, because a top-secret communications channel was required for relaying the message. No such secure channel was available, however, so the communications system searched endlessly for relays with the needed top-secret clearance. The *Liberty* never received the message.

It can plausibly be argued that the *Pueblo* and *Liberty* fiascoes

45. Daniel V. Gallery, *The Pueblo Incident* (Garden City, N.Y.: Doubleday, 1970), p. 7.

were simply signs of a maturing command system working out the bugs inherent in any complex organization. No repeats of this particular type of breakdown have occurred recently, and this might be an indication of improved performance. On the other hand, there is some likelihood that procedures have been successfully worked out only in a peacetime information situation when the communications system was not flooded with competing messages. On full alert, however, the peacetime procedures designed to produce a smooth working command arrangement would be placed under great pressure.

Erosion of the Common Carrier Network

The original idea behind the creation of the NCS in 1963 was to tie together the government's communications system using the common carrier network. Over twenty years, however, the common carriers have been altered considerably by technological and regulatory changes. As a result, the connectivity, survivability, and reliability of the single most important defense communications system in the nation has declined significantly.

The federal government obtains more than 85 percent of its total communication needs, and 94 percent of its most critical circuits, through leases of common carrier communication lines.[46] The Bell system of AT&T supplies three-fourths of these, with independent companies supplying the remainder. The common carriers are thus absolutely vital to U.S. command and control, and almost every U.S. system we have mentioned relies on them in some way.

Tactical warning systems such as the DSP satellites relay their information over telephone lines. Even the emergency conference calls of the president and military leaders rely on these circuits. Nearly all of NORAD's incoming and outgoing information uses the common carriers.[47] The BMEWS, DEW Line, and Pave Paws radars depend on them as well. The presidential NEACP aircraft, the Look-

---

46. U.S. Department of Defense, "Analysis of the Effects of AT&T Divestiture upon National Defense Security and Emergency Preparedness," June 1981, p. 5.

47. Ibid., p. 6.

ing Glass alternate command post of SAC, and the SAC and JCS alerting networks are equally dependent on leased telephone lines. Most important, the president depends heavily on the vast redundancy of the telephone system to establish communications with the major military commands.

The only defense communication system independent of the telephone network consists of point-to-point radio links. The VHF and UHF communications of the NEACP and other command aircraft can relay with each other, but VHF and UHF wavelengths can only be used for short-range communications. Other frequencies can be blocked out by nuclear radiation effects. For command and control of nuclear forces, long-range communications are required, and these are provided by linking the VHF and UHF transmissions with the telephone system.

Over the past twenty years, switching technology has changed from older electromechanical dvices to computerized switches, which are more vulnerable to EMP effects. More important, economies of scale have altered the shape of the Bell network, making it much more concentrated. Microwave transmissions now handle a large portion of long-distance calls, both civilian and military, and the network is far less distributed and redundant than it was twenty years ago. Calls are routed automatically, not by the shortest or most reliable route but the "least cost path." Consequently, calls tend to be routed through a handful of critical switching or microwave transmission nodes that are surely known and targeted by the Soviet Union. Less than twenty-five critical nodes handle the great bulk of military communication.

The other reason for the decline in the common carriers' role in national security is the increased competition in the telecommunications industry.[48] The cost of undertaking national security improvements in the telephone system was traditionally passed on to consumers. In the mid-1970s federal regulatory changes made this increasingly difficult. Moreover, the agreed breakup of AT&T in 1982

48. See Stanford Research Institute, "Basic Telecommunications Issues Affecting U.S. National Security and Survival," (Arlington, Va., 1980).

into local operating companies ("Big Bell"), and an interconnecting
Long Lines Division (which, with Bell Laboratories and the Western
Electric production facilities, constitutes "Baby Bell") makes long-
term network planning for defense a very low priority.

These developments have eroded the usefulness of the common
carrier system for the command of nuclear forces. In turn, efforts
have been made to replace it with an expanded number of mobile
point-to-point radio systems. The result has not been a substantial
improvement in communications under a wartime information regime. Rather, it has only compensated for the eroding military capabilities of the common carriers. Moreover, there are strong reasons
to believe that under wartime conditions, the new mobile point-to-
point communication systems are not an adequate replacement.

Greater Vulnerability

Command centers, computers, radars, satellites, aircraft, communication lines, and other physical pieces of the system of command and
control proved to be more vulnerable than was anticipated when these
systems were designed. The experts appreciate the physics of vulnerability, even if they don't understand them, so much so that piecemeal
physical vulnerability reduction forms the centerpiece of most discussions of command and control.[49]

Satellites can be hardened against blast, command posts can be
made mobile because of advances in microelectronics, and exotic
kinds of communications can be used to skirt the peculiar problems
of the nuclear war environment. But there are twin dangers in taking
this kind of approach to the command of nuclear forces. First, and
most obvious, without a rudimentary understanding of the organization, and the process it goes through to go on alert, it is not possible
to allocate resources wisely and decide what should be hardened or

49. An especially good account is Desmond Ball, *Can Nuclear War Be Controlled?*
(London: International Institute for Strategic Studies, 1982); see also Bruce G. Blair,
"The State and Future of C³I," Ph.D. diss., Yale University, 1983.

made redundant. Satellite hardening is a case in point. Over the last few years much has been made of the fact that Soviet satellites can destroy American low-altitude satellites. However, nearly all American satellites tie in to ten or fewer ground stations, which are far more vulnerable to direct attack than the satellites themselves. If the Soviets are interested in direct attack of the American command system, they will have no difficulty destroying the ground stations. Effort spent on satellite hardening would be inefficient.

The more troubling danger in approaching command and control from the question of the physics of vulnerability is that it distracts attention from far more critical problems. In the American failure to predict surprise military operations, in the fiascoes of the *Liberty* and *Pueblo*, or in any other postwar command failing, the major factor was never a broken communication link or piece of equipment. The real problems have been things like crossed lines of authority, confusion, inability of standard operating procedures to solve problems, and an ineffective integration of political and military decision making. Certainly, survivable communications are desirable, if they are cost effective. But the common infatuation with the communications engineering aspects of command and control is all too reminiscent of the drunk who looks for his lost keys under the streetlight because that is where he can see the clearest.

EQUILIBRIUM TENDENCIES AND CRISIS STABILITY

Nuclear threats can be conveyed by the institutions, operating practices, and codes of behavior inherent in a military organization every bit as much as by explicit threats declared by a national leader. Declared threats focus the enemy's attention; they can act as a warning shot across the bow; and, for nuclear forces at least, these threats are fairly well understood. A Soviet action that violates vital U.S. interests risks nuclear retaliation. An invasion of Western Europe, a nuclear attack on the United States, perhaps a major invasion of the Middle East, are all situations in which stated American policy threatens to resort to nuclear attack, either on the Soviet Union itself or on its offending forces.

But what can we say of the other kind of threat? The institutions established to command nuclear forces, their operating practices, and their codes of behavior convey threats of their own. Complex organizations have certain built-in tendencies, directions they naturally move toward when subjected to different controls and levels of excitement. We can think of these tendencies as their internal dynamic response to outside stimuli, producing a new equilibrium or balance between internal forces and outside conditions. In peacetime, for example, nuclear command organizations have a strong tendency to avoid accidental war, so much so that when aberrations arising from Canada geese or malfunctioning computers provide indications of enemy attack there is effectively no chance that the organization will in fact authorize return fire. Far from launching a nuclear weapon, most operators in the system do not even believe there is an attack directed at the United States; they merely grind through a set of precautionary procedures which raise the alert and vigilance levels of the forces. In peacetime the equilibrium tendency of nuclear command organizations is then to minimize the possibility of unauthorized nuclear fire. This equilibrium may be so strong, in fact, that we should worry about the system's vulnerability to surprise attack in peacetime.

For a given level of threatening stimulation there can be more than one equilibrium tendency. At a particular level of tension and alert there may be pressure to go to even a higher alert level as a precautionary measure, yet there could be a countervailing pressure to step down to a lower alert level for fear that events are going beyond the control of political (or even military) leaders. No one can say for sure which equilibrium tendency will prevail, for there is thankfully little experience of operating nuclear command organizations at the highest alert levels. The most that we can do is to attempt to discern the competing set of equilibrium tendencies which could occur, in effect, trying to trace the dynamic responses possible without trying to predict exactly what would happen in a given situation.

Soviet institutions of command have their own tendencies toward equilibrium, which could interact with the American ones, making the equilibrium achieved a function of both institutions' actions. In simpler terms, a Soviet decision to go on full alert compels the United

States to respond with an alert of its own. This is dictated by the vulnerability of American and NATO nuclear forces, and the structuring of the warning and intelligence networks as mechanisms integrated vertically with the forces themselves.

In the powerful dynamics of a severe crisis, national leaders may have roles analogous to those of the European royalty in 1914. Instead of steering their national security establishments into positions of bargaining leverage over the enemy, those leaders were moved by the dynamics of mutually reinforcing alerts to search desperately for alternatives to war, chiefly through attempts to dampen the unwinding alerting process facing them. The tendency toward equilibrium led their armies to mobilize and attack. Force generation and force application had merged. While some leaders, like the Kaiser, turned over the decision-making authority to their staffs, other leaders tried to hold back their alerts, all the while sitting on an exploding powder keg.

For today's mature nuclear forces, a declaration of alert above some level reinforces the need to go on still higher alert. One principal reason for this was discussed in chapter 3. Authorizations to use nuclear forces must be distributed above a certain alert level lest the enemy's spoiling attacks paralyze the entire national security apparatus.[50] The need to make authorizations quickly once a certain level of alert is declared is seen most clearly in the coupling of strategic and theater nuclear operations, most especially in Europe. Soviet SS-20 and Pershing 2 missiles have short flight times and paralyzing damage can be wrought by the Pershing if it is targeted at the Soviet High Command bunkers around Moscow. A Pershing attack on the Soviet High Command would take only twelve minutes from launch to impact and would be comparable to a Soviet attack on Washington and SAC headquarters.[51] The tendency toward equilibrium would be to issue, at best, contingency second-strike or launch-under-attack firing orders. At worst, authorization would be linked to strategic

50. This conclusion is also observed by John D. Steinbruner in "National Security and the Concept of Strategic Stability," *Journal of Conflict Resolution* 22 (September 1978): 411–28.

51. See "Four Minutes before a Pershing Strikes," *Boston Globe*, January 29, 1982, p. 11.

warning, and this would lead to individual interpretation of indicators and extreme crisis instability.

Other pressures for issuing contingency firing authorizations come from the threat posed to the FB-111 bombers in Britain, the spread of QRA aircraft throughout Western Europe, and especially the dispersal of tactical nuclear weapons from their storage igloos. Additional interactions will push toward destruction of or interference with enemy satellites. Many of these satellites are nothing more than high-altitude artillery spotters that call in more accurate missile fire on targets. The Soviet RORSAT and EORSAT programs are probably intended to direct Soviet Backfire bombers and cruise missiles against American aircraft carriers. This suggests that it is probably a mistake to think of alerting as a continuous progression of tightly directed political actions. Certain "natural" levels of equilibrium probably exist that are characterized by sudden jumps in the readiness to go to war.

While the reciprocal actions described may push toward more intense force interactions, leading to war initiation or escalation to higher levels of violence, a powerful countertendency also exists. One of the greatest reasons why the World War I analogy of mobilization leading to war may not serve as an adequate prediction lies in the different perceptions held by political and military decision makers about what they are getting into. Bertrand Russell recalls in his autobiography how the nations of Europe marched into the Great War with brass bands. No one will go into World War III with brass bands blaring. Nothing seems safer than a prediction that everyone will be scared out of their wits about the prospect of nuclear war, and this can be a powerful counter to the upward mobilization spiral.

A sudden jump in alert levels might be followed by a period of political leaders coming to their senses. This is exactly what occurred during the Cuban missile crisis. However, as noted in chapter 2, the nuclear forces of 1962 were primitive compared to those of today. Furthermore, the Soviet forces did not go on alert at that time. One-sided alerts of any magnitude are intrinsically more controllable than mutual alerts. Most troubling is the likelihood that in the future Soviet nuclear forces will be more active than they have been in the past.

As their general staff acquires more authority over day-to-day operations and as their command system further matures the United States will have to deal with an opponent who no longer rolls over and plays dead at the least sign of an American alert. It is not at all clear that the United States is facing up to the problem of living in a world where there are two highly reactive nuclear command organizations. For one thing it may no longer be as safe to de-alert the forces as it was in the past because there could be no guarantee that it would be reciprocated. Although it is unpleasant to consider, a mutual high alert followed by one side's unilateral step down to lower alert could entice the more vigilant force to attack.

Were Soviet and American forces actually at war, either conventional or limited nuclear war, then interactions between them would be extraordinarily intense. Although a step down in escalation could occur it is hard to imagine that this would be easy, let alone controllable by political leaders. Multiple equilibrium tendencies would still exist, but more and more of them would lead to some form of all-out escalation once a few nuclears fly when both commands are on full alert. Nonetheless, vulnerabilities might arise from desperate political leaders ordering last-minute interventions into long-planned military operations, upsetting finely tuned coordination, and effectively locking the forces either totally or partially into inaction. Haphazard political and military actions designed to control the uncontrollable could compound disaster, as could the pathological strategies arising from communications breakdowns described in chapter 4. In sum, many new equilibrium tendencies never before dreamed of could appear in a crisis once a certain alert or stimulation threshold was crossed. As in many complex organizations, stability is maintained only by not letting the system get too far out of whack.

AMBIGUOUS COMMAND

Pressure to issue contingency firing orders can take different forms and extend to different levels of the command. The embedding of tactical nuclear weapons in conventional force structures means that firing authority could penetrate down to battlefield units in a European nuclear war. On the other hand, for ICBM forces the system of alternate command posts and headquarters of various units makes it highly unlikely that firing authority would ever be given to individual launching crews. The shape of the management mechanisms for nuclear forces can make a great difference in how authority flows in a command.

Authority to use nuclear weapons, or any other kind of military authority, by nature cannot be precisely delimited ahead of time. The nature of delegated military authority also dictates that contingencies for taking actions cannot be specified in advance. It rather turns over decision-making power to another agent. An astronomical number of possible contingencies could arise from command structure breakdown. Thus, delegation of authority rather than a detailed specification of what should be done in all circumstances is required. Theories of delegation and agency are therefore highly relevant to the command of nuclear forces.

For the United States an important constraint that prevents excessively detailed instructions for nuclear-firing authority from being given is likely to be the sensitivity of the subject matter. If President Eisenhower was troubled by the need to bypass the constitutional process for going to war, how much more sensitive would it be to lay out elaborate specifications between a president and his generals without congressional advice or approval. Such a discussion defies comprehension at any level of security classification, for the same reason that NATO leaders would be unable to sit down and specify the amount of nuclear destruction they would find "acceptable." In a democracy, decisions that appear to undermine the legitimacy of the institutions and laws that are the foundation of the government's power cannot be made.

Details about exactly how much discussion on these sensitive matters does take place are necessarily sketchy. Nonetheless, the accounts of those close enough to be informed invariably point to presidential benign neglect.[52] Presidents just have too many other things on their minds, and one would guess that Soviet premiers are equally

52. See, for example, Gulley, *Breaking Cover*, pp. 213–32; and the remarks of General Brent Scowcroft at the Aspen Institute Arms Control Seminar, August 1982.

busy people. Even when it comes to knowledge of prepared war plans, the pressures of office take their toll, and matters of nuclear war have a low priority. A former director of the White House Military Office, where the responsibility for these matters rests, a man who served under all the presidents from Lyndon Johnson through Jimmy Carter, said about their knowledge of the Football:

> No new President in my time ever had more than one briefing on the contents of the Football, and that was before each one took office, when it was one briefing among dozens. Not one President, to my knowledge, and I know because it was in my care, ever got an update on the contents of the Football, although material in it is changed constantly. Not one President could open the Football—only the warrant officers, the military aides and the Director of the Military Office have the combination. If the guy with the Football had a heart attack or got shot on the way to the President, they'd have to blow the goddamn thing open.[53]

One must seriously doubt that even if a leader in the United States or the Soviet Union did take detailed interest in these matters that this, alone, would make much of a difference. Once again, people do what they are organized to do. If a national leader was greatly concerned about nuclear-firing authority being used accidentally or inadvertently in a crisis, he could issue a memorandum to all of his commanders revoking all of their authority in this domain, and he could even go further by issuing orders *never* to fire off a weapon no matter how many bursts they thought they saw. But how effective could this really be? By not addressing the decapitation problem, and by imposing such an order on either a safety catch and trigger type of command system or a system rigged for massive preemption, the order would likely be ineffective. The problem is not that subordinates are eager to disobey their superior, but rather that such a memorandum represents a strategy fundamentally at odds with the vast command system built over the decades.

Since the details of the exact conditions of when and how nuclear weapons would be employed cannot be specified in advance and cannot be centrally controlled by any single individual, an ambiguity in command arises. The causal world in which many military com-

53. Gulley, *Breaking Cover*, p. 225.

manders live is obscure. Lines of authority are clear only in principle, not in practice. Command procedures are opaque because commanders are told that only the president can authorize nuclear usage, but they also know that there may not be time for such a message to be transmitted, and they know that the layers of peacetime nuclear controls will almost guarantee delays in carrying out such an order. At the same time, they are expected to perform their military assignments without a hitch. The deeper into the unusual conditions of a high alert or a controlled nuclear exchange the more likely ambiguous command is to gain importance. Although the subject is fraught with uncertainties, it is still possible to suggest certain features of ambiguous command, based on the institutions, operating patterns, and behavior codes of national security organizations. Any organization contains a body of systematic knowledge, based on the precepts, procedures, and rules preprogrammed into it. As precepts, procedures, and rules evolve and accumulate over time, they may lead to decisions and reactions being taken without full comprehension of their rationale or justification.

Ambiguous command over nuclear weapons was discussed previously in the context of a war in Europe. There, the decentralization of the European battlefield is a factor that is used to enforce the NATO threat that nuclear weapons would actually be used to defend against a Soviet attack. A similar factor exists for strategic forces to deter a command structure attack. The numbered armies, air forces, and navies that fall below the primary command posts and the alternates to the primary centers are all commanded by persons of lower military rank. An attack on the alerted American command structure would then do more than destroy the safety catch holding back retaliation. It would turn over authority to perhaps dozens of lower-ranking officers. This propensity for cascading authority is an aspect of the system that deters Soviet attack on the command structure, because any such attack would induce a spread of nuclear use authority, and would induce it *downward* in the organization. Here, the Soviets would face a nuclear war system that apparently was going berserk, with which it might be impossible to negotiate a cease-fire agreement.

The difficulty of specifying exactly who is in charge and who commands the nuclear force is a problem not limited to the aftermath of a command structure attack that has separated the forces into isolated islands. Daniel Ellsberg describes investigations he undertook on this question in the early 1960s at the behest of the then-commander of Pacific Forces, Admiral Harry Felt:

> Craziness is not the most immediate and serious problem. Misunderstanding and misguided judgment by one of the thousands of people is a much more serious possibility. For instance, during the study for CINPAC I questioned a particular major in Kunsan, Korea, who had on his little airstrip, possibly closer to Communist territory than any other airstrip in the world, 10 F-100's, each of which had slung under it a 1 megaton bomb. This kind of weapon was not meant to be carried underslung; it had too high a risk of going off if it were dropped or if there was an accident. This man had under his command in that little strip ten of those, the equivalent of five World War II's.
>
> He told me what his orders were and if Jimmy Carter were to ask his counterpart today what his orders were, I'm sure he'd get the same answer—"I can't alert those planes, even for their safeguarding; I can't let them take off, let alone execute without direct orders" (in those days from Osan, his higher base, or Kadena in Okinawa, or possibly Tokyo). The reason for those orders was that if he, on his own judgment, merely safeguarded his planes by having them take off (which other people did do more or less routinely), his weapons might go off. And if his weapons went off, all communications would go out in that area. The last thing that people would know was that in the course of an alert, either a false alarm or a real war, a thermonuclear explosion had just gone off on one of our bases. Their belief that the war was on and that they would get no further messages, including execute messages, would then follow.
>
> So I asked the major, "Quite aside from accidents, what would you do about your orders?" Since I had authority from Admiral Felt, he answered me: "Despite my orders, I'm the commander of this base. It is the oldest principle of war that a commander has the right and authority to protect his troops. If I thought my troops were in danger, for example, if I heard of an accident, that is, an explosion, somewhere else in the Pacific during an alert, I would send them off."
>
> And I said, "And what do you think they would do?"
>
> He said, "Well, you know what the orders are. They would go to a rendezvous area, reconnoiter, circle, until they got an execute order

to carry out their plans, and if they did not get an execute order, they would return. Those are their orders."

"And how would that work?" I asked.

"I think they'd come back. I think most of them would. Of course, if one of them broke out of that circle and headed for his target, I think the others would follow, and they might as well," he added philosophically, "because if they go, we might as well all go."

Of course the major in Kunsan didn't claim *he* had been authorized to alert his planes; but he did refer to the President's delegation to Admiral Felt, which he clearly took as precedent. At higher intermediate levels of command, like the Seventh Fleet, I was told by Atomic Control Officers that there existed secret delegations from CINPAC, paralleling the delegation to CINPAC by the President.[54]

Perhaps the greatest source of ambiguous command arises in control of the at-sea SSBN force. Communications are intrinsically difficult for the submarines, and the command channels are inherently vulnerable to enemy attack. Given a threat to these communication lines, it is entirely conceivable that the command would be turned over to negative control measures. This means that nuclear agency would be delegated to the submarines, subject to a periodic signal indicating that headquarters was alive and functioning. This is sometimes called a "fail-deadly" command system, because a failure of headquarters to transmit the proper code at the proper time would be construed as turning over command authority to the armed unit. It is clearly a dangerous practice and is never used in peacetime.

In one U.S. war game played in the 1960s, however, the Soviets were postulated to have interfered electronically with communication lines in an attempt to force American submarines to reveal their positions. The response of the American team was to give very serious consideration to the employment of fail-deadly policies for maintaining deterrence. In the game a fail-deadly policy could come into effect by the United States authorizing the submarines to launch their weapons unless they received an order not to do so at some periodic interval. For example, weapons would be launched unless a coded

54. "Interview with Dr. Ellsberg," p. 2.

signal were received at four-hour intervals. In the opinion of the game's designer, resort to fail-deadly control was judged "plausible if fail-safe procedures appeared in an extreme crisis to jeopardize national security more than protect it."[55]

The difficulties of limiting nuclear war once some weapons have actually exploded is compounded by the fact that ambiguous command will be overlaid onto a disconnected, broken-up control system in which information and authority have become decentralized by reason of the attack. Under these conditions, isolated forces could continue to salvo, effectively destroying any tacit cease-fire that had developed. As described in chapter 4, the decentralized information could drag the entire command into continuing the attack if it was perceived that escalation was inevitable. At the level of the separated island of forces, there would be conflicting pressures—to wait for orders from higher authority or to salvo everything in the house.

The latter tendency cannot be underestimated, especially when it is realized that an average person does not pull the nuclear trigger. Under ambiguous-command conditions, even relatively small stimuli could tip the balance of the decision one way or another. The individual or group of individuals in the command who will make this choice will have substantial grounds for firing their weapons. At the highest political levels of government a leader may be so terrified of escalation as to refuse to take decisive action. But at the middle levels of the military command, these officers might be overwhelmed by the shock and rage following confirmation of enemy attack.

The positive benefit from firing nuclear weapons is an inherently unpleasant subject. No one wants to go down in history as the person who annihilated tens of millions of innocent civilians. But at a middle-level command, or even at lower levels on the nuclear European battlefield, even a purely military attack would effectively be an attack on the families of those officers in the middle level of command.

This stems from geography: military bases in the area contain

55. "A Political-Military Exercise of Naval Communications during a Nuclear Crisis," Detex II Games, Center for International Studies, Massachusetts Institute of Technology, February 1964, p. II-6.

the families of the servicemen and officers on duty there. These are not ordinary families, however, for their family heads will be on duty in a nuclear exchange. Much has been made of the "use them or lose them" philosophy—that is, of the pressure to launch weapons before they can be destroyed by the enemy. However strong this is, the sure knowledge that a man's children have been incinerated would be a much stronger pressure for loss of control, especially under circumstances of ambiguous command. Whether it be a German QRA pilot with a one-megaton bomb capable of reaching Leningrad, or a Soviet submarine crew informed that Murmansk, and hence their families, had been wiped out, one cannot expect of them a reluctance to launch weapons; revenge would be a powerful incentive to do so. If there is an ambiguous or even a rumored delegation of authority, the likelihood of a frenzied orgy of pulling every trigger possible should not be discounted.

There is a lesson in all of this for crisis stability: command and control strategies must account for the incentives in one's own command. Far too much emphasis is often placed on secret written statements of delegated authority. A balance must be reached that gives members of a command good reason not to take actions prematurely. It is in the beliefs of command members that the ultimate sources of crisis stability probably lie. The reason that Soviet Yankee submarines off the Atlantic coast or Pershing 2 missiles in Europe are such intrinsically dangerous weapons is not the physical damage that they can do to the White House or the Kremlin. Rather, it is that each of these weapons injects ambiguity into the enemy command. The existence, not the use, of these weapons compels commanders to anticipate that their political high commands are not likely to survive more than five minutes in a nuclear war. This fear is transmitted to lower echelons of the command organization by rumor and after-hours discussions, and an expectation develops throughout the command that attacks on political leadership are likely. In a war, or even in an intense alert, the command will then see the smallest disruption or unusual action in this context. Ad hoc verbal understandings will develop as the alerting process begins to manage the potential loss of political leadership. This will necessarily entail a rapid devolution of command authority once the shooting starts, even if the political centers are not attacked.

Not only do the beliefs of one's own command matter, but so do enemy beliefs. For this reason, declaratory threats to strike the enemy's command structure are among the most dangerous and short-sighted policies imaginable. In the early 1960s declaratory nuclear strategy emphasized the preservation of enemy cities in a war in order to lessen the trigger-happiness of the enemy command. Threats to decapitate the enemy command structure reinforce the ambiguity of control over nuclear weapons, because they convince the military that early attack will be made against their already vulnerable command and control system. Their reaction is not likely to be one of intimidation. Rather they will be forced to adopt a range of extremely dangerous operating policies, such as launch under attack or a more extensive predelegation of firing authority within the military.

The most dangerous aspect of the adoption of such policies is that it is apt to happen independently of political review. The sensitivity of the subject is hardly conducive to a free exchange of ideas. Are a Soviet general and Secretary Andropov likely to discuss frankly the necessity of the military to undertake ad hoc methods of firing off the nuclear forces? For this reason, open threats to destroy the Soviet High Command may backfire and create a much more trigger-happy force.

DECAPITATION

One thing emerges repeatedly when we examine nuclear command and control: there are seemingly insurmountable barriers to maintaining political control in a strategic war. The breakup of communications after attack leads to decentralized assessment and to joint decision making among the isolated islands of forces, with pathological strategy implications. War plans themselves are not structured for centralized political control. Rather, they are based on preplan attacks in which a dead-reckoning control mechanism further increases the likelihood of unstoppable salvoing in a communications-disrupted environment. The European nuclear forces are almost intrinsically un-controllable; in fact they derive their deterrent effect from this.

Three schools of thought attempt to deal with this state of affairs. For actually *fighting* a nuclear war, the first argues, measures to improve command and control should be undertaken in advance, to increase the likelihood that some political control can be enforced on a strategic war. Satellites should be further hardened, mobile control trucks purchased, and more redundant communication lines set up. These measures are all easy to take, it is argued, and since control in nuclear war is likely to be difficult, therefore now is the time to take steps in this direction. The scope of control could range from allowing for the possibility of war termination short of attacks on populated areas to a quest for victory in some classical military sense.

The danger in this line of reasoning is that it might end up bumbling into a nuclear war with a vague belief in its controllability, only to result in uncontrollable escalation. The only thing worse than an uncontrollable force is a political leadership that mistakenly believes it has a controllable force.

The second school of thought believes that problems of control in a war are so overwhelming as to be effectively insoluble. The *desire* for warfighting command and control, it argues, should not be confused with the capability to do this. A robust command system is always ten years away in the future. At any given time, there are promises and pleadings to get started on this task, and some small improvements might be made, but even five years of effort would still leave the dream ten years away. Nuclear war, then, is uncontrollable.

This line of thought poses quite a different danger. Rather than believing nuclear war can be limited, it suggests the contrary. The strategy that is consistent with this belief in the uncontrollability of war can be described as follows: You will only get one shot at the king, and it had better be a devastating one. The top military leaders in the United States and the Soviet Union are not fools, and they are not unaware of the vast deficiencies of each other's command systems. For this very reason there is a strong bias against excessively complicated strategies that, at bottom, nobody believes are going to work. What is attractive about this strategy is that it turns the well-recognized deficiencies in command and control to one's advantage in a manner consistent with simplicity. If only one shot at the king is allowed, point the pistol at his brain, not at his body. If one knows that assessment and communication systems will break down, that European forces cannot be controlled, and that there are many other problems with the nuclear system, the best strategy may be to so paralyze and disrupt the enemy's command structure that his retaliation will be ragged and ineffective. In broad terms, this means a precursor decapitation attack against the command system, followed by a massive strike on the enemy forces.

Before we take a closer look at the decapitation strategy let us briefly point out a third school of thought in response to these issues. Many people find the subject so distasteful and morally contaminated as to preclude giving it any attention whatsoever. They take the attitude that there can be no such thing as a "good" nuclear strategy, and only general nuclear disarmament can offer any hope of security. One unfortunate drawback of this view is that it does not stop the study of these unpleasant problems, but only leaves it by default to narrow-minded planners. Indeed, one of the major reasons that mature command systems look the way they do is that their design has been left to provincial specialists. Since the prospects for disarmament do not look good, perhaps the best mankind can hope for is to learn to live with the pervasive presence of nuclear weapons.

Of all these alternatives, the decapitation strategy unfortunately may offer the best hope of escaping annihilation. The Soviet and American arsenals are so large and dispersed that a coordinated attack cannot hope to destroy enough of them to limit the retaliatory strike. But if such attacks were executed in conjunction with strikes against the command system, many additional weapons might be paralyzed into not retaliating. They could then be destroyed in later follow-on attacks, or they might remain dormant permanently. As others have noted, a command-structure attack would not only eliminate central coordination; it might offer some small chance that no retaliation would follow.[56]

56. John D. Steinbruner, "Nuclear Decapitation," *Foreign Policy* 45 (Winter 1981–82): 16–28.

A command-structure attack would place only a small targeting burden on a general countermilitary attack. About one hundred additional weapons would do the trick. It would target four or five weapons on major command posts and would further destroy the principal telephone switching centers, satellite ground stations, radars, and warning and intelligence data fusion centers. The national capitals, Washington and Moscow, would naturally be especially urgent targets. They would have to be destroyed before the political leadership could issue firing orders to their forces. Since the Yankee SSBNs and Pershing 2 missiles have the ability to reach national command sites in a few minutes, these weapons could take advantage of the slightest foul-up in issuing orders.

A command-structure attack could also exploit the serendipities of nuclear phenomena. Ten high-altitude, high-yield nuclear bursts might be launched in conjunction with attacks on the national capital in order to generate strong EMP waves that could knock out communication and electrical power systems. Ground bursting of weapons would throw up radioactive dust, which could foul airplane engines and disrupt reconstitution of the bombers. Although the detailed physics of these attacks are not understood, the attacks involve so few weapons that it might be considered worthwhile to attempt them. The Soviet Union reportedly maintains special high-yield nuclear warheads on its SS-18 missiles, and almost surely these are intended for command-structure attacks.

The success of a decapitation attack would depend on many factors. The victim's alert level at the time of the attack and the beliefs of his commanders would both be important. Ambiguity over command is a potential source of retaliation, yet ambiguity might be preferable to receiving a well-prepared full SIOP retaliation.

But just as top military leaders are unlikely to be foolish enough to rely on complicated strategies and complex command systems that are not apt to work in a war, so too are they unlikely to be indifferent to the threat of a command structure attack. They can take countermeasures that are almost dictated by the structure of the problem.

Earlier, in describing the nuclear command mechanism, we discussed the relation of the alternate command posts to the primary command centers. The Looking Glass aircraft, the emergency rocket communication system (ERCS), and other alternates all could be used to send out firing orders in the event of an attack on the primary command centers. Detailed information on the procedures for using these control mechanisms is one of the U.S. government's most closely held secrets. Information about which location the president would go to, which communication lines he would use, how much predelegated authority would be given to provincial commanders, and which communication system would be selected for sending firing orders are all shrouded in much deeper secrecy than that surrounding the technical characteristics of the weapons themselves. Comparable secrecy surrounds the Soviet command system.

The reason for this secrecy is not hard to fathom. Keeping such information secret gives an asymmetric advantage to the United States, in that to destroy our command system the Soviets would need just this information. For example, if the exact location of ERCS missiles were known, an appropriately designed Soviet attack could foreclose this avenue for sending out launch orders.

At the top of the government the procedures for spreading out authority to issue firing orders represent, potentially, the weakest link in the retaliatory chain. A tailored precursor attack by the Soviets could isolate U.S. nuclear forces from the authority needed to use them and paralyze the American arsenal. If the Soviets knew all of the procedural and predelegation details, they could launch an optimal isolating attack, to be followed up by a massive attack on the weapons themselves. What makes a command-structure attack so difficult is the fact that the Soviets do not know precisely who has nuclear authority in an emergency and, more important, how this authority would flow at the highest levels of government in a crisis. Both the vast Soviet command and its U.S. counterpart could be switched from fail-safe to fail-deadly control in an intense crisis by means of a thirty-second telephone conversation between the national leader and one of his generals. Since nuclear-firing orders are based on code words, the military officers who fire the weapons will never know if their orders are predelegated or direct. Indeed, they won't care as long as all the code words are in the proper order. A national leader can simply give a prearranged code word to a general, who in the event of a surprise attack will inject it into the command system to be amplified and retransmitted by every radio in the military system.

The Soviets cannot readily know whether plans call for the commander of SAC to go down with the ship if attacked or to make secret preparations to evade destruction by moving to a secret location that only he and a handful of assistants are aware of. Nor can they know where the redundancy of the telephone system could be used to couple him to unlaunched weapons. The Soviets also cannot easily know whether a long-dormant commercial satellite is actually a disguised "dark satellite" containing coded firing messages for ICBMs and bombers that could be activated from any one of numerous secret transmitters located on innocuous military posts or civilian locations.

Were all of this information available to Soviet targeteers they could plan a potentially paralyzing precursor attack on America, to be followed by more standard attacks on isolated military units. The point is that information asymmetry—in the form of knowledge about predelegation, authority flows, secret locations, dark satellites, alternate command post arrangements, and other things—and the inability of the Soviets to acquire this knowledge at a reasonable price create a deterrent against a command-structure attack. Indeed they would be a deterrent against any sort of nuclear attack on the United States. The Soviets cannot know that an attack will not trigger a chain reaction of cascading firing authorizations that will send a spasm that will cause the arsenal to retaliate. *The asymmetric information conditions are what protect the command structure, rather than any hardening of command and control systems to withstand the physical effects of nuclear attack.* This may explain why such intense secrecy surrounds the subject of command and control. Without it, a parity of information could develop, permitting carefully designed attacks to destroy the enemy's ability to retaliate by isolating forces from their needed authority. The idea of information asymmetry also suggests that for protecting a command system, relying more on a smooth flow of authority ought to be a higher priority than improvements in or expansion of communications hardware.

7 New Directions

It is both satisfying and perplexing to look at the process of how nuclear forces do what they do. It is satisfying because our intuitive, gut reaction is that the operation of anything so large and complicated must be dangerously unstable. Deterrence, second strike, and limited nuclear war are concepts that are logical but incomplete. The job of management and command is to turn these concepts into actuality— that is, into processes. Extending the analysis of nuclear forces to include process is also satisfying, because we are examining truly fundamental problems, not problems that are stripped of so much vital detail that our resulting conclusions are meaningless.

But as satisfying as the investigation of command problems is, it is perplexing because frequently we don't like what we find. More realistic analyses of nuclear war result, but these results are often so unpleasant and the problems are so seemingly insoluble, that we are perplexed about the next step. This is a danger in any venture of this sort. Our analysis of nuclear forces from the perspective of command and control does lead to the right questions. But there are no easy answers to these questions.

The questions and problems may be so unpleasant, in fact, that the next step is only too predictable. Instead of thinking through the questions, we might revert to slogans and then, because of our inability to come up with persuasive answers, rely on vague concepts. We might even conclude that there should be an index of forbidden knowledge. Peace through Strength or Ban the Bomb can go a long way in substituting for thought and sidestepping the hard questions. Some problems are just too hard to ever solve; attacking them is like

238

battering our head against a brick wall. It might, therefore, be better to remove the issue from the policy agenda by ignoring it rather than trying to think it through. I believe that this is what has happened in the management of nuclear forces. There is a pervasive sense among both critics of nuclear weapons and strategists inside the security establishment that questions of how nuclear weapons would really be used are questions of irremediable insanity. What passes for a strategic debate is little more than construction of a facade of nuclear logic to permit getting on with the day-to-day job of deterrence. The most that can be said for this practice is that creating a veneer of rationality in the discussion of nuclear strategy is a ritual used to convince opponents that we are serious about deterrence. In many instances the motivation is even harder to identify, serving only as a psychological defense mechanism against what is, at bottom, an issue of madness. After thinking about nuclear war, we may conclude that studied evasion is not such a bad solution at that. Evasion might function as a lubricant, giving us a perspective that enables us to get on with the task of buttressing deterrence, without being bothered or slowed down by the problem of how to govern such highly dangerous forces.

If we follow a logic that emphasizes the process of how nuclear forces go on alert, how situations are assessed in wartime, and how command and control ties all of these pieces together, we can focus our attention on questions that cannot be answered with "technical fixes." Technical fixes have their place, but they belong in a more supporting role. The problems that do come to center stage are those of organizational design for life in a world in which immensely dangerous arsenals form the backdrop for the routine daily business of diplomacy. At any moment these forces can be triggered onto alert, and decades of sleepy, unexamined confidence that "it can't happen here" would disappear.

In broadest terms, the danger facing the world is that the superpowers have institutionalized a major nuclear showdown. They have built the most complex technological apparatus ever conceived, without thinking through its purpose or how to control it. The resulting conflict system is strongly reminiscent of the institutionalized conflict mechanisms of the early twentieth century. World War I was a war waiting to happen at any time in the decade before 1914. Remarkably enough, during the very time when the general staffs of Europe were working out the interlocking mobilization programs, a feeling of security and complacency dominated popular and elite opinion. Although the war was waiting to happen, the fact that it *hadn't* happened was taken as a sign that all was well. Bertrand Russell tells of how the absence of conflict during the Victorian Age lulled people into confidently projecting peace into the indefinite future. Skirmish wars aside, they felt that no one would be so irrational as to initiate a major war. The abrupt suddenness of World War I surprised everyone, yet in retrospect, almost nothing else could have occurred, given the institutionalized mobilization plans and firepower developed in the preceding decade.

In World War I military forces completely *failed* to serve national interests. There is a lesson in this. Raw military strength alone does not unfailingly guarantee either peace or security. Can anyone believe that World War I would not have occurred if France mustered ten additional divisions? Peace through strength may be wise counsel, but it oversimplifies some terribly complex problems. Those who counsel strength at the expense of all else in the nuclear age are not addressing the full question of national security. It is one thing to risk the lives of millions of people to meet a national security objective. But it is quite another thing to kill 200 million people frivolously, for no real purpose or reason. The nuclear forces of the superpowers are capable of doing just this, and they can do so less because of their firepower than because of the instabilities of their command structures.

THE ROLE OF NUCLEAR STRATEGISTS

There is a peculiar divergence between idea and outcome in the American study of nuclear forces, which helps explain how the world has reached its present precarious position. An idea is what strategists talk about; an outcome is what gets built. On the one hand, the intellectual strategies offered as paths to greater security have been getting more and more sophisticated over the past twenty years. The first relatively simple strategies consisting of deterrence through all-out attack were soon tempered by plans to withhold certain kinds of targets from attack. Later, plans were made to bargain with the Soviet Union in the middle of a war through so-called "limited nuclear options." Most recently, beginning in the late 1970s and continuing to the present, the notion of a protracted nuclear war has become the new centerpiece of nuclear strategy.

Yet while nuclear strategies have been getting more complicated, the ability to carry out *any* of these strategies has been declining, because the necessary system of command and control has not been constructed. It has not been built because no one has any idea of how to build it. Instead, an ever-widening chasm between strategic ideas and the command structure's ability to carry them out has developed.

Remarkably, little attention has been focused on this gap between idea and outcome. The tendency has been quite the opposite, that is, to meet a failure in outcome not by concentrating efforts there but by devising an even more complicated nuclear strategy that places ever-greater demands on the command structure. In the mid-1970s a White House document known as National Security Decision Memorandum (NSDM) 242 enunciated a requirement for American nuclear forces to be able to wage limited attacks on the Soviet Union. For all of the reasons we have spelled out in earlier chapters there are strong reasons to believe that any such attacks would initiate an uncontrollable cascading sequence of actions and reactions. However, no major or even minor command restructuring followed the issuance of this document.

In 1980, PD-59, the presidential directive that required American nuclear forces to wage a *protracted* nuclear war against the Soviet Union, was issued. The requirements it set on the command structure are far more demanding than the mere ability to launch limited attacks. A protracted nuclear war, for example, would require that virtually all of America's forces be connected to a centralized command even *after* they had absorbed many thousands of Soviet nuclear explosions. PD-59 met all of the difficulties of waging a limited war not by any improvements in our ability to do this, but rather by setting forth a strategy whose demands on the command system were an order of magnitude greater.

During the same period, a more critical question was universally ignored. Instead of asking whether nuclear *war* can be controlled, it is more relevant to ask whether nuclear *alerts* can be controlled. If forces cannot safely be put on alert without the alert process becoming so provocative and dangerous that the alert order is tantamount to a declaration of war, then two dangers follow. First, alerts may directly lead to war, through accident or inadvertence—or through compelling an opponent to preempt merely to protect himself. A full dispersal and alerting of theater nuclear weapons in Europe would surely force the Soviets to think about this. Second, the dangers of alerting may be so apparent as to paralyze political leaders into taking no action whatsoever. Here, virtually all room for maneuver would be removed and political leaders, especially in Europe, would be faced with a decision of being either "red or dead."

Yet throughout the debates of NSDM-242 and PD-59, not a single study was made of the safety of going on alert, and especially not of a two-sided alert. Instead of asking whether a protracted alert was possible, the debate centered on waging a protracted nuclear war—something for which the gap between concept and actuality is larger than the Grand Canyon.

In a recent book Lawrence Freedman provides a telling argument. Nuclear strategizing, he says, has become so abstract and incestuous that it has only a tenuous connection with the real security problems of nations.[1] We could carry Freedman's arguments a step further by observing that ever more difficult demands have been placed on nuclear forces, and especially on command systems, regardless of their success or failure in meeting earlier strategic demands. Indeed, the tendency has been for strategy to so far outstrip capabilities that an illusion of control may develop among the specialists who attend to these matters.

Such illusions may be endemic to certains kinds of problems. For example, in the reinsurance business, the term "innocent capacity" has been coined to describe the systematic tendency of some

1. Lawrence Freedman, *The Evolution of Nuclear Strategy* (New York: St. Martin's, 1981).

companies to make naively optimistic projections about future losses. These projections cause them to underreserve capital to cover losses and result in widespread bankruptcies after a catastrophic event like a hurricane or tornado. The term *innocent* is used to convey a sense of naivete and foolishness, rather than fraudulent behavior. Reinsurance capacity to handle major losses is innocent before the catastrophe hits; after the disaster, the company will presumably lose its innocence. In the same way, no amount of analysis or persuasion may make much of a difference for altering the basic trends in nuclear forces. Perhaps only a disaster or near-disaster arising from a nuclear showdown can really expose the planners' innocent capacity to control events.

SOME NEW DIRECTIONS
THROUGH ARMS CONTROL

Although a disaster is one time-honored way to change directions, it is, fortunately, not the only way to go about this when it comes to national security. The present reliance on tightly coupled nuclear forces to backstop American and Soviet security interests did not come about overnight. It did not stem from a single unfortunate decision to do this or that, or to emphasize one kind of weapon over another. It arose from a series of changes that were individually small, each of which was thought to make an improvement in the existing state of affairs. The changes, whether in the synergistic interactions of the warning system or in the deployment of thousands of nuclear weapons to Europe, were cumulative. Only after the nuclear force system had grown to maturity can it be seen that the new situation is potentially disastrous.

Yet if a series of individually small changes can lead to the present situation, so can it lead away from it, toward nuclear forces that are "safe" at least in the sense that they do not risk killing millions of people frivolously. The incremental arms control approach offered here is not likely to be speedy, nor is it as exciting as a dramatic proposal to eliminate nuclear weapons altogether. But it does have the advantage that it can be institutionalized, and it can therefore grind away at problems individually.

What are needed are nuclear "rules of the road" to govern the operation of forces and alerts. Most important, we need to focus on *operational issues* rather than rely solely on cuts in the quantities of weapons possessed. For the next decade at least, major catastrophes can best be averted through controls on the *operations* of nuclear forces.

In broad terms, in our arms control efforts we should emphasize the use of information about operating patterns to control the most dangerous points of contact between American and Soviet nuclear forces. Exact formulations are difficult to analyze in detail, but there are many examples where small individual changes in operational practices would substantially improve command stability. Such changes would also reduce the incentive for preemptive attack. It is more than plausible that neither side will consciously try to use nuclear war as an instrument of statecraft or national policy. Therefore, measures that are designed to control the interactions of the forces of the two nations address what is the most likely cause of World War III—the escalation of a crisis into a major confrontation and ultimately to war.

Certainly one of the greatest pressures for early release of needed firing authorizations arises from weapons with short flight times that can attack national command centers. The Soviet Yankee SSBNs and the proposed Pershing 2 missile are weapons which can decapitate a national command structure in a few minutes' time. The likely, and quite effective, response to these weapons is to move the command toward launch-under-attack doctrines or to greater degrees of pre-delegated authority to use nuclear weapons. The mere existence of such weapons injects enormous ambiguity into a command system, for even if political authorities do not make a formal response to the threat such as to issue extensive predelegations, military commanders will have expectations created in peacetime that such a decapitating attack is likely. Such expectations may induce ad hoc, informal arrangements when the forces are placed on alert, as military commanders search for ways to bolster the protection of the vulnerable points in their retaliatory abilities. Purely verbal arrangements of an ad hoc variety may be agreed to once an alert is declared, and they may be undertaken without the knowledge of higher political authorities. With the Soviet penchant for secrecy and compartmentalized channeling of information, this sort of thing could be especially endemic inside the Soviet command.

The obvious course of action for arms control in this particular example is to structure a Soviet-American agreement around banning short-time-of-flight weapons or restricting deployments of systems that can reach national command centers. It might mean, for example, trading deployment of the Pershing 2 missile for a curtailment of Soviet SSBN operations near America's coastlines. In 1982, Leonid Brezhnev actually proposed talks about pulling back nuclear submarines from coastal areas. This kind of agreement would be verifiable, and it would serve notice that the entry of Soviet submarines into coastal waters would be an action outside the rules of the game for safe operation of strategic forces. The value to the United States of increasing the minimum warning time from five to twenty-five minutes is almost beyond calculation. It would sharply increase the survivability of the American bomber force and would greatly lessen the problem of ambiguous command authority arising from the threat of decapitation. Similar benefits would accrue to the Soviet Union.

Another measure that would enhance stability in a crisis or a limited conflict would be a unilateral declaration of "no first strikes against national command centers." The declaration would presumably include a ban on indirect attacks on command centers (such as high-altitude EMP attacks to disrupt communications). It is hard to see what the United States could gain from declaratory threats to attack the Soviet command system early in a conflict. Not only would such an attack eliminate the governmental entity we wish to negotiate with, it would also drive the Soviets into launch-under-attack policies or more extensive predelegation of firing authority. The centralized peacetime Soviet command system is sure to be a more decentralized command once its forces are placed on alert. Misunderstanding this shift in the Soviet command system is a sure prescription for catastrophe. As the scale of Soviet military operations increases, and their general staff increasingly controls operational matters, the Soviet com-

mand will be affected increasingly by organizational, not merely political, factors. The United States must take this into account and
avoid reckless threats that only induce Soviet counterthreats that weaken
U.S. command stability.

Unilateral declarations on operational matters are controversial
because they are intrinsically unverifiable. But they do have important
uses, especially if accompanied by arms talks oriented around com-
municating what each side considers vital.[2] Arms talks directed at
establishing transparency of force operations, so that each side is better
able to see patterns and activities in their most realistic context, would
be a useful first step for establishing nuclear rules of the road. They
would be an extremely useful forum for the United States to convey
its concern about interference with or attack of its warning and assessment sensors. Similarly, the Soviet Union could be encouraged
to harden some of the weak points in its system of command and
control. If, for example, American intelligence agencies detected accidents in Soviet military exercises, things such as the incorrect sending of firing orders from one unit to another, these mistakes could be
pointed out in the privacy of the arms control forum. It is easy to
believe that American intelligence officials may have better knowledge
of such mistakes than Soviet political leaders.

Reemphasizing the operational aspects of arms control would
also produce a framework within the government for evaluating new
weapon programs. This approach would point out areas of study that
have received little or no attention because of the past emphasis on
quantitative limitations in force levels. War termination would receive
greater attention than war initiation. "High-speed arms control" would
be a fit subject for study and analysis, something which is not the
case today. This term refers to preplanned ways to defuse a crisis
quickly. It includes measures like sequential surfacing of SSBNs to
demonstrate their positions, restriction of alert bombers to U.S. airspace, and permitting Soviet observers into U.S. command posts as

---

2. Such talks are proposed in the excellent discussion of arms control found in
Joseph S. Nye, Jr., "Restarting Arms Control," *Foreign Policy* 47 (Summer 1982):
98–113.

a way to convey intentions. Our point is not that these ideas are good regardless of context, but that a broad framework needs to be established for deciding which actions are useful in particular situations. As things stand now, none of the actions will receive consideration, and it is dangerous to believe that any of them could be thought out in the midst of a crisis.

There can be no absolute guarantees of security in the nuclear age, but there can be traffic signs and precautionary tactics to guide the superpowers through politically inspired confrontations. Even so, the world may have to rely on a measure of good luck, on playing for the breaks, in order to reach a less dangerous era. But until a time arrives when all nuclear weapons are banned from the face of the earth the prudent path to both security and survival lies through understanding how to manage and govern these forces.

Index